THE WIRIYAMU M

THE WIRIYAMU MASSACRE

AN ORAL HISTORY, 1960–1974

Mustafah Dhada

BLOOMSBURY ACADEMIC
LONDON • NEW YORK • OXFORD • NEW DELHI • SYDNEY

BLOOMSBURY ACADEMIC
Bloomsbury Publishing Plc
50 Bedford Square, London, WC1B 3DP, UK
1385 Broadway, New York, NY 10018, USA

BLOOMSBURY, BLOOMSBURY ACADEMIC and the Diana logo
are trademarks of Bloomsbury Publishing Plc

First published in Great Britain 2020

Cover design by Tjaša Krivec
Cover Image © Mustafah Dhada

Bloomsbury Publishing Plc does not have any control over, or responsibility for,
any third-party websites referred to or in this book. All internet addresses
given in this book were correct at the time of going to press. The author
and publisher regret any inconvenience caused if addresses have changed
or sites have ceased to exist, but can accept no responsibility for any such changes.

A catalogue record for this book is available from the British Library.

A catalog record for this book is available from the Library of Congress.

ISBN: HB: 978-1-3501-1993-2
PB: 978-1-3501-1996-3
ePDF: 978-1-3501-1998-7
eBook: 978-1-3501-2000-6

Typeset by Deanta Global Publishing Services, Chennai, India
Printed and bound in Great Britain

To find out more about our authors and books visit www.bloomsbury.com
and sign up for our newsletters.

CONTENTS

List of Photos viii

List of Maps ix

List of Tables x

Foreword *Jeanne Penvenne* xi

Preface xix

Acknowledgments xxxii

Introduction 1

    Portugal's Colonial Wars and Mass Violence 1

    The Erasure of the Five Villages 9

    The Outing 13

1   The Colonial War and the Wiriyamu Triangle 19

    Tete's March to the South 21

        Cabo Delgado, Malawi, and the Tete Front 23

        Political Mobilization and the Church 27

        The Wiriyamu Triangle and Raimundo Dalepa 30

        The Manica-e-Sofala Front 32

        Dissent and the Final Attack 34

    Frelimo's Arrival in the Triangle 36

        Spiritual Life and Frelimo's Arrival 38

        Wiriyamu and the End 41

    The Loss of Homes and Cattle 44

    Operation Marosca and the Aftermath 47

        Burning Huts and an Act of Compassion 52

        The Night after the Massacre and the Second Cleanup ... 54

        Inquiry, Training, and Reflections on War 57

        Violence on Girls and Informants 61

        My Family and Their Return to Portugal 62

    Chico, the Secret Agent, and His Death 65

        How He Went 67

2   The Anatomy of the Massacres 69

    Chaworha's Demise 71

        We Gathered to Clap 73

        When I Woke Up 75

Contents

Deliverance 76

Into Exile and Back 77

Today 79

Juawu's Killing Fields 80

The Premonitions That Went Unheeded 82

Signposts to War 83

The Ending Begins 85

Seeing Is Believing 86

My Escape 87

I Ran from the Wiriyamu Fires 89

In the Morning before the Massacre 90

The Massacre as It Happened 90

The Escape from the Fire 92

An End of Sorts 93

The Flames of War and the Spirit of My Tears 94

The Loud "Woorh . . . Woorh . . . Woorh . . ." 95

The Spirit of My Tears 96

Djemusse's Lengthy Erasure 97

3 **Gathering and Surveying the Evidence** **101**

Family Life, Data Collection, and Torture 102

Wiriyamu—Near Escapes 103

Rescue and the Tortures 108

Evidence Gathering, Cover-Up, and Coercion 110

Chaworha Survivors and Their Stories 111

Lists Are Formed; Concerns Are Expressed 113

The Escape and the Cover-Up 115

Checking Bodies from the Air 118

Surveying the Dead 119

Interrogation and the Mobbing Journalists 121

Not Wiriyamu Again! 126

4 **The First Public Outing of the Wiriyamu Narrative** **127**

How I Smuggled the Report 128

The Bulge 130

The Revelations 133

The Wiriyamu Narrative Escapes Undetected! 137

Expulsions 138

5 **The Final Revelation** **141**

Development Issues, Father Adrian Hastings, and the Opposition 142

Adrian and the Detractors 144

Wiriyamu and the People of London   146
    After the Story Came Out   148
The Final Revelation and Vatican II   150
    Caetano and the Wiriyamu Revelation   153
    Political Neutrality and the Press   156
    To the UN and Back   159
    Wiriyamu and the Portuguese Revolution   163

6   The British Fact-Checkers   165
Knipe Combats Fake News   167
    Experiencing Africa   168
    Into the Bush and Back   170
    Expulsion and Returns   172
How the Portuguese Foiled One Fact-Checker   175
    The Bouncer and Knipe's Return!   176
    Williamo and Departures   177
"The Story Checks Out!" Said Peter Pringle   180
    How I Got the Story Out   181
    The South African BOSS and the Attempted Blackmail   185
    Hastings, Loudon, and Gaster   186

7   The Final Act—Witness Protection   189
An Eyewitness Confirms the Place and the Events   190
    The Massacre   192
Mixone's Rendition on a Suzuki Motorbike   195
    Contacts with Frelimo—and My Nemeses   196
    The Visitor from London and Hiding Mixone   198
    The Pendulum Swings   201
    To Spain and Back   204

Conclusion   207

Works Cited   209
Glossary   215
Index   217

PHOTOS

Photo 1   Abidu Karimu, Chaworha. Photo by Mustafah Dhada, © 1995   xxvii

Photo 2   Senhor Elídio, Tete city. Photo by Mustafah Dhada, © 1995   xxvii

Photo 3   *The London Times*, Wiriyamu revelation. Personal archives.
Photo by Mustafah Dhada, © 1995   2

Photo 4   Bulachu Pensadu Zambezi, Wiriyamu. Photo by
Mustafah Dhada, © 1995   36

Photo 5   Vasco Tenente Valeta, Wiriyamu. Photo by
Mustafah Dhada, © 1995   44

Photo 6   Chico Kachavi, Tete. Identity card photo, public domain.
Used with permission from a family member   65

Photo 7   António Mixone, Chaworha. Photo by
Mustafah Dhada, © 1995   71

Photo 8   Domingo Kansande, Cantina Raul, Tete. Photo by
Mustafah Dhada, ©1995   102

Photo 9   Padre Domingo Ferrão, Tete. Photo by
Mustafah Dhada, © 1995   110

Photo 10   Miguel Buendia, Maputo. Photo by Mustafah Dhada, © 1995   128

Photo 11   Alberto Fonte Castellã, Changara. Photo by
Mustafah Dhada, © 1995   137

Photo 12   Father Adrian Hastings, Leeds. Photo by
Mustafah Dhada, © 1995   150

Photo 13   Michael Knipe, London. Photo by Mustafah Dhada, © 1995   166

Photo 14   Peter Pringle, New York. Photo by Susan Meiselas, © 2011.
Used with permission   180

Photo 15   Padre Vicente Berenguer, Maputo. Photo by
Mustafah Dhada, © 1995   190

Photo 16   Padre José Sangalo, Madrid. Photo by
Mustafah Dhada, © 1995   194

MAPS

Map 1 The Wiriyamu triangle. Map by Mustafah Dhada, © 1973   xviii

Map 2 Church missions and place names in Tete. Map by
Mustafah Dhada, © 1973   5

Map 3 Chieftaincies of the Wiriyamu triangle. Map by
Mustafah Dhada, © 1973   7

TABLES

Table 1 Interview List   xxi

Table 2 List of Massacre Victims   xxviii

FOREWORD

No scholar has more deeply engaged with the Wiriyamu Massacre of December 16, 1972, than Mustafah Dhada. No one has more firmly insisted on placing the people, the place, and the corroborated events and processes on the record, nor steadfastly confronted efforts to diminish the evidence or its significance.[1] His book *The Portuguese Massacre of Wiriyamu in Colonial Mozambique, 1964–2013* won the American Historical Association's coveted Martin A. Klein Prize (2017) for the most distinguished work of scholarship on Africa published in English during the previous year.[2] It garnered widespread praise for intrepid and meticulous oral, archival, and field research, a rare willingness to open the intimate details of the research processes to scholarly scrutiny, and the passion that drove Dhada's endeavor. Dhada's work was distinguished by its capacity to sustain multiple narratives in a common register, insist on historicity, and confront historical horrors and their implications for all involved. Tellingly, he dedicated the book: "To Those Who Perished at Wiriyamu, I Hope They Find a Place to Rest Here."[3]

This book, with all the hallmarks of Dhada's earlier work—easy transitions across space, close detail, and deep explication of methods—not only makes a truly impressive case for the value of oralcy and its embedded dynamics, but, by setting out compelling testimony from such a broad range of people, he draws readers directly into these events and their nuanced and layered complications. Each narrative casts its own special light on one or another aspect of the overall story. Whether revealing a village's relationship to the protective or predatory lion spirit, probing the impact of Vatican II on Mozambique's Bishop Dom Sebastião Soares Resende, or exposing the duplicitous conduct of the infamous Portuguese apologist Jorge Jardim, the narrators incrementally provide the pieces that readers, with Dhada's support, come to experience as a whole.

Dhada set daunting challenges for himself in both the *Portuguese Massacre of Wiriyamu* and *An Oral History*. Kathleen Sheldon's review of the first aptly quoted from the cover of Arundhati Roy's novel *The Ministry of Utmost Happiness*: "How to tell a shattered story? By slowly becoming everybody. No. By slowly becoming everything."[4]

---

[1]Bruno C. Reis and Pedro A. Oliveira, "Cutting Heads or Winning Hearts: Late Colonial Portuguese Counterinsurgency and the Wiriyamu Massacre of 1972," *Civil Wars* 14, 1 (2012): 80–103; Mustafah Dhada, "The Wiriyamu Massacre of 1972: Response to Reis and Oliveira," *Civil Wars* 15, 4 (2013): 551–8; Bruno C. Reis and Pedro A. Oliveira, "Reply to Mustafah Dhada," *Civil Wars* 15, 4 (2013): 559–62.
[2]*The Portuguese Massacre of Wiriyamu in Colonial Mozambique, 1964–2013* (London: Bloomsbury Academic, 2015), www.historians.org/awards-and-grants/past-recipients/martin-a-klein-prize-recipients.
[3]*Portuguese Massacre*, p. v.; K.B. Wilson, "On Truth About Truths in Mozambique's Liberation Struggle," *Journal of Southern African Studies* 43, 4 (2017): 846–8, 846.
[4]Kathleen Sheldon, "Review of *Portuguese Massacre*," *International Journal of African Historical Studies* 50, 1 C (2017): 545.

The multiple narratives that piece together this shattered story hinge on people's memories, but often their words and perspectives emerge as embedded in the landscape: the riverbeds, the boulders, the *machambas*, the tamarind and baobab trees. Indeed, everybody and everything in the Wiriyamu triangle must be pieced together.

The baobab in the Wiriyamu village was much more than a mnemonic device for oral narration or a crucial shelter. In the obscene language of the Portuguese Special Forces, so much else could be "cleaned up," but not the tree. The powerful and feared Polícia Internacional e de Defesa do Estado (PIDE, International Police for the Defense of the State)/Direção-Geral de Segurança (DGS, General Directorate for Security) villain Chico Kachavi ordered his commandos: "*Aphani Wense!! Aphani Wense.*" [Kill them all! Kill the lot leave no one alive. No witnesses—they will denounce us].[5] The tree witnessed all that had taken place around it, and the tree remained.[6] Survivors who narrated their denunciations sometimes referenced the baobab.[7] In this way, Dhada's oral history evokes poet/historian Landeg White's *Ultimatum, a Novel*, in which White elided history and fiction, tapping the Shire River to narrate the stories that played out on and along its banks in the 19th century.[8] The Wiriyamu baobab and the Shire River endure. They provide the landscape for denunciation—they are part of everything. For East and Central Africa, Ranger, Alexander, McGregor, Bender Shetler, and others underscore the mutual inscription of landscape and history, violence and memory, and the gendered ways of history telling.[9] People, their words, and the physical places of their lives entangle in ways that endure.

This work cedes center stage to oral narratives. It is about time. In his review of *Portuguese Massacre*, Manuel Bandeira Jeronimo questioned Dhada's "unrestrained confidence in the heuristic potential of oral history and revelatory powers of ethnographic fieldwork . . .," arguing that "History is not the register of testimonies *in situ* or the echo chamber of previously unheard voices, however crucial and inclusive they may be. History is not memory."[10] Indeed, history is not memory; at least it is not only memory, but Dhada's previous work, and this work in particular, firmly locate the importance of the ways people recall their past and assign meaning to it. Moreover, Dhada honors what people are not willing to remember and recount. On the day of the massacre, Enéria Tenente was in Wiriyamu to visit her family. In one of the most difficult narratives to

[5]See, "The Erasure of the Five Villages," under Introduction; and, António Chuva Culher's interview.
[6]Detailed repeatedly in Antonino Melo's testimony.
[7]See, interviews by Enéria Tenente, Kudangirana, Magaissa, Baera, and Djemusse, Michael Knipe, Padre Vicente Berenguer, and Padre José Sangalo.
[8]Landeg White, *Ultimatum* (Gwynedd: Cinnamon Press, 2018). See also, Landeg White, *Livingstone's Funeral* (Gwynedd: Cinnamon Press, 2000).
[9]T. O. Ranger, *Voices from the Rocks, Nature, Culture and History in the Matopos Hills of Zimbabwe* (Oxford: James Currey, 1999); Jocelyn Alexander, JoAnn McGregor and T. O. Ranger, *Violence & Memory: One Hundred Years in the "Dark Forests" of Matabeleland* (Oxford: James Currey, 2000); Jan Bender Shetler, *Imagining Serengeti: A History of Landscape Memory in Tanzania from the Earliest Times to the Present* (Athens: Ohio University Press, 2007).
[10]Miguel Jeronimo, "Mustafah Dhada. *The Portuguese Massacre of Wiriyamu in Colonial Mozambique, 1964–2013*," *American Historical Review* 122, 3 (2017): 967–8.

read, Enéria Tenente tells us how she narrowly escaped being burned to death with her mother and other villagers: "Memories of death and dying women and children still haunt me . . . I will not go to Wiriyamu . . . I do not want to give that fire more kindling."[11] Some of the narrators who survived the massacres in the Wiriyamu cluster of villages carried burn marks and bullet wounds on their bodies, but all carried images in their minds that they did not want to recall but could not escape. Most never returned to their villages.[12]

In honoring people's words, the limits of their narrations, their ways of knowing and telling, and the physical setting before, during, and after the events of December 16, 1972, Dhada incrementally moves the center and guides students of history into a greater appreciation of the heuristic potential of performance and oralcy. In the early 1990s, Ngugi wa Thiong'o argued for the centrality of African common parlance, assignation of meaning, and vernacular languages.[13] History should register testimonies *in situ*, name, record, fully engage "previously unheard voices," and take seriously the work that some disciplines call "deep listening" or "deep hanging out."[14] Anthropologists, ethnomusicologists, and others recognized performance and song as historical narratives long before historians.[15]

Dhada's work further unsettles assumptions regarding archives. Archival, print, and iconic sources are too often imagined to surpass forms of oralcy. In the manner of feminist scholars, however, we should seriously consider why the written record should not be interrogated in light of oralcy as often as oral testimony is tested in light of the written record.[16] These oral narrations broadly document efforts to erase evidence of the banality of widespread violence in Portuguese-held colonial Africa. The Portuguese and South African intelligence forces, PIDE/DGS, and South Africa's Bureau of State Security (BOSS) may have conceptualized the horrific counterinsurgency strategies documented here, but everyone from the hapless conscript to the military commanders was implicated in the colonial wars' merciless bloodshed. Adrian Hastings' narrative revealed that even the cohort of military officers who overturned Portugal's dictatorship in 1974 recognized that inquiries into the massacres would implicate too many people.[17] Dhada found that "the copy of the military commission of inquiry is missing from the folder in the Portuguese National Defense Archives."[18] Can history and memory be

---

[11]See Enéria Tenente's testimony in, The flames of war and the spirit of tears.
[12]See Kalifornia Kanniveti's testimony in, Juawu's killing fields.
[13]Ngugi wa Thiong'o, *Moving the Centre: The Struggle for Cultural Freedoms* (Portsmouth: Heinemann, 1993).
[14]Clifford Geertz, "Deep Hanging Out," *The New York Review of Books* 45, 16 (1998): 69–72.
[15]For this region Leroy Vail and Landeg White's work on performance and song was transformative, *Capitalism and Colonialism in Mozambique; A Study of Quelimane District* (Minneapolis: University of Minnesota Press, 1980); Jeanne Marie Penvenne co-authored with Bento Sitoe, "Power, Poets and the People—Mozambican Voices Interpreting History," *Social Dynamics* 26, 2 (2000): 55–86.
[16]Susan Geiger's classic essay raises this point: "What's so Feminist about Doing Women's Oral History?" *Journal of Women's History* 2, 1 (1990).
[17]See Adrian Hastings' testimony in, The final revelation and Vatican II.
[18]See "The Outing" subsection of this book's Introduction, especially the last footnote.

erased by the removal of sheets of paper? History is exciting detective work, whether in the archives, in the library, in the press, or among historical actors, but this book will definitely serve as a model for scholars seeking to decolonize history, build confidence in oralcy, and enhance the partnership of ethnographic and historical methods.

Historians struggle to hear and understand "previously unheard voices," and to rearrange dominant narratives into the kaleidoscopic patterns that emerge in complicated vernacular conversations. Dhada aspires to bring forward testimony from those whose voices were previously unheard: "data-gatherers and their transmitters, victims before their erasure, survivors, massacre perpetrators and priests."[19] In so doing he directly confronts the qualities and shortcomings of his research. Trauma and the gendered distribution of daily reproductive work partially explain why women's testimony is limited. Since the mid-1990s when he was in the field, scholars have built a much greater understanding of oralcy and gender.[20] Steven Feierman's work on the creation of invisible histories revealed that women's common practices and ways of voicing their concerns were likely to be missed or misrepresented because the sources historians use did not understand, see, or value them. Helen Bradford drew attention to layered androcentric assumptions that led scholars to misunderstand women's roles in centrally important, complex phenomena and processes, even when historical evidence was fairly complete.[21] Finally, Jan Bender Shetler observed that "women possessed not just another version but wholly different kinds of knowledge about the past . . . men and women share neither styles of oral narration nor types of knowledge about the past. Men and women occupy separate spheres in their daily routines, sharing the same world but participating in different, though intersecting, sets of discourses about that world . . . A gendered analysis of oral tradition is necessary for finding its historical meaning."[22] Even scholars who recorded women's testimony while sharing the separate spaces of their quotidian work have to sort out their words and their potential meaning.[23]

Since I began my historical research in Portugal and Mozambique in the 1970s, I repeatedly confronted the erasure of African people and their experiences in archival and print sources. The historical actors whose agency interested me were broadly

[19]Mustafah Dhada, *The Portuguese Massacre of Wiriyamu in Colonial Mozambique, 1964–2013* (London: Bloomsbury Academic Press, 2015), 10.
[20]Barbara M. Cooper, "Oral Sources and the Challenge of African History" and Kathleen Sheldon, "Writing about Women: Approaches to a Gendered Perspective in African History," in John Edward Philips, ed., *Writing African History* (Rochester: University of Rochester, 2005).
[21]Stephen Feierman, "Colonizers, Scholars and the Creation of Invisible Histories," in Victoria E. Bonnell and Lynn Hunt, eds., *Beyond the Cultural Turn: New Directions in the Study of Society and Culture* (Berkeley: University of California Press, 1999), p. 209; Helen Bradford, "Women, Gender and Colonialism: Rethinking the History of the British Cape Colony and Its Frontier Zones, c. 1806–70," *Journal of African History* 37 (1996): 351–70.
[22]Bender Shetler, *Imagining Serengeti*, 11–12.
[23]Heidi Gengenbach, *Binding Memories: Women as Tellers and Makers of History in Magude, Mozambique* (New York: Columbia University Press, 2005); Arianna Huhn, "The Tongue Only Works Without Worries: Sentiment and Sustenance in a Mozambican Town," *Food and Foodways: Explorations in the History and Culture of Human Nourishment* 21, 3 (2013): 186–210.

absent and almost always unnamed. Sometimes they were "counted" as though they were commodities—they were just so many "blacks." Their personhood was erased. I could read the language of the paper track and was trained to work with it, but it was of limited use. When I was finally able to meet and converse with the Mozambican people at the heart of my research, I had mediocre language skills and was inexperienced to the point of being clueless. Incrementally I learned to listen more carefully and was able to absorb and understand more. Mozambicans conveying their truths through oralcy and performance often upended my expectations about narratives and images. I increasingly welcomed being surprised and puzzled. Scholars and students at many stages will profit from the insights Dhada shares with us here, about both doing research and grappling with oral narratives.

This book will engage a broad audience, but it has special value as a teaching text. When I was a historian at Tufts University, Massachusetts, my goal was to meet students where they were and try to bring them to their fullest potential. Depending upon a reader's interests and background, the experiences related here are differentially "accessible." Dhada presents all the narrators' experiences with authority and dignity, so a reader's potential stretch to understand less accessible texts is well supported. Not every reader will be familiar with quotidian lives of agropastoral villages in Southeastern Africa, where elders and spirit mediums enter sacred forests to engage the lion spirit's dangerous or protective energy and direct it to positive ends. They may resist notions that villagers should have understood unusual wind energy around the region as a premonition of the massacre and taken heed. Readers will relate to fear, efforts to spare one's family, mourning for murdered family members, and rejoicing for those who were spared.

Some of these narratives are extremely difficult and clearly merit a "trigger warning," under the criteria faculty are encouraged to adhere to in North American universities. They reveal monstrous murder, torment, and the power of men with weapons to wreak carnage. The term "hearts and minds campaign" was used by the Portuguese and other powers fighting guerrilla wars, to capture their wartime counterinsurgency efforts to win the populations that sheltered the guerrillas over to the side of the colonizer. It was appropriated in chilling terms in Portuguese Army Commando Antonino Melo's narrative. Melo confirmed:

> We were trained to be stone-cold—to kill a person at that time was normal. We were trained for that purpose and prepared to be psychologically ready to kill. The psychological training we received as commandos shaped our minds and hearts. They were the enemy. We had to shoot them or else; it was either them or us. We did what was needed to be done. We could not leave anything behind. You were told to clean up and you did just that; therefore, killing a person was normal.[24]

The term "cleanup," like the term "ethnic cleansing," is a euphemism for murder. Melo and his troops returned to murder any survivors. At Wiriyamu, the evidence of their

---

[24]See Antonino Melo's interview in, Operation Marosca and the aftermath.

murder was hidden, "cleaned up" by burying what remained of rotting corpses in mass graves.

Frelimo Commander Hama Thai conveys his recollection of August 8, 1973, in similarly chilling terms. Hama Thai's base, strategy, and soldiers had been betrayed by fellow Frelimo officer Zeca Calilate. Instead of facing abuse of power charges within Frelimo, Calilate turned himself over to the Portuguese and revealed all. In light of the security breach Hama Thai acted quickly. However, instead of rapid withdrawal and relocation, he went on the offensive, planning a daring and devastating attack on a patrol column of Portuguese soldiers. Hama Thai took pride in his success: "I just can't forget that day, August 8, 1973! It was carnage, total carnage."[25]

Indeed, the attack resulted in total carnage, but it was an ambush by armed Frelimo soldiers of armed Portuguese soldiers. It was not the kind of sadistic execution of unarmed and innocent civilians that the PIDE and Portuguese special forces conducted in the Wiriyamu triangle. The commandos mocked innocent villagers as monkeys or "girlfriends" and forced them to clap and run before they shot them dead like clay pigeons. This level of violence was simply unimaginable to the villagers. Many explained their inability to take in what was unfolding before them with the words: "We had no knowledge of war," "We did not know what a war looked like," "I never knew war."[26] The narratives of violence give one pause.

Other narratives are broadly accessible and unfold like a fast-paced mystery novel, an account of espionage and of journalistic daring. As one of the key agents recording evidence of the massacre, Domingo Kansande reveals quick thinking and courage, as he evades some of the most dangerous PIDE agents and eventually survives 45 days of PIDE torture.[27] Padre José Sangalo similarly navigates threats to evidence collection and at one point literally absconds with António Mixone, the young boy whose firsthand evidence was a lynchpin for the report to reveal the massacre. Sangalo was as determined to keep Mixone out of harm's way as the PIDE were to capture him. Like Kansande, Sangalo also suffered PIDE torture, but he knew that, thanks to his white privilege and status as a Catholic padre, they would go only so far. They would not kill him, at least not on purpose. Sangalo avoided involving any of his African colleagues in risk taking, knowing their situation was much more dangerous.

The narrative dramas span remote areas of Tete, border crossings into Zambia, Tanzania, and South Africa, and the transfer of evidence and strategies to reveal the evidence in Rome and London. The narratives of international investigation, journalism, PIDE's seizure of evidence files, and the intimidation of international and national actors are lively and accessible. The role of the Catholic Institute for International Relations (CIIR) personnel and networks, which enabled the dramatic timing of *The London Times*' article coinciding with Marcelo Caetano's visit, can be paired with readings of archival

---

[25]See General Hama Thai's interview in, Tete's march to the south.
[26]Enéria Tenente's interview in, The flames of war and the spirit of tears.
[27]See Domingo Kansande's interview in, Family life, data collection, and torture.

press material from CIIR or ALUKA-based pieces by Adrian Hastings and others.[28] The book is a model for teaching African ALUKA history through a range of primary sources, and particularly promising for foundation courses that consider historiography, theory, and methods.

Finally, the narratives, maps, photographs, and bibliography combine to secure the history of the Wiriyamu massacres and the process whereby they were revealed. The military commission file of inquiry may have gone missing, and the perpetrators of mass violence may not be brought to justice because too many military careers are still at stake, but those who read this book will have a much better idea of what is being hidden and why. Dhada's closing paragraph argues that the book reveals "unalienable truths," that "the integrity of the narrative is impregnably solid," and that "Wiriyamu the event and Wiriyamu the revealed narrative [are] incontestably true."[29] If his first book gave the victims of Wiriyamu a place to rest, this book gives pride of place to the narrators, evidence collectors, journalists, and fact-checkers, whose work he so carefully curated. It too promises to become a classic.

Jeanne Penvenne
Professor of History, Emerita
Faculty of Arts & Sciences
Tufts University, Massachusetts

---

[28]ALUKA holds digitized archival materials on PIDE's operations in colonial Mozambique that are held in Torre do Tombo. See https://www.aluka.org.
[29]See the concluding lines of this book.

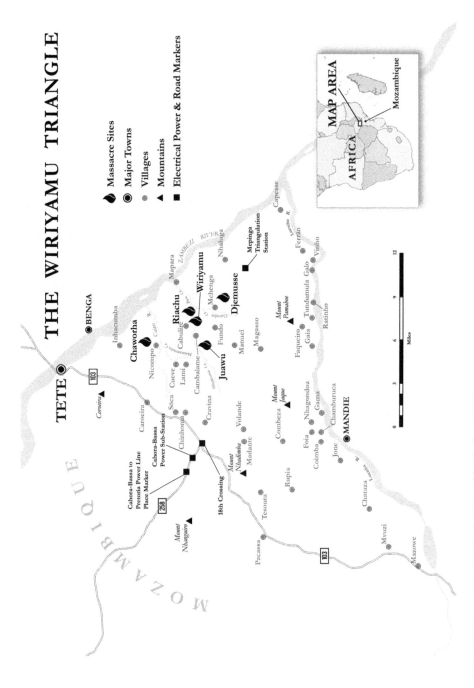

Map 1 The Wiriyamu triangle. Map by Mustafah Dhada, © 1973.

PREFACE

The shaping of this monograph

On March 1, 2015, at 2:58 p.m., I dashed a manuscript on the Portuguese massacre of Wiriyamu in colonial Mozambique off to my publishers, extolling its virtues as an eminently qualified text for advanced undergraduates and graduates on the history of African decolonization.[1] Almost immediately after I pressed "send," I was consumed by self-doubt. What if it was of no interest to students? I had no culture of evidence to back the claim I had just made in my blurb to the publishers! Thirty days later, the opportunity to test the claim presented itself during the spring quarter in my course on the history of African decolonization. Select chapters of the unpublished manuscript were put on the reading list for the students enrolled in the course, accompanied by three interview transcripts, all three dealing with the genesis of the story as revealed in *The London Times*.[2] Their verdict was unanimous: The manuscript could benefit from a collection of primary source interviews prefaced by a discussion on methods used to get them to talk; one, in their view, would allow them to get closer to the events with minimal interpolation; and the other, the preface that is, would reveal strategies used to get informants to talk about Wiriyamu.

I set to work on my students' wish list—and intimated as much in a codicil inserted in the monograph before it was sent to print in early 2016. I envisioned a heavily redacted set of fifteen tape-recorded interviews accompanied by a skeletal introduction on Wiriyamu, followed by a rationale for publishing it. The conclusion was to be equally austere in that it would outline in a summative fashion the thematic contents of the fifteen interviews.

Anonymous peer reviewers, to whom the publishers sent the project proposal, were equally unanimous but cautious—for different reasons. The project though publishable as proposed—and that was the cautious bit—deserved a wider audience, they averred. Their carefully worded set of thirteen measures proved hard to ignore. They thought the proposal needed these carried out in order for it to be a broadly appealing book. The least notable among the measures recommended were the inclusion of photographs, maps, tables, and a glossary of terms and acronyms and the excision of a number of artifacts in the text, for example, idealized tropes of African landscapes, conceptual ambiguities, allusive references to genocide museums too peripheral to the

---

[1]Dhada, *The Portuguese Massacre*.
[2]One chapter tackled literature review, one was on oral research methods, and the third dealt with the events that brought the massacre to light. See, Dhada, *The Portuguese Massacre of Wiriyamu*, 11–41 and 111–25.

story on Wiriyamu, and unclear explanations of transcription techniques I had used for the proposed book.

The most notable measure they proposed was to consider the project as a stand-alone book. For that they suggested a robust fact-based introduction of the Wiriyamu story even at the risk of repeating the contents of the earlier monograph, but in the context of nationalism, counterinsurgency, mass violence, and public disclosure of the narrative. They also urged me to increase the number of interviews—fifteen testimonies was viewed to be too narrow to aim for a broader readership, to identify lacunas important for evaluating the text's academic merit, and to indicate its "fit" among testimonial works on mass violence, be they precolonial, colonial, or postcolonial. Two peer reviewers echoed the student demand mentioned earlier—a discussion on the oral methods I had used to get the interviewees to talk.

Notes on the book's structure and content

Thereafter, this wish list of students and peers reshaped of the project to include a fulsome introduction. Borrowing heavily on the materials used in the previously published work,[3] this introduction outlines the events before, during, and after the massacre, linking it to political changes in Portugal—but with a twist. Twenty-seven key individuals are woven into the fabric, partly to familiarize readers with their names before they reappear as interviewees, and partly to contextualize the role they played in the Wiriyamu story. The introduction ends with a short rationale justifying the book as a primary source of evidence on the massacre.

Twenty-four out of a total of twenty-nine tape-recorded interviews populate the book's landscape. They cluster around seven themes: the colonial war, Tete, and the Wiriyamu triangle; the anatomy of the Wiriyamu massacre; evidence gathering and on-site verification of the killing fields; the first public outing of the massacre narrative; the subsequent and highly successful revelation of the story in *The London Times*; the fact-checking efforts that followed the story as revealed in London; and the witness-protection measures taken to hide a key survivor of the massacre. Each of the seven thematic groups comes equipped with an italicized mini-preface guiding readers to the contents that follow. Informed by the format that Totten and Ubaldo's book adopts for eyewitness accounts of the Rwanda genocide,[4] each interview in a given thematic group is watermarked right at the top, identifying the interviewee; the date, place, and duration of the interview; the language used; interpreters employed where I was not the main interviewer; and redactions made to the transcripts.

---

[3]One chapter tackled literature review, one was on oral research methods, and the third dealt with the events that brought the massacre to light. See, Dhada, *The Portuguese Massacre of Wiriyamu*, 11–41 and 111–25.
[4]Samuel Totten and Rafiki Ubaldo, eds., *We Cannot Forget: Interviews with Survivors of the 1994 Genocide in Rwanda* (New Brunswick: Rutgers University Press, 2011).

Table 1 Interview List

Interviewees	Date(s) yyyy mm dd	Duration hh mm ss	Place	Language	Interpreter	Redactions
General Hama Thai	1995 04 28; and 05 11	1h 26m 54s	Maputo	Portuguese	None	Light
Bulachu Pensadu Zambezi	1995 05 14–26	1h 57m 46s	Tete	Portuguese/Nhungwe	Abidu Karimu and Senhor Elidio	None
Antonino Melo	1995 07 02–05	9h 10m 23s	Lisbon	Portuguese	None	Light
António Kachavi	1995 05 20	1h 2m 22s	Tete	Nhungwe	Abidu Karimu and Senhor Elidio	None
António Mixone	1995 05 15 and 24	3h 17m 46s	Chaworha	Portuguese/Nhungwe	Abidu Karimu	None
Kalifornia Kaniveti	1995 05 14–26	0h 57m 10s	Juawu	Nhungwe	Abidu Karimu	None
João Xavier	1995 05 14–26	1h 25m 22s	Wiriyamu	Portuguese/Nhungwe	Abidu Karimu	None
António Chuva Culher	1995 05 26	2h 28m 2s	Wiriyamu	Portuguese/Nhungwe	Abidu Karimu	None
Enéria Tenente	1995 05 25	0h 50m 0s	Wiriyamu/Riachu	Nhungwe	Abidu Karimu	None
Vasco Tenente	1995 05 25	1h 2m 13s	Wiriyamu	Portuguese/Nhungwe	Abidu Karimu	None
Kudangirana, Magaissa, Baera, and Djemusse	1995 05 26	1h 32m 55s	Djemusse	Nhungwe	Abidu Karimu	None
Domingo Kansande	1995 05 17	0h 46m 3s	Changara	Portuguese	None	None
Padre Domingo Ferrão	1995 05 16	2h 25m 43s	Tete	Portuguese	None	Moderate

Table 1 Interview List

Interviewees	Date(s) yyyy mm dd	Duration hh mm ss	Place	Language	Interpreter	Redactions
Irmã Lúcia Saez de Ugarte	1995 05 19	0h 47m 45s	Tete	Portuguese/Spanish	None	None
Miguel Buendia	1995 03 14 and 21; 04 04 and 14	4h 30m 29s	Maputo	Portuguese	None	Heavy
Alberto Fonte Castellã	1995 05 17	1h 21m 11s	Changara	Portuguese	None	Heavy
Mildred Neville	1996 03 nd	1h 7m 59s	London	English	None	Light
Hugh O'Shaughnessy	1996 03 26	0h 53m 55s	London	English	None	Light
Adrian Hastings	1996 03 nd	3h 0m 0s	Leeds	English	None	Light
Michael Knipe	1996 03 nd	1h 30m 59s	London	English	None	None
Christopher Wain	1996 03 25	0h 52m 32s	London	English	None	None
Peter Pringle	2013 03 27; 2014 04 15; and 2015 03 15	5h 30m 17s	New York	English	None	None
Padre Vicente Berenguer	1995 03 02, 06, 20, 27; 1995 04 03, 06, and 10	6h 4m 56s	Maputo	Portuguese	None	Heavy
Padre José Sangalo	1995 06 11–21	3h 51m 11s	Madrid	Portuguese/Spanish	None	Very Light

The interviews included here were held between 1994 and 2015. Seven were conducted in Portuguese; six in English; four in Nhungwe, which required translators; five in a mixture of Portuguese and Nhungwe, which were assisted by Portuguese-language informants; and two in a mixture of Portuguese and Spanish.

There is now a wealth of information on doing narrative and oral research,[5] which informed the interviewing process adopted here as "interactional events." The interviews themselves followed a simple procedure, meaning the recorded tapes were first transcribed verbatim and then brought into English where necessary.[6] I then eliminated onomatopoeias; embedded *in italics* interview questions into the texts or eliminated them altogether; excised sensitive information, at the interviewees' request; redacted chunks tangential to the Wiriyamu story where appropriate; inserted interpolations in block parentheses to help clarify the meaning of the text under review; and made a final check against the original transcriptions to project the original voice of the interviewees as much as possible.

While the vast body of literature on oral historiography and memory studies informed this project,[7] the techniques applied for interviews included here, as opposed to the approaches taken during fieldwork to dig up evidence about the massacre, were kept simple with an eye to learning from doing and adapting along the way[8]: Team leaders and trainees on-site were told to let interviewees know they were being recorded and to seek their permission to publish the interview once done.[9]

Let them choose where they want to be interviewed, and then begin with personal background and professional training; ask them to talk about their experience and primary knowledge of the events that transpired at Wiriyamu; end the interview by soliciting any thoughts and feelings they would like to share with the world at large; keep questions to the minimum; allow narratives to flow even if tangential to the story line, you are there for their benefit, it is their time to speak; listen without activating normative filters; treat each informant as a human archive of memories

[5]Molly Andrews, Corinne Squire, and Maria Tamboukou, eds., *Doing Narrative Research,* 2nd ed. (Los Angeles: Sage, 2016).

[6]For attendant problems tied to this process, see, Marilena Papachristophorou, "Orality, Transcription and Construction of Data," *Indian Folklore* 4, 1 (2003): 13–15.

[7]Most influential works used for the initial phase of the project included: Paul Thompson, *The Voice of the Past: Oral History* (Oxford: Oxford University Press, 1988); Jan M. Vansina, *Oral Tradition as History* (Madison: The University of Wisconsin Press, 1985); and, Robin George Collingwood, *The Idea of History* (Oxford: Oxford University Press, 1994). See also, *An Oral History Bibliography: A Research Guide by the Columbia University Center for Oral History,* accessed February 10, 2019, https://library.columbia.edu/content/dam/libraryweb/locations/ohro/The%20Oral%20History%20Bibliography%20--%20A%20CCOH%20Publication.pdf; Liz H. Strong, Mary Marshall Clark, and Caitlin Bertin-Mahieux, eds., *Oral History Transcription Style Guide* (New York: Columbia University Center for Oral History Research, 2018); *Introduction to Oral History* (Waco: Baylor University Institute for Oral History, 2016); and, Linda Shopes, *Web Guides to Doing Oral History* (Murfreesboro: Oral History Association, 2012).

[8]Kathryn Roulston, Kathleen deMarrais, and Jamie B. Lewis, "Learning to Interview in the Social Sciences," *Qualitative Inquiry* 9, 3 (2003): 643–68.

[9]Chich Hoong Sin, "Seeking Informed Consent: Reflection on Research Practice," *Sociology* 39, 2 (2005): 277–94.

and memorial data, and respect the memorial contents of what you hear and see, and try to leave these unstirred; use pauses as an opportunity to redirect the oral text; and phantomize your presence—that is to say, keep yourself practically invisible at all times.

They were reminded,

Remember interviewing informants can become an interactive process, perhaps even a dialogue, and you should be open to view the exchange between yourself and your informant with that framework in mind; keep the eye on the ball though, data-mining, but be mindful not to reduce the interviewing process into a predatory relationship, not if you can help it.

That was it, in a nutshell!

The majority of interviews appear here in their entirety; others are redacted ever so lightly to excise materials peripheral to the story. Four interviews, however, are heavily truncated with regard to material related to missions: They are with Padre Vicente Berenguer, Miguel Buendia, Padre Alberto Fonte Castellã, and Michael Knipe. Five tape-recorded interviews failed to make it into the book because their subject matter was in its entirety unrelated to the Wiriyamu story, though they remain crucial to our understanding of Church–state relations during the period of the Wiriyamu massacre. These interviews are with Father Joseph of Zóbuè Seminary and the adjoining mission; Padre Giacono Palagi and Padre Claudio, both of Verona Missions; Padre Francisco Correia, head of the Jesuit Mission in Maputo; and Padre Enrique Ferrando, founder of the Burgos Mission in Mucumbura.

The original ferric oxide tapes from which the interviews are drawn are practically inaudible now. Serious efforts are afoot to rescue them, and this effort is headed by one of the best digital sound designers in Hollywood.[10] Although all respondents understood the interviews would be published either intact or in a redacted format, each complete text was sent to the appropriate author for review. The few that responded, suggested edits, further redactions, and corrections—and these were incorporated into the collection presented here. For transcripts of interviewees now deceased and those without an editorial response, I took the precaution of excising sensitive information likely to have met their disapproval were they on this side of the veil or had they responded to my query.

Readers will note the book reuses maps and photographs from the earlier monograph but omits fifteen images that could have enhanced the text's visuals. These images proved costly to obtain, but most of them are easy to procure from the Internet using Google Images or similar image and video search engines. The images in question are of General Hama Thai, Kalifornia Kaniveti, João Xavier,

---

[10]Marc Aramian of Crunch Entertainment, accessed February 3, 2019, www.marcaramian.com.

António Chuva Culher, Enéria Tenente, Vasco Tenente, Kudangirana, Magaissa, Baera, Djemusse, Irmã Lúcia Saez de Ugarte, Mildred Neville, Hugh O'Shaughnessy, and Christopher Wain. I have excluded one image that I took of Captain Antonino Melo. He is seated on his living room sofa with members of his family, who I felt justly deserved protection from needless public exposure since they were not party to Wiriyamu.

Fifty-four published scholars—some active in this field of inquiry; others, lay readers—helped me decide which of the three photographs to use for this book's front cover: One photograph was of a Portuguese soldier in commando uniform pointing a bayoneted gun at an imaginary victim in the bush. The second photo, which I took of survivors of the last massacre in Djemusse, identified where each survivor stood as they faced a gauntlet of soldiers ready to fire on them. The last image, which I also took, portrayed António Mixone, the massacre survivor at Chaworha, facing the grave of the first victim with a makeshift cross as a headstone. Mixone is seen in the photograph recalling the events of that day to Abidu Karimu, my field research coordinator. Mixone placed the cross to memorialize the events and bear witness to a life lost as head of the local church he helped found in a new location in Wiriyamu some distance away from Chaworha. The majority of scholars and lay readers voted for the Mixone image because of "the centrality of memory and remembrance as themes of the book."[11] "It fits well with oral history . . . is dramatic and specific . . . and with an explanation note would be perfect . . ."[12] And, because the book "contains many stories and many characters, not just the Portuguese soldiers who shot down Mozambicans . . . (placing) . . . actors in balanced spaces, with the dead in the middle."[13]

Two tables help readers with a statistical overview on Wiriyamu: One is a list of interviews included in the book, and the other is a list of massacre victims in the Wiriyamu triangle. Demographic data on the triangle are in footnotes with indications of where to find these in the earlier monograph. Names of former priests appear in both formats, e.g., Padre Júlio Moure and Júlio Moure, Miguel Buendia and Padre Miguel Buendia, Father Adrian Hastings and Adrian Hastings.

The interviews included here formed a small part of a larger reconstructive investigation of the events of that day and the three-day manhunt that followed it, which resulted in 385 dead, identifiable by name and where they had died.[14] The reconstruction work was dynamic, engaging a large body of informants, many of whom

[11]Kathleen Sheldon in an e-mail message to author, July 23, 2019.
[12]Peter Pringle in an e-mail message to author, July 23, 2019.
[13]Jeanne Marie Penvenne in an email to author, July 23, 2019.
[14]This project entailed twenty-eight tape-recorded interviews, eighteen of which were used in the previous book; ninety-six recorded field notes; and 102 data sources recorded in annotated fragments during fieldwork. 216 carefully curated respondents supplied data on Wiriyamu's demographic agronomy, while qualitative data for the project came from an additional pool of thirty informants. Of the oral sources culled, fifteen undergirded the narrative on Wiriyamu's military context in Tete. The anatomy of that day's massacre was pieced together from details provided by twenty-four respondents supported by a group of fact-checkers who worked closely with 216 affected families already mentioned: 107 of these respondents

proved willing to go from place to place to identify key events, and then to wait while my team and I measured distances and jotted down data fragments on bone remnants; boulders, trees, dry creeks, riverbeds; old footpaths; burial sites; who was killed where; who had how many goats, chickens, pigs, cows, goat and cow pens, houses and their location, plus number of wives and children; and remnants of a dais used for rituals to invoke rain.

Were you standing here when you saw him? May I ask you to go where you stood, and you tell me where I should be to spot the place he was as he walked towards Johnny. May I? Did you actually see a soldier pound a child in a pestle with a mortar? If so, can I ask you to tell me where? Where were you standing when you saw it, so I can measure the distance between you and the pestle? Where were you standing in the file before they started shooting? Do you remember who was ahead of you and who was behind you? Was their house here or there? How big was the house? Can you show me?

Sharp-eyed readers will spot a lacuna or two in the book. Very unlike Selma Leydesdorff's work on women's voices on the Bosnian genocide,[15] only three informants in this book are women: Irmã Lúcia Saez de Ugarte, a nurse who treated a survivor's wounded shoulder and then surveyed from the air the killing fields of Wiriyamu; Enéria Tenente, a survivor from the hut set on fire by an exploding grenade in the village of Wiriyamu proper; and Mildred Neville, who hosted Father Adrian Hastings' public discourse on Wiriyamu in London. There is no simple explanation for this slim offering. This type of query-driven forensic reconstruction was designed to identify the who and how of the 385 killed and did not lend itself terribly well to tape-recording sessions with informants tethered to seats, wires, and microphones. The fieldwork days were long and involved, and took informants away from their own economic necessities for daily sustenance in a society largely dominated by patriarchy. The men delegated their obligations predominantly to the womenfolk, many of whom identified as potential interviewers of fellow women survivors.

Those that stayed put had the means to do so, either because they had children that could pick up the chores left unattended or because their participation ensured their voices were heard, and it mattered to them to have their say on record. "I want my children to know what happened," said one informant, then a young girl rescued by the Portuguese commander from the jaws of a burning hut. Unfortunately, her recorded tape oxidized before I could retrieve the text as a transcript. Enéria Tenente fell into this

---

came from Chaworha, thirty from Wiriyamu, thirty from Juawu, fourteen from Riachu, and thirty-five from Djemusse.

[15] Selma Leydesdorff, *Surviving the Bosnian Genocide: The Women of Srebrenica Speak,* trans. Kay Richardson (Bloomington: Indiana University Press, 2015).

Photo 1 Abidu Karimu, Chaworha. Photo by Mustafah Dhada, © 1995.

Photo 2 Senhor Elídio, Tete city. Photo by Mustafah Dhada, © 1995.

category, that is, of an informant who took her testimony seriously in the project and was willing to sacrifice time and domestic chores to that end.

One other factor entered the mix behind this lacuna—my response to eyewitness accounts by women. At one point during Enéria's testimony, she recoiled from describing her escape from the blazing fire.

"I would never want to go back to Wiriyamu. Every time Wiriyamu is mentioned, I see my mother. Then my eyes don't shut; every blink brings her alive. She stands in front of me *parada*—motionless. Memories of death and of dying women and children still haunt me. I cannot wipe away the memory of how the heat of guns and burning grenades lit up the roofs of our homes. I cry but cannot close my eyes. If I do, I see flames; I see moving arms, stretched high, screaming for the sky to help."

That recollection triggered childhood trauma from my colonially induced separation from my own mother, which I did not care to revisit at the time, nor admit publicly then, but I do so now, and I have sought repeated professional help to overcome the ensuing trauma.[16]

We stopped the session that day, left fieldwork for rest and recreation, and then regrouped after a series of long debriefing sessions on how to proceed. In the subsequent sessions, as indicated in the earlier monograph, we successfully averted such episodes.

Table 2 List of Massacre Victims

Location	Adult male	Adult female	Young male (1 month–15 years old)	Young female (1 month–15 years old)	Fetus (1–9 months)	Total
Chaworha	32	27	38	19	2	118
Juawu	12	14	20	9	0	55
Wiriyamu	7	14	9	11	0	41
Djemusse	27	34	27	16	0	104
Riachu		1				1
In the triangle unspecified location	10	13	28	14	1	66
Total	88	103	122	69	3	385

[16]This is now a burgeoning field of inquiry given the dramatic rise of returning veterans from the war across the globe. Marwa Shoeb, Harvey Weinstein, and Richard Mollica, "The Harvard Trauma Questionnaire: Adapting a Cross-Cultural Instrument for Measuring Torture, Trauma and Posttraumatic Stress Disorder in Iraqi Refugees," *International Journal of Social Psychiatry* 53, 5 (2007): 447–63; and, Donna L. Schuman, Karen A. Lawrence, and Natalie Pope, "Broadcasting War Trauma: An Exploratory Netnography of Veterans' YouTube Vlogs," *Qualitative Health Research* 29, 3 (2018): 357–70.

My interpreters, Abidu Karimu and Senhor Elídio, their assistants, and field research workers were impacted too by this testimony and took extra precautions from then onward not to trigger such episodes in us and in our informants.

This explanation in no way mitigates the small number of female voices in the book. Had I been better educated and self-aware of the corrective importance of gender equity in historiography more so than perhaps I am today, I am sure I would have found ways to include women survivors to voice their ordeals and those of 171 women who perished in Wiriyamu. After all, they constituted 44.53 percent of the total 385 dead.[17] Their lives mattered, and they deserved to be heard, as did the voices of those that survived! They are both now, to my utter professional remorse, buried as data elements that undergirded Chapter 9 of the previous monograph, which brought the Wiriyamu triangle alive as a thriving community before the massacre.[18]

The literature in this field of erasures is now awash with texts on precolonial, colonial, and postcolonial violence both in general[19] and in specific case studies.[20] It covers a swathe of territory ranging from studies on the My Lai massacre[21] to that in Nanking,[22] the Armenian genocide,[23] the Herero–Nama genocide,[24] the decimation of millions in

---

[17]The total tally of 385 *named* dead excludes "casualties during the three days manhunt, Jane and John Does untraceable due to memory loss, and victims brought to the DGS headquarters for in-depth interrogation. Of the 385, 118 died in Chaworha, 55 in Juawu, 41 in Wiriyamu, 104 in Djemusse, and one in Riachu. The location of the rest cannot be specified." "The massacre wiped out 30 percent of Chaworha's population. Djemusse suffered the second heaviest casualty followed by Juawu. Djemusse's demographic erasure stood at 27% and that of Juawu at 14. 29%. Wiriyamu suffered the lightest causality, followed by Riachu. 89% of Wiriyamu survived the onslaught. Riachu's near intact escape is deceptive in that its casualties are likely to remain buried in the list for the fallen at unspecified locations. That list of casualties constitutes 27% of the total number killed." Dhada, *The Portuguese Massacre of Wiriyamu*, 159–72 and 190–97. The monograph gives the estimated population in the triangle as well, see tables two to seven, 181–90.

[18]See, Dhada, *The Portuguese Massacre of Wiriyamu*, 139–59.

[19]Ben Kiernan, *Blood and Soil: A World History of Genocide and Extermination from Sparta to Darfur* (New Haven: Yale University Press, 2007); Robert Gellately and Ben Kiernan, eds., *The Specter of Genocide: Mass Murder in Historical Perspective* (Cambridge: Cambridge University Press, 2003); Timothy J. Stapleton, *A History of Genocide in Africa* (Santa Barbara: Praeger, 2017); Martin Thomas, *Violence and Colonial Order: Police, Workers and Protest in the European Colonial Empires, 1918–1940* (Cambridge: Cambridge University Press, 2012); Martin Thomas, Bob Moore, and L. J. Butler, *Crises of Empire: Decolonization and Europe's Imperial States,* 2nd ed. (London: Bloomsbury Academic Press, 2015).

[20]Jocelyn Alexander, JoAnn McGregor, and Terence Ranger, *Violence and Memory: One Hundred Years in the 'Dark Forests' of Matabeleland* (Oxford: James Currey, 2000); and Heike I. Schmidt, *Colonialism and Violence in Zimbabwe: A History of Suffering* (Oxford: James Currey, 2013).

[21]James S. Olson and Randy Robert, *My Lai: A Brief History with Documents* (New York: Bedford/St Martin's, 1998).

[22]Iris Chang, *The Rape of Nanking: The Forgotten Holocaust of World War II* (New York: Basic Books, 2011).

[23]Electronic archives at www.armenocide.de holds all German materials on the Armenian Genocide in English translation. See also University of Minnesota's online archive: www.chgs.umn.edu/educational/; as well as www.chgs.umn.edu/educational/.

[24]David Olusoga and Casper W. Erichsen, *The Kaiser's Holocaust: Germany's Forgotten Genocide and the Colonial Roots of Nazism* (London: Faber and Faber, 2011).

the Congo, the so-called free state under Leopold II,[25] the Mau Mau rebellion,[26] and the genocides in Rwanda,[27] Bosnia,[28] and Cambodia.[29] As Ben Kiernan's *Blood and Soil* cited earlier suggests, this list is by no means systematic or omniscient; it continues to grow as we enter the age of killer drones.[30]

This study, however, fits a niche in the field of eyewitness accounts,[31] more specifically between Totten and Ubaldo's 224-page monograph of eleven survivor interviews of the 1994 genocide in Rwanda,[32] and Svetlana Alexievich's eyewitness accounts[33]—with notable differences; the voices in this book cover a wider range of events before, during, and after the massacre. Whereas Alexievich's texts are, to quote one anonymous reviewer of this book proposal, "a polyphonic rendering of the human experience of war and violence," which is to say her texts actively interpolate the voices of informants with hers, this book gives the voices on Wiriyamu ample room to speak at will, allowing readers to live the experience from primary sources in one fluid rendition. In addition, the book includes the voice of the commanding officer on the role he played in the massacre, allowing readers to experience both sides of the coin, insurgent and counterinsurgent.

With all this said, it is worth remembering that Wiriyamu was neither unique in the annals of colonial or postcolonial counterinsurgency, even in a contemporaneous context,[34] nor was it a behavioral aberration in Portugal's pacification campaigns that

---

[25]Adam Hochschild, *King Leopold's Ghost: A Story of Greed, Terror, and Heroism in Colonial Africa* (New York: Mariner Books, 1999).

[26]David Anderson, *Histories of the Hanged: The Dirty War in Kenya and the End of Empire* (New York: W. W. Norton, 2015); and Caroline Elkins, *Imperial Reckoning: The Untold Story of Britain's Gulag in Kenya* (New York: Holt Paperbacks, 2005).

[27]Phillip Gourevitch, *We Wish to Inform You That Tomorrow We Will Be Killed With Our Families: Stories From Rwanda* (New York: Picador, 1999); and Information, Intelligence and the U.S. Response at www.gwu.edu/%7Ensarchiv/NSAEBB/NSAEBB117/index.htm. Evidence of global inaction is to be found at www.gwu.edu/%7Ensarchiv/NSAEBB/NSAEBB53/index.html. See also the electronic repository for Rwanda related materials at www.gwu.edu/%7Ensarchiv/NSAEBB/NSAEBB119/index.htm. Additional Rwanda genocide related documents consisting of 4,705 declassified documents that address the situation in Rwanda are to be found at www.rwandadocumentsproject.net/gsdl/cgibin/library.

[28]Leydesdorff, *Surviving the Bosnian Genocide.*

[29]See the classic text, François Ponchaud, *Cambodia: Year Zero* (New York: Penguin Books, 1978). Primary materials can be reviewed at Cambodian Genocide Databases (CGDB), https://gsp.yale.edu/cambodian-geno cide-databases-cgdb.

[30]See, Amrit Singh, *Death By Drone: Civilian Harm Caused by U.S. Targeted Killings in Yemen* (New York: Open Society Foundation, 2015).

[31]Samuel Totten and William S. Parsons, eds., *Centuries of Genocide: Essays and Eyewitness Accounts* (New York: Routledge, 2012); *The River Ran Red,* directed by Michael Hagopian (1988); *The Devil Came on Horseback,* directed by Ricki Stern and Anne Sundberg (Break Thru Films, 2007); Ponchaud, *Cambodia*; and *Shake Hands with The Devil: The Journey of Romeo Dallaire,* directed by Peter Raymont (White Pine Pictures, 2004).

[32]Totten and Ubaldo, eds., *We Cannot Forget.*

[33]Svetlana Alexievich, *The Unwomanly Face of War: An Oral History of Women in World War II* (New York: Random House, 2017); Svetlana Alexievich, *Zinky Boys: Soviet Voices from the Afghanistan War* (New York: W. W. Norton, 1992); and Svetlana Alexievich, *Last Witnesses: An Oral History of the Children of World War II* (New York: Random House, 2019).

[34]Helen Lackner, *Yemen in Crisis: Road to War* (London: Verso, 2019).

presaged the last colonial war on its three fronts in Africa.[35] Further, it was inevitable, given the context of the armed struggle, Portuguese counterinsurgency, and the repeated failures of the local leadership in the Wiriyamu triangle to navigate the conflicting demands between two adversaries, Frelimo and the Portuguese army. What was unique to Wiriyamu was the confluence of forces that brought it to light six months after it happened. Here, Wiriyamu tipped the balance in favor of the Luso-African liberation movements when, nine months after the revelation, Portugal's very own men-at-arms disembowelled Caetano's regime of its African possessions.

---

[35]Felícia Cabrita, *Massacres em África*.

ACKNOWLEDGMENTS

This book has leaned heavily on my students and peers, who instigated me to write it and then helped me reshape the way it is presented here. I want to single out my undergraduate students of the History of African Decolonization course of spring quarter 2015 and 2016 at California State University, Bakersfield (CSUB). They helped me transcribe sections of the interviews, which are excluded here, regrettably. Their input in and outside the classroom, however, informed the structural spine of the penultimate draft of this book. Peer reviewers, on the other hand, proved instrumental with their copious and carefully crafted suggestions, which, when acted upon, markedly strengthened the book's final objective to reach a wider audience. They rightfully own the strength of this book. I am happy to own the rest!

CSUB's History Department granted release time for one course during the spring semester 2017 to get the bulk of the transcription redone, and the department's Historical Research Group facilitated discussions on getting this work to reach a broader audience. The Office of the Dean of Arts and Humanities funded my travels to pitch a seminal chapter of this book on oral methods at a conference panel of the American Historical Association (AHA), in January 2017.

Three entities funded this work: the Fulbright Commission, 1994–1995; Foundation for Science and Technology (FCT/MEC) Portugal, Programa Operacional Competitividade e Inovação'2 2020, PTDC/CVI-ANT/6100/2014, POCI-01-0145-FEDER-016859; and the Office of the Provost, CSUB, 2017–2018, then headed by Dr. Jenny Zorn. Paula Maria Meneses of the Centro de Estudos Sociais (CES), Universidade de Coimbra, procured additional funds from the above-referred FCT grant to underwrite part of my research stay in Lisbon.

My undergraduate students of the History of African Decolonization course of spring quarter 2019 edited the penultimate draft of this text as part of their course assignment. Jasmine Armstrong, applied history intern and graduating senior assigned to this project, edited and checked the footnotes of the final version of the manuscript presented to Bloomsbury for the second peer-review process. Two consummate professionals handled this monograph with utmost care and compassion for the spoken and the written word. One was Maria Batty who copy-edited the final page proofs of the book, and the other was Rennie Alphonsa, Senior Project Manager, Deanta Global, http://www.deantaglobal. com, who oversaw the digital processing of the text from start to finish with flawless integrity. I am utterly grateful to both. Needless to add, neither my students nor my peers or those mentioned elsewhere on this page are responsible for omissions and errors; I am.

Mustafah Dhada
Professor of History, CSUB
Associate Researcher, Center of Social Studies, Coimbra University
dhada@mindspring.com

INTRODUCTION

Portugal's Colonial Wars and Mass Violence

On April 25, 1974, Portugal's armed forces ousted Marcelo Caetano from power, ending the colonial wars in Africa. Until then Portugal had successfully fought back demands for transparency in its colonies with a formidable strategy of global silence on its colonies, by deploying diplomatic sophistry and counter-information.[1] Contemporary historical works place *O Movimento das Forças Armadas* (MFA), the Armed Forces Movement, at the center of this event, as liberators freeing Portugal from Caetano's political incarceration. The role of women, incidentally, is resoundingly absent in the majority of contemporaneous accounts on the revolution![2]

Two significant historical events coaxed Portugal's imperial discourse away from Caetano's corporatist politics and polity,[3] toward its own liberation; Portugal's complex exposure to the African liberation wars was one such set of events.[4] The liberation wars, in Guinea-Bissau in particular, tutored many officers into questioning Portugal's *raison d'être* in Africa. Included in this group was no less than Guinea-Bissau's governor general, António Sebastião Ribeiro de Spínola, whose text, *Portugal e o Futuro*, gave voice to those who felt the war, though militarily winnable, was politically lost.[5]

---

[1]William Minter, *Portuguese Africa and the West* (New York: Monthly Review Press, 1972).
[2]Hugo Gil Ferreira, *Portugal's Revolution: Ten Years On* (Cambridge: Cambridge University Press, 2011); Rona M. Fields, *Portuguese Revolution and the Armed Focus Movement* (Santa Barbara: Praeger, 1975); Douglas Porch, *Portuguese Armed Forces and the Revolution* (Stanford: Hoover Institution, 1977); and Insight Team of *The Sunday Times, Insight on Portugal: The Year of The Captains* (London: Andre Deutsch, 1975).
[3]Howard J. Wiarda, *Corporatism and Development: The Portuguese Experience* (Boston: University of Massachusetts Press, 1977).
[4]Patrick Chabal, *Amílcar Cabral: Revolutionary Leadership and People's War* (Cambridge: Cambridge University Press, 1983); Mustafah Dhada, *Warriors at Work: How Guinea Was Really Set Free* (Niwot: University Press of Colorado, 1993); Sayaka Funada-Classen, *The Origins of War in Mozambique: A History of Unity and Division*, trans. Masako Osada (Cape Town: African Minds, 2013); John A. Marcum, *The Angolan Revolution, Vol 1: The Anatomy of an Explosion* (Cambridge: MIT Press, 1969); John A. Marcum, *The Angolan Revolution, Vol 2: Exile Politics and Guerrilla Warfare, 1962–1976* (Cambridge: MIT Press, 1978); and A. J. Venter, *Portugal's Guerrilla Wars in Africa: Lisbon's Three Wars in Angola, Mozambique and Portuguese Guinea, 1961–74* (Southhill, UK: Helion, 2013).
[5]António Sebastião Ribeiro de Spínola, *Portugal e o Futuro*, (Lisbon: Editora Arcádia, 1974).

Photo 3 *The London Times*, Wiriyamu revelation. Personal archives. Photo by Mustafah Dhada, © 1995.

The other set of events was the Mozambique Catholic Church's revelations of Portugal's complicity in colonial mass violence, which compounded the gravity of this discontent in Spínola's text. These revelations, in particular of the Wiriyamu massacre, shattered the credibility of Caetano's carefully engineered global silence on its abuse of human rights in Africa,[6] and ended Portugal's rule in colonial Mozambique.

---

[6]Adrian Hastings, *Wiriyamu* (London: Search Press, 1973).

In fact, the end of the Portuguese empire in Mozambique began and ended with mass violence. It started with the slaughter of protestors demanding better wages and labor conditions in Mueda,[7] northern Mozambique, on June 16, 1960, and ended seventeen months after the wholesale carnage of civilians suspected of harboring insurgents in Wiriyamu on December 16, 1972.

Four years after Mueda, several nationalist organizations came together to form the Frente de Libertação de Moçambique (Front for the Liberation of Mozambique, Frelimo),[8] under the leadership of Dr. Eduardo Mondlane, an American-educated sociologist whose formative education had been sponsored by the Swiss and American Protestant missionary societies.[9] Frelimo subsequently demanded Portugal free Mozambique peacefully or face an armed struggle. Portugal refused, viewing Frelimo and its demand for independence as a communist-inspired conspiracy, threatening the very core of Portugal's mission in Africa, namely, to propagate and protect Western civilization.[10]

One cleric within the empire thought differently—Dom Sebastião Soares de Resende, bishop of the diocese of Beira, which initially included the then-district of Tete, where Wiriyamu was located. Born in Porto and educated as a philosopher in Rome, Resende was a sensitive, sentient soul, serious about his role as a priest and prelate, conservative

---

[7]"Reunião de indígenas perturbada por agitadores estrangeiros que foram repelidos," *O Século*, June 19, 1960; Alberto Joaquim Chipande, "The massacre of Mueda," *Mozambique Revolution* 43 (1970): 12–14; "Mueda evocada em Portugal," *Notícias* June 13, 1981; "Mueda: memórias de um massacre," *Tempo* 609 (June 13, 1982): 24; *Notícias* (June 19, 1982); Yussuf Adam and Hilário Alumasse Dyuti, "Entrevista: o massacre de Mueda— falam testemunhas," *Arquivo* 14 (1993): 117–128; Michel Cahen, "The Mueda Case and Maconde Political Ethnicity," *Africana Studia* (Porto) No. 2 (1999): 29–46; Guilherme Almor De Alpoím Calvão, Comandante da Marinha reformado e ex-combatente na Guerra Colonial, "Quantos Morreram em Mueda?" *Jornal Público* June 16, 2002; "Quantos Morreram En Mueda," Macua.org, accessed December 16, 2011, www.Macua.Org/ Quantos_Morreram_Em_Mueda.htm; Joel Neves Tembe, "Uhura na Kazi: Recapturing MANU Nationalism through the Archive," *Kronos* 39 (November 2013): 257–79; and Paolo Israel, "Mueda massacre: The musical archive," *Journal of Southern African Studies* 43 (6): 1157–1179, DOI: 10.1080/03057070.2017.1382186. See also John A. Marcum with Edmund Burke III, Michael W. Clough (eds.), *Conceiving Mozambique* (London: Palgrave Macmillan, 2018), pp. 19–21. He highlights what he calls the Mueda massacre counter-story by Michel Cahen.

[8]Centro de Estudos Africanos (CEA), Universidade Eduardo Mondlane, Pasta 967. 5 25/I. The groups were the Mozambican African National Union (MANU), the National Democratic Union of Mozambique (UDENAMO), and the National African Union of Independent Mozambique (UNAMI).

[9]Teresa Cruz e Silva, "The Influence of the Swiss Mission on Eduardo Mondlane (1930–61)," *Journal of Religion in Africa* 28, 2 (1998): 187–209; Alf Helgesson, *Church, State and People in Mozambique: An Historical Study with Special Emphasis on Methodist Developments in the Inhambane Region* (Uppsala: Studia Missionalia Upsaliensia, 1994), p. 442; Teresa Cruz e Silva, "Igrejas Protestantes no Sul de Moçambique e nacionalismo: O Caso da 'Missão Suíça' (1940–1974)," *Estudos Moçambicanos*, 10 (1992): 19–39; and Teresa Cruz e Silva, *Protestant Churches and the Formation of Political Consciousness in Southern Mozambique (1930-1974)* (Basel: P. Schlettwein Publishing, 2001). For background on Mondlane see: *Panaf Great Lives, Eduardo Mondlane* (London: Panaf, 1972); Herbert Shore, "Resistance and Revolution in the Life of Eduardo Mondlane," quoted in Eduardo Mondlane, *The Struggle for Mozambique* (London: Zed Press, 1983), pp. xii–xxxi; Barry Munslow, *Mozambique: The Revolution and Its Origins* (Harlow: Longman, 1983), pp. 62, 66, 69, 81, 89, 98–105, 107, 110–11, 114–15, 119, and 139; and Livio Sansone, "Eduardo Mondlane and the Social Sciences," *Vibrant— Virtual Brazilian Anthropology* 10, 2 (2013): 73–111. Archival materials on Mondlane consulted in the Herbert Shore Collection, Oberlin College included: Series 1. "Biographical Files, 1950s–2003," and Series 4. 1952–1966. Subseries 1, "Writings by Eduardo Mondlane, 1952–68, n.d.," Box 1. Catalogue of materials in the collection accessed December 16, 2012, can be viewed at http://tinyurl.com/l4kgxm3.

[10]"News in Brief: Portuguese Africa," *Africa Report* 11, 2 (1966): 30–31.

in temperament, and a believer in the Portuguese imperial mission in the colonies. He arrived in Beira in 1943. Over time, however, he grew troubled by what he saw, particularly concerning social inequality and the economic conditions of the majority of his black congregants in the diocese.[11] Once exposed to new thinking under Vatican II,[12] which saw the Church as a ministry for social advancement, he embraced its teaching wholeheartedly and ceased to identify his prelacy with the Portuguese empire, which viewed the Church as a promoter of the colonial state policy.[13]

Thereafter, Tete witnessed a change under his leadership. He hired a slew of foreign-born and foreign-educated missionaries aligned with his vision of a progressive church for the colony. Notable among the new hires were White Fathers, staffing the seminary in Zóbuè, the mission nearby, and missions in Lundo and Muraça; and the Burgos Fathers, who were secular priests seconded from their respective dioceses on the Spanish mainland to serve in Tete's remote areas, most notably Unkanha, Marara, Mucumbura, Mutarara, and Changara, and in more accessible locations, namely the city of Tete, nearby Matundo, and the coal-mining town of Moatize—to name but three.[14]

Meanwhile, Frelimo's armed struggle began in earnest, rapidly spreading insurgency in the north of Mozambique. By 1968, four years into the colonial war, it opened a new front in Tete, from which it had to withdraw almost immediately. Neighboring Malawi opposed Frelimo's logistic activity on its territory; and without its support, the front was unsustainable.[15] A year later, both Frelimo and the Portuguese military establishment underwent dramatic changes in leadership, which resulted in changes in military strategy and tactics on both sides. Frelimo elected a new leader, Samora Machel, a seasoned military commander trained in guerrilla warfare, with a clear vision of the armed struggle to further the party's liberation agenda. The Portuguese government, on the other hand, appointed a new commander, Kaúlza de Arriaga, a trained engineer, well

---

[11]These observations are abstracted from his writings. See, in particular, Sebastião Soares de Resende, *Os Grandes Relativos Humanos em Moçambique* (Porto: Livraria Nelita Editora, 1957); Sebastião Soares de Resende, *Responsibilidades dos Leigos* (Porto: Oficinas Gráficas da Sociedade de Papelaria, 1957); Sebastião Soares de Resende, *Problemas do Ensino Missionário* (Beira: Tip. EAO, 1962); and Sebastião Soares de Resende, *Um Moçambique Melhor* (Lisbon: Livraria Morais Editora, 1963).

[12]Documents of the Second Vatican Council are electronically available in Vatican archives at www.vatican.va/archive/hist_councils/ii_vatican_council/.

[13]A. Carlos Lima, *Aspectos da Liberdade Religiosa. Caso do Bispo da Beira* (Lisbon/Braga: Diário do Minho, 1970); Gulamo Tajú, "Dom Sebastião Soares de Resende, Primeiro Bispo da Beira: Notas Para Uma Cronologia," *Arquivo, Boletim do Arquivo Histórico de Moçambique* (October 1989): 149–76; Carlos A. Moreira Azevedo, "Perfil biográfico de D. Sebastião Soares de Resende," *Lusitania Sacra* 2 6 (1994): 391–415; Carlos Lima, *Caso do Bispo da Beira, Documentos* (Porto: Civilização, 1990); and Arquivo Histórico Diplomático (AHD), D. Altino Ribeiro Santana, *Bispo da Beira, 1973–74*, PT/AHD/MU/GM/GNP/RNP/0456/07052. To save valuable print space only the accession codes of PIDE documents are cited from hereon.

[14]"Mozambique in London," *The Tablet Archives*, accessed December 24, 2013, http://preview.tinyurl.com/o99ctgj. See also, Eric Morier-Genoud, "The Catholic Church, Religious Orders and the Making of Politics in Colonial Mozambique: The Case of the Diocese of Beira, 1940–1974" (PhD diss., State University of New York, 2005).

[15]*Africa Report*, 1 (1967): 30.

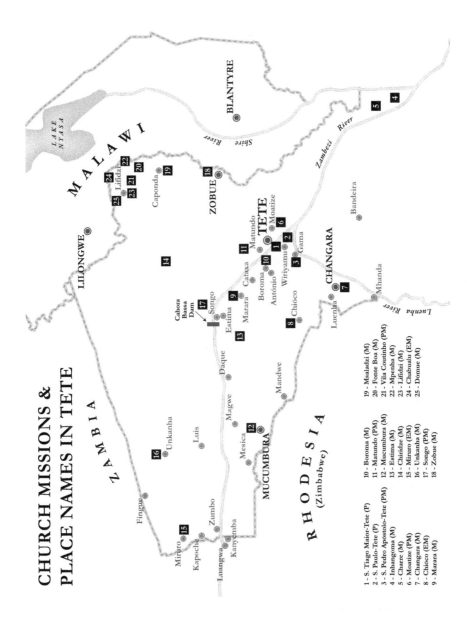

CHURCH MISSIONS & PLACE NAMES IN TETE

1 - S. Tiago Maior-Tete (P)
2 - S. Paulo-Tete (P)
3 - S. Pedro Apóstolo-Tete (PM)
4 - Inhangoma (M)
5 - Charre (M)
6 - Moatize (PM)
7 - Changara (M)
8 - Chióco (EM)
9 - Marara (M)
10 - Boroma (M)
11 - Matundo (PM)
12 - Mucumbura (M)
13 - Estima (M)
14 - Chiridze (M)
15 - Miruro (EM)
16 - Unkanha (M)
17 - Songo (PM)
18 - Zobue (M)
19 - Msaladzi (M)
20 - Fonte Boa (M)
21 - Vila Coutinho (PM)
22 - Mpenha (M)
23 - Lifidzi (M)
24 - Chabualu (EM)
25 - Domue (M)

Map 2 Church missions and place names in Tete. Map by Mustafah Dhada, © 1973.

5

versed in counterinsurgency,[16] who was given a free hand in bringing Frelimo's guerrilla war to a close; and he nearly did, when upon his arrival in Northern Mozambique, he mounted a formidable assault on Frelimo bases in northern Mozambique under Operation Gordian Knot. That operation resulted in deep losses for Frelimo, but not total annihilation.

Its surviving units regrouped to launch a tri-frontal offensive, two in northern Mozambique, and one in Tete. By this time, Zambia had gained independence under Kenneth Kaunda, a keen supporter of liberation for the entire region of southern Africa, which included Mozambique. With that logistical support assured, Frelimo appointed several commanders to lead the front in Tete. Notable among them were Major General Bonifácio Massamba Gruveta, General Mariano de Araújo Matsinhe, Lieutenant General António Hama Thai, and Commandant Raimundo Dalepa, to mention but four. The latter two commanders were charismatic and skillful warriors, with a keenly developed understanding of Portuguese counterinsurgency. Together, they came to dominate the Frelimo guerrilla landscape in Tete, with Dalepa focusing around Unkanha, Mucumbura and Luenha, south of Wiriyamu, liberating Lieutenant General António Hama Thai to advance toward Mozambique's midriff, just north of Beira.

The Church's socially transformative work in Tete worked in Frelimo's favor once its leaders opened the Tete front in 1970, three years after Bishop Resende's death. Tete churches' black congregants were already sensitized to issues of human rights and human dignity under the rubric of Vatican II, exactly the same set of issues with which Frelimo was fighting to liberate Mozambique. Once in Tete, the Frelimo forces gained momentum, spreading from the Unkanha Mission headed by Padre Alberto Fonte Castellã to south of the river Zambezi in and near Mucumbura, where Padre Ferrando, a visionary Burgos priest, had founded a Catholic mission. Within two years, Frelimo spread throughout Tete,[17] threatening Portugal's key installations: the military regional headquarters in Tete; the Cahora Bassa dam, approaching completion; the Moatize coal mines; and the main highway leading to Beira and Rhodesia, which Ian Smith had by then declared unilaterally independent.

In the face of this insurgency, Arriaga placed Colonel, later Brigadier, Armindo Videira, a protégé of his, in charge of counterinsurgency, an ideal choice in his view.[18] Videira had a distaste for compromises and for taking prisoners, preferring to engage in preemptive strikes to eliminate suspected enemy bases, rendering these areas into fire-free zones. In a fascist empire under dictatorship, Videira had a free hand to do just as he pleased. The only restraints on him were the church missions in the vicinity staffed

---

[16]General Kaúlza de Arriaga, *História das Tropas Páraquedistas Portuguesas* 3, BCP 21, CTP. 1, accessed January 1, 2010, http://preview.tinyurl.com/qzeovqb.

[17]PT/TT/D-F/001/00004, December 15, 1971.

[18]A brief biography on Brigadier Videira is to be found in *Operacional: Defesa, Forças Armadas de Segurança*, accessed June 13, 2012, http://preview.tinyurl.com/l7jdxrv; and Gen. Kaúlza de Arriaga, *História das Tropas Páraquedistas Portuguesas* 3, BCP 21, CTP.1, accessed January 1, 2010, http://preview.tinyurl.com/m8bfh94. Additional information can be gleaned from two blog sites, both catering to the military alumni, accessed November 18, 2011, http://preview.tinyurl.com/kpgcds4; and http://estrolabio.blogs.sapo.pt/2011/02/07/.

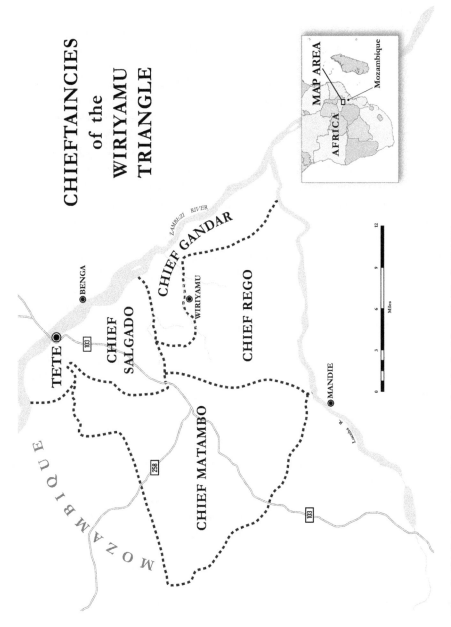

Map 3 Chieftaincies of the Wiriyamu triangle. Map by Mustafah Dhada, © 1973.

predominantly by non-Portuguese priests and nuns, nearly all subscribing to the values underpinning the Vatican II doctrine on social change, nearly all opposed to Videira's form of nihilistic counterinsurgency.[19]

Once in the driver's seat, Videira transformed Tete's theater of war into a battleground for colonial mass violence. A year after Frelimo's entry, Tete then witnessed a series of massacres, one at Estima and one near the Catholic Mission of Mucumbura, both of which the Burgos Fathers documented with meticulous care, and with which they confronted the colonial authorities. In the face of protests from priests in the area, the Mucumbura Mission was ordered closed, liberating Portuguese counterinsurgency from priestly restraints.[20] By then, Dalepa's forces had moved nearer Tete, to a base around Luenha, with the intention of establishing a more direct logistical supply route linking Zóbuè with Luenha, south of Wiriyamu, where António Hama Thai's forces were poised to attack Portuguese army convoys.[21] In October Dalepa enlisted Wiriyamu's help, and one goat herder, Bulachu Pensadu Zambezi, took note of his entry into the village. Aware of this new insurgent peril on their doorsteps, the Portuguese surmised the chieftaincies of the Wiriyamu triangle to be an insurgent-infested node. On December 16, 1972, they moved to destroy it.

They summoned Antonino Melo, a young commander of a specially trained counterinsurgency unit to appear in Zona Operacional de Tete (ZOT), the Portuguese army's regional headquarters in Tete city. He got there at six-thirty in the morning. He was told to take the men of his unit and get rid of insurgent fighters, who were believed to be embedded in Wiriyamu in a cluster of five villages south of the city, wedged in a triangle between the main road linking Tete and Changara, the Zambezi River to the southeast, and Luenha, the tributary south of the Zambezi River. Thus began Marosca, which failed to eradicate Dalepa's men, killing instead 385 civilian men, women, and children, and destroying livestock and granaries in the five villages identified as Chaworha, Juawu, Wiriyamu, Djemusse, and Riachu. The total tally excluded casualties unaccounted for during the massacre, casualties from the three-day manhunt that followed the massacre, and victims brought to the police headquarters for in-depth interrogations. Seven months later, *The London Times* published the story on its front page.

Had Melo arrived at ZOT earlier than six-thirty, he would have bumped into Domingo Kansande, a young seminarian heading, via ZOT, into the triangle to visit his family near the Changara Catholic Mission, then headed by Padre Vicente Berenguer. That evening both men were in the region, but they failed to cross paths. Melo and his men had camped some distance from the place of the carnage. Unbeknownst to him, Kansande spent the next two days near Melo's encampment surrounded by escapees and survivors. With a pencil in hand, he jotted down on a butcher's paper the names of the men, women, and children killed during the Marosca cleanup. That is how the first incomplete list of the dead was compiled, which went on to feed *The London Times'* story.

---

[19]Thomas H. Henriksen, *Revolution and Counterrevolution: Mozambique's War of Independence 1964–1974* (Westport: Greenwood Press, 1983), p. 130.
[20]Enrique Ferrando, interview by author, Madrid, Spain, 1995.
[21]PT/TT/PIDE/D-A/1/2826-10, June 11, 1973.

Melo's cleanup was routine. They and their cohorts had conducted hundreds of these before Marosca and continued to do so after it. It was like any other cleanup operation, quick and to the point. Normally, they returned to base after a cleanup and then were airlifted to rest and recuperate at a resort before a new deployment. This time, after the Wiriyamu erasure they were sent to the Gorongoza mountains south of Wiriyamu, where another carnage of civilians occurred during their stay in Inhaminga.[22] The only unusual aspect of this cleanup at Wiriyamu was the presence of a small unit of the Portuguese secret police assigned to Melo's men to interrogate the villagers on the insurgent whereabouts. Two police operatives familiar with the area led this band of interrogators. They were Johnny Kongorhogondo and Chico Kachavi. Soon after the cleanup, a female squad of insurgents assassinated Kachavi with a couple of grenades lobbed through a bathroom window, killing him as he showered to get ready for a party that evening where he was listed to perform as the lead drummer.

The Erasure of the Five Villages

We know very little about Marosca. The Portuguese archives are silent. The little that we do know comes to us from survivors, commanders, colonial soldiers, priests, and a nun familiar with the case. At around eleven in the morning, the mother of António Mixone, a survivor of the carnage at Chaworha, noticed a red flag flapping on a pole at the perimeter of her village. She had not seen it until that morning, and neither had António, for that matter. The flagpole spooked her. Could this be the start of something ominous? She was right. A logistics unit of Portuguese counterinsurgents had planted these around the five villages to identify their perimeter from the air. In the meantime, fifteen miles north of Chaworha, Padre Domingo Ferrão, young Domingo Kansande's mentor, was getting ready for his afternoon break. He grabbed a book and notepads and headed to his favorite tree under which to read and write. At around noon, Ferrão heard jets roaring toward the triangle. They then bombed the perimeter, forcing people to flee inward, just as Melo's men and police interrogators attached to his unit prepared to land for the cleanup. In the meantime, the counterinsurgent unit that had put up the flags assumed its logistic backup position around the perimeter to hunt down people fleeing from the triangle.

What followed then is well documented in recent texts but is worth repeating here in its abstracted format to render this book a stand-alone text.[23] Briefly, upon arrival in Chaworha, Chico and Johnny summoned everyone to assemble near the Chief's quintal—yard. The immediate sequence of the events after this is unclear. People

---

[22]Enrique Ferrando, the founder of the Catholic Mission in Mucumbura, confirmed Melo's claims in that such cleanups were a practiced norm in Portuguese counterinsurgency in Tete. Felícia Cabrita, a Portuguese journalist, later affirmed such massacres formed part of Portugal's counterinsurgency in all of its African colonies during the liberation wars of the 1960s and early 1970s.

[23]Mustafah Dhada, "The Wiriyamu Massacre of 1972: Its Context, Genesis, and Revelation," *History in Africa* (2013): 1–31; Mustafah Dhada, *The Portuguese Massacre of Wiriyamu in Colonial Mozambique, 1964–2013* (London: Bloomsbury Academic, 2015).

assembled gradually as uniformed men ferreted them out of their homes. That is how two survivors, the Mixone brothers, were discovered as they prepared to flee. The crowd in Chaworha grew, said Mixone. Johnny stood beside Chico. Why had they refused to move to a Portuguese fortified village in Mpharhamadwe? they were asked. Chief Chaworha replied that they had done no such thing; they were waiting a response assuring them access to water and grazing land for their animals. Chaworha's response failed to appease the interrogators.

The assembled were then asked to clap their hands and told, This is it. They were about to die. They should prepare to meet their Maker. Pandemonium ensued once shooting began. Fifty-three among the assembled near Chief Chaworha's yard fell. As the rest ran to escape, Chico bellowed, "*Aphani Wense! Aphani Wense!* Kill Them All. [Leave no one alive. No witnesses]." The armed men in uniform were ordered to split in two. One group gathered the bodies in a pyre. Aided by "capim" grass, the pyre was set on fire. The other group formed a semicircle within shooting range to kill escapees. António was on the edge of the pyre as was one of his brothers. Both had fallen, unconscious but unhurt. António regained consciousness as the heat of the burning flesh nearby woke him up. He made a dash for it as did his youngest brother, Domingo. Four others escaped from the pyre. The Portuguese armed men, "black and white," fired in their direction. One bullet hit António on the shoulder. Ignoring the wound, he continued to run until he got to Chief Matambo's village. The next day a close relative in the Portuguese militia arrived and took him to have his shoulder wound looked at by the nun Irmã Lúcia Saez de Ugarte, who worked at Tete's hospital.

The killings at Juawu were clinical. Kalifornia Kaniveti, a survivor, ran as the carnage got underway. He slung a goat on the back of his neck and two infants in each arm and descended the mound crossing the squiggly foot track that led to the main road. He then heard a helicopter behind him. He stooped low to avoid the blades, but kept running until he fell, dropping his goat and children. The helicopter above stopped too, hovering nearly motionless. He got up and ran and kept running only to stop again, this time to drink some water from a stream before crossing it. The helicopter then left him there. Kaniveti returned to the site a few days later. He found the place deserted. Dogs and predators were there, pecking on the rotting meat. He did not dare go to the Wiriyamu village. He took two goats with him and dashed back to Mpharhamadwe, where he settled eventually. He never returned to Juawu.

The killings at Wiriyamu were as swift as those at Juawu, but a bit more nuanced. While Melo's men ignited huts brimming with people, Melo himself directed the shoving of people into Tenente Valeta's hut, one of the largest in the village. The task proved easy since many were already there for a social event. At one point a young girl, then under ten, held Melo's leg in a tight grip, refusing to let him go. Melo didn't have the heart to send her into the hut that was about to be set on fire. Instead he ordered his men to retrieve her mother from the hut and told them both to flee.

With several unpinned grenades thrown in, the hut was slammed shut just as the grenade blast lifted up the thatched roof. Many perished in that hut and the village. Several of the survivors told the world of their escape. With a swift cleanup complete just before sunset, Melo and his men headed to set up camp a distance from the site, hunting escapees on the way.

Djemusse's cleanup took longer. Chico and Johnny played a central role here as interrogators. Where were they hiding Frelimo? Did they know their bases? "Reveal what you know or die," recall Kudangirana, Magaissa, Baera, and Djemusse, four survivors from Djemusse. At some point a helicopter arrived but hovered above ground on the left of the baobab tree that framed Djemusse's entrance to pick up a handful of "confessors" for in-depth interrogations at the police headquarters. One eyewitness heard the cries of torture victims emanating from the blood-splattered walls of a police cell: "No, please, no more. Please stop. I don't know any terrorist. *Para, para Chico, por amor de Deus.* Stop, stop Chico, for the love of God."

By sundown the interrogations had outlived their usefulness. There were no more "confessions" to be had. The uniformed armed men split in two; one formed a wide gauntlet, while the other group stood in a semicircle to cull escapees for the final kill. Upon instruction, Djemusse's people formed a line facing their smoldering homes. The armed men ordered the assembled to run for their lives, which they did. It is unclear how many escaped. One zigzagged straight into a smoldering hut. He did not feel the heat, and the smoke probably saved his life. The soldiers, in the end, joined their unit command for the overnight camping to prepare for the next three days' manhunt. Data on the killings in Riachu, the last of the five Wiriyamu villages, are practically non-existent except for fragments suggesting a number of casualties.

On Sunday, December 17, Melo and his men got up early for the three-day manhunt. Survivors fled in three directions, toward Raimundo Dalepa's guerrilla base, northward to join those already settled in the fortified village of Mpharamadwe, where the Portuguese colonial administration wanted them to be and live in the first place, and toward the bus station on the main road leading to Tete. Kansande headed back to see his mentor, to see Padre Ferrão, the list of the dead in his pocket. He took the back roads to avoid detection. By the time he reached the parish school compound in Tete, Mixone and survivors like him had already gathered in small groups at the hospital where Irmã Lúcia did her best to treat the wounded, referring several of them, Mixone included, to see Padre Ferrão and tell him what had happened the day before. To Irmã Lúcia, what she had heard from survivors as she treated their wounds smacked of Mucumbura all over again, but much, much worse. She did not want to get involved in this "mess." She feared she was under police surveillance and could easily fall prey to torture.

Padre Vicente Berenguer was then heading the Changara Mission, as noted earlier. That morning he got up early to prepare for the Sunday mass, during which his congregants and students publicly prayed for the departed souls of Wiriyamu. That is how Padre Berenguer got the news. He knew the place well; he could identify it by a baobab tree, its trunk etched with the name of the main village, one of the five affected by the massacre. Padre Berenguer took the next bus to Tete to find out more about the killings. The bus stopped at the crossing that led to the mouth of the triangle, whence refugees were pouring begging for a free ride on the bus to Tete. The struggle to accommodate them all in a bus nearly full of passengers was a clear sign of the magnitude of the tragedy that had unraveled the night before, and that was still unfolding as the first day of the three-day manhunt got underway. Padre Berenguer took note of the scene, mumbling to himself, "Something has got to be done about this."

Berenguer reached Tete. Padre Ferrão had not seen Mixone yet but was in the thick of interviewing survivors gathered near the hospital and the mission, creating a preliminary list of the dead. He subsequently expanded it to include additional details, which Kansande procured for him with repeated visits to the triangle. The Burgos Fathers had compiled a similar report during the massacre at Mucumbura that had preceded Wiriyamu, and this report had listed the names of individuals killed and where they fell. Using the Mucumbura report as a model, Padre Ferrão produced two lists, which were ultimately revealed in *The London Times*.[24] The first list was on Chaworha and catalogued the names, ages, gender, and marital status of the victims.[25] The second list on Wiriyamu was completed on Saturday, January 6, twenty-one days after the massacre, and included data culled from several sources: the young seminarians and churchgoers from Changara;[26] villagers from several locations near Wiriyamu on the western banks of the Zambezi River; black and white soldiers who, horrified by the events, came forward with information on the killings; and survivors variously located in the triangle. Subsequently, twenty-six stenciled copies were produced for the second edition of the report. All the bishops in the colony received a copy, as did heads of missionary congregations in the colony.

The Burgos Fathers in Tete asked the newly appointed bishop of Tete to raise the matter with Tete's military governor, who assured the priests via the bishop that the matter would receive appropriate attention. Unhappy with the results of the meeting, the bishop escalated the matter up the chain of command during a legal briefing in Lourenço Marques, now Maputo, with the lawyers handling the case of Portuguese-born priests from Macúti, Beira, who had been incarcerated for protesting the Portuguese conduct of war from the church pulpit. The least they could do, he averred, was to bury the putrid dead in the triangle, which posed a public health hazard.[27] On Friday, January 5, 1973, the priests got what they asked for, in a manner of speaking. On the direction of Dr. José Paz, the local medic, Irmã Lúcia flew over Wiriyamu to see for herself the state of the public hazard, which then led the army to bury some of the exposed dead in a communal grave; others too decomposed were dragged into a pile and burnt.

The Tete missionaries waited to hear from the military governor, who ignored the plea to look into the atrocities and act accordingly. The Tete priests concluded they needed to draw international attention to the atrocities before the events ran cold. Two priests led the way to this end: Padre Júlio Moure and Padre Miguel Buendia, a recent arrival to Mozambique, stationed briefly at the Muraça Mission left vacant by the White

[24]Father Adrian Hastings, interviews by author, Oxford, London, and Leeds, 1977, 1978, 1979, 1981, and 1996.
[25]Mustafah Dhada, "The Wiriyamu Massacre of 1972: Its Context, Genesis, and Revelation," *History in Africa* 40, 1 (2013): 45–75.
[26]Padre Vicente Berenguer, interview by author, Maputo, 1995.
[27]Ibid.

Fathers, who two years earlier had left the colony in protest of Portugal's military conduct in counterinsurgency.

The Outing

Padre Miguel Buendia was already under threat of deportation, as were Padre Moure and Padre Berenguer, for their vocal opposition to the regime's counterinsurgent conduct in Tete. Finally, the dreaded day arrived, February 6, 1973. Buendia and Moure had two weeks to pack and go. Both did just that and headed to the Burgos house in Beira before their prospective departure the next day. On Tuesday, February 20, at noon, they were ready to head for the airport. Just then a Jeep drove to the house, with Padre José Camba, a fellow Burgos Father, who had driven 124 miles from his mission house in Chimoio ostensibly to say goodbye thirty minutes before their departure for the airport. In reality, he had come to hand over a sealed envelope containing the Wiriyamu report. Buendia was instructed to deliver the package to Father Artazcoz in Madrid. The report, however, was incomplete, for it excluded the list of those killed at Chaworha. Haste and an opportunity to smuggle the report out of the colony may well have underpinned this omission. A few weeks later another copy of the report was smuggled out, undetected by the colonial airport authorities. This time Padre Castellá carried it hidden in his underpants, and it was a more complete version.

Miguel Buendia clutched the packet all the way to Lisbon on board the plane, which arrived in Lisbon the next morning, where he transferred to a flight to Madrid. Once there he did as instructed and delivered the report to the director of the congregation in Madrid. In the meantime, Padre Bertulli, heading the White Fathers, who was in Rome, had received the two reports, one on Chaworha and the other on Wiriyamu. On May 12–13 he broached the matter with a high-ranking official of the Portuguese government present at a public meeting in Kamen, Germany. The Portuguese response was disavowal. Bertulli felt stonewalled and approached *Cablo Press*, which published the texts in their entirety on Monday, June 4, 1973.[28] Bertulli also forwarded a copy to Amnesty International, which received it on Monday, June 11.[29] In the end the *Cablo* piece failed to garner public attention as the fathers had hoped, because of its limited circulation.[30] Back in Madrid, Miguel Buendia and Padre Moure began to lose hope.[31] What they wanted was to attract international press coverage and get the United Nations involved.[32] That is when Hastings entered the narrative.

[28]"Esclusivo: Massacri Nel Mozambico," *Cablo Press* June 4 (1973): 5–11.
[29]Amnesty International, *Annual Report 1973–1974* (London: AI, 1974), pp. 63–4.
[30]"Esclusivo: Massacri Nel Mozambico," *Cablo Press* June 4 (1973): 5–11.
[31]Miguel Buendia, interview by author, Maputo, 1995.
[32]Ibid.

Some 1,192 miles from Madrid, Father Adrian Hastings was at Selly Oaks College, Birmingham, busy preparing for a lecture tour in Ian Smith's Rhodesia.[33] Hastings departed for Harare, then Salisbury, in April. During the lecture tour, the fathers stationed in Rhodesia informed him of the massacres. When probed for additional details, they told him to get in touch with the Burgos' headquarters in Spain. This he did. He was scheduled to deliver a seminal paper on the Church's new thinking on ecumenical matters at an intercommunion conference in Salamanca, Spain, in the middle of June and took the opportunity to raise the matter first with Father Artazcoz in Salamanca and then with Father Anaveros in Madrid. The two meetings occurred the week of June 18. At the Madrid meeting he was shown the documents that Miguel Buendia had smuggled out of Beira. Hastings felt that both the Burgos Fathers as churchmen and the document were genuine. He asked Anaveros for a copy, which they sent to him on Wednesday, June 27. Hastings received the texts three days later. The Chaworha report was missing from the batch of two reports they had sent, one of which was on Mucumbura and the other on Wiriyamu.

The Mucumbura report, Hastings felt, had already been aired; the report on Wiriyamu was more recent and justly deserving of publication in an English daily newspaper. On Thursday, July 5, he cabled Madrid seeking permission to publish. Anaveros replied the following day giving him the go-ahead. By then Hastings had already decided on which paper to contact for the story—*The London Times*.[34] Hastings could not have timed it better. The Tory government of Edward Heath was about to host Caetano in London to celebrate the 600th anniversary of the Anglo-Portuguese Alliance.[35] Hastings was at the time serving as a member of an influential committee on education of the Catholic Institute of International Relations (CIIR), which was planning to organize a public discourse on the imperial alliance. The CIIR wanted a substance-driven examination of the Anglo-Portuguese Alliance.[36]

Two CIIR committee members, Mildred Neville and Hugh O'Shaughnessy, had asked Hastings to spearhead a discussion on the role of the Church in the alliance. Hastings proposed the CIIR focus on the massacres. Mildred feared the narrative would dominate the CIIR proceedings. Hastings disagreed. The story needed airing at the CIIR and publication on the front page of *The London Times*, no less!

Hastings called *The London Times* on Friday, July 6, late afternoon. Fortuitously, William Rees-Mogg, the chief editor, was not in at that late hour; his deputy was, Louis Heren. Heren himself was by then highly skilled at nurturing stories of momentous

[33]Adrian Hastings and Ingrid Lowrie, eds., *Christianity and the African Imagination: Essays in Honour of Adrian Hastings* (Leiden: Brill Academic Publications, 2013).

[34]Hastings, interviews, 1977, 1978, 1979, 1981, 1995, 1996.

[35]See the following issues of *The London Times*: March 16 (1973): sec. 8a; May 17 (1973): sec. 18h; and May 23 (1973): sec. 6h. Additional information on the alliance and reactions to it are to be found in, Staff, "Motions by Tory MPs support Caetano visit," *The London Times*, July 12 (1973): sec. 16a. The Foreign and Commonwealth Office archives contain approximately fifty documents on the commemorative aspect of this alliance. For details, see bibliography in Dhada, *The Portuguese Massacre of Wiriyamu*, 199–200.

[36]Hastings, interviews, 1977, 1978, 1979, 1981, 1995, 1996.

human interest, having spent a ten-year stint as the paper's foreign correspondent in Washington, DC, where he had seen the debacle of the My Lai massacre. He asked Hastings to forward the texts, which Hastings did on Saturday. Heren got the package on Monday, and his subsequent return call to Hastings that evening proved ominously thunderous for the story's outing. On July 10, 1973, 206 days after the event, *The London Times* ran the story; five days later, *The London Sunday Times'* Insight Team followed suit with extensive background coverage on the massacre.[37] Back in Lisbon, Caetano was six days away from landing at Heathrow, which was now heavily fortified with police[38] to protect him from public protests.[39]

Portugal denied the story and attacked it as fake news.[40] *The London Times* and *The London Sunday Times* fought back and dispatched three fact-checkers to Tete: Michael Knipe, Christopher Wain, and Peter Pringle. By then Portugal had already prepared an abandoned village with charred huts northwest of the triangle as an alternative to Wiriyamu to counter Hastings' claims. Tete did indeed have a place locally known as Williamo; perhaps the priests and Hastings were referring to this village, and, if so, the village in question was too small a place to accommodate a freshly executed carnage of the magnitude claimed in *The London Times*. Truth-seekers, Portugal added, were welcome to tour Williamo to check the facts for themselves.[41]

Knipe spent three days in Tete where he was escorted to the fictitious site, Williamo. Knipe filed his story suggesting just that—that he had found the place called Williamo to be small and insignificant, with little evidence of freshly discharged bullet casings.[42] By this time, the secret police had intensified surveillance, just as Knipe was getting closer to the truth, as he sought out Tete's missionaries and nuns directly connected to the case.[43] Before he could interview them for a follow-up story, the Portuguese swooped in and ejected him from Tete. A similar fate awaited Wain. He too failed to get close to Wiriyamu and interview survivors. Hastings, on the other hand, had left London for New York on July 19, 1973, to testify on Wiriyamu before the United Nations Special Committee of 24 on Decolonization.[44]

---

[37]"Mozambique—The priest's fight," *Sunday Times*, July 15 (1973): 17.

[38]"Heavy police precautions as Dr. Caetano begins his visit to Britain today," *The London Times*, July 16 (1973): 1.

[39]"An unwelcome visit," *Sunday Times*, July 15 (1973): 16.

[40]Anonymous, *"Wiriyamu" or a Mare's Nest* (Lisbon: Ministry of Foreign Affairs, 1973); "Lisbon inquiry rejects massacre story," *The London Times*, August 20 (1973): 1; and A. M. Rendel, "Embassy issues angry reply," *The London Times*, July 11 (1973): 1.

[41]"Memorando enviado por Kaúlza de Arriaga a Pimentel dos Santos," n.d.; and Kaúlza de Arriaga in an interview with Michael Knipe, quoted to the author by Knipe. Michael Knipe, interview by author, London, 1996.

[42]*Cable: 1973Lourenn00559_b, 1973*, August 14, 14, no. 46 (Tuesday).

[43]Michael Knipe, "Mozambique secret police keep an eye on correspondent from *The London Times*," *The London Times*, July 25 (1973): 1.

[44]David Wigg, "Priest gives massacre details to UN committee," *The London Times*, July 21 (1973). Frelimo representatives at the meeting included the party's ideologue, Marcelino dos Santos, who at one point during his delivery commended Hastings for his great contribution "to the movement against oppression." "We appreciate your courage," he added. "Portuguese converge on Lisbon to welcome Dr. Caetano back home," *The London Times*, July 20 (1973).

Days after Caetano's departure from London, Peter Pringle followed Knipe. Given how the Portuguese had managed to steer earlier investigators away from the real Wiriyamu and given how they had ejected Knipe out of Tete before he could get to the evidence, Pringle planned his journey with characteristic care. He went to Spain first. The Burgos Fathers and their network prepared him on how to outmaneuver the secret police.[45] From there Pringle went straight to Lisbon on his way to Mozambique via Beira. He then spent three days in Tete and quickly unearthed the appropriate sources, thereby establishing the veracity of the story—and the location of the massacres.

Armed with a trove of evidence, Pringle sprinted out of Hotel Zambêzia where he was staying to interview Tete's bishop. A vigilant secret police agent lay in wait for him and whisked him away for interrogation. The chief of secret police Joaquim Sabino and his associates took away his notes, recordings, and photos. He was then ordered to leave Tete. They promised to return his materials upon his departure from Mozambique. They never did.[46] While they were busy reviewing his materials, Pringle pushed a roll of film at the edge of the desk toward him and slipped it in his jacket pocket.[47] Those photos when published were a visual proof that something violent had transpired in Wiriyamu.

Pringle returned to London and filed his story,[48] with a follow-up, which appeared in *The London Sunday Times* on August 3, 1973, and which was subsequently picked up by *The London Times*. The evidence existed; the place existed and would continue to exist as long as eyewitnesses and survivors remained alive and beyond the reach of the Portuguese secret police. One such survivor nearly didn't make it—António Mixone. The BBC had picked up one of Pringle's stories. Padre Sangalo was in Tete, at his one-room home in Matundo, when he heard the news on the BBC on his wireless radio. It mentioned Mixone by name. They, Padre Burgos and Padre Ferrão, had been discussing Mixone's safety a few days earlier. This time he got even more worried. He knew Mixone's life was in danger. He got up early the next day and delivered him to safety—that is, into the hands of Frelimo—returning to Matundo only to find the Portuguese secret police engaged on a manhunt for Mixone. By then, he had crossed the border into Zambia on his way to Tanzania to be debriefed by Frelimo. In August, the Portuguese secret police, after consulting with the Bishop of Tete, apprehended Padre Sangalo on charges of aiding and abetting the enemy. He was interrogated in the presence of informers and subsequently put on a plane bound for Lisbon and then Madrid.[49] On August 6, 1973, two priests arrived at the offices of *The London Times*: Padre Vicente Berenguer and Padre Júlio Moure. Both said they knew exactly where Wiriyamu was and vouched for the story.

[45]Berenguer, interview, 1994 and 1995; Hastings, interviews, 1977, 1978, 1979, 1981, 1995, 1996; and Buendia, interview, 1994 and 1995.

[46]Peter Pringle, interview by author, New York City, 2012.

[47]Pringle, interview, 2012.

[48]Peter Pringle, "Secret police seize my Mozambique tapes," *Sunday Times*, July 29 (1973): 1.

[49]Peter Pringle, Father Padre José Sangalo, and Burgos Fathers, "My ordeal with the secret police—and my bishop," *Sunday Times*, December 9 (1973): 9; and PT/TT/PIDE/D-F/001/00023, August 22, 1973.

Nine months after the revelations, Caetano's regime fell.[50] The new regime, once established, acknowledged fully the veracity of *The London Times'* narrative.[51] By then, the United Nations had already documented the story on its own by cataloging the evidence,[52] which it then published as a report seven months after the coup, on November 22, 1974.[53] That is how the Wiriyamu narrative was revealed, dismissed, denied in parts as fake news, and contested with manufactured evidence.

*

Several texts now address the Wiriyamu story—and the chronology of their appearance merits a brief note.[54] Early texts affirming the story relied on published documents, some primary in nature. Scholarly works, after the revelation in *The London Times* in 1973, continued to appear until the 1980s when its factual presence gave way to works of fiction,[55] which filled the gaps left open in the narrative, notably in works by Father Adrian Hastings, the UN's Wiriyamu investigation committee,[56] British historians and journalists,[57] and anti-colonial advocacy groups.

Discourses among veterans and commanders continued as expected, split between deniers[58] and redemption-seekers, among whom was none other than Antonino Melo, the commander of Operation Marosca, which decimated Wiriyamu.

Melo's agony found public expression in the form of a journalistic inquiry,[59] which once published saw a rash of subsequent works after the 1990s, all fiction-based. One such work, published in 2010, placed the events against a background of coexistence between colonialists and their adversaries, implying there were good relations in the region just before Wiriyamu turned to ashes.[60]

---

[50]António de Spínola, *Portugal e o Futuro: Análise da Conjuntura Nacional* (Lisbon: Editora Arcádia, 1974), p. 247.

[51]Foreign Staff, "Army report confirms Wiriyamu Massacre," *The London Times*, April 24 (1974): 8.

[52]Tim Jones, "UN hearing on Portuguese atrocity reports begins," *The London Times*, May 15 (1974): 5.

[53]"UN report accuses Portugal of atrocities," *The London Times*, December 10 (1974): 1.

[54]*Terror in Tete: A Documentary Report of Portuguese Atrocities in Tete District, Mozambique, 1971–1972* (London: IDAF, 1973); Adrian Hastings, *Wiriyamu: My Lai in Mozambique* (London: Orbis, 1974); Adrian Hastings, "Reflections upon the War in Mozambique," *African Affairs* 292 (1974): 263–76; Amnesty International, *Annual Report 1973–1974*, pp. 63–4.

[55]Williams Sassine, *Wirriyamu* (London: Heinemann, 1980); Farida Karodia, *A Shattering of Silence* (Oxford: Heinemann, 1993); Ricardo de Saavedra, *Os Dias Do Fim* (Lisbon: Editorial Notícias, 1995); Lídia Jorge, *A Costa dos Murmúrios* (Lisbon: Publicações Dom Quixote, 2008); and José Rodrigues dos Santos, *O Anjo Branco* (Lisbon: Gravida, 2010).

[56]United Nations Commission of Inquiry, 1974.

[57]Kevin Parker, "Wiriyamu and the War in Tete, 1971–1974" (MA thesis, University of York, 1982); Felícia Cabrita, "Os Mortos Não Sofrem," *Revista Expresso*, December 5 (1992); Felícia Cabrita, "Wiriyamu, Viagem ao Fundo do Terror," *Revista Expresso*, November 21 (1998); and Felícia Cabrita, *Massacres em África* (Lisbon: A Esfera dos Livros, 2008).

[58]Paulo Oliveira, "Kaúlza de Arriaga e o 'Peso de Wiriamu,'" *Público*, February 4 (2004).

[59]Cabrita, "Os Mortos Não Sofrem"; Cabrita, "Wiriyamu, Viagem ao Fundo do Terror"; and Cabrita, *Massacres em África*.

[60]Rodrigues dos Santos, *O Anjo Branco*.

Thereafter, we heard nothing—and for good reason. The story had served its purpose: to expose Portugal's conduct of war in Africa. The story, too, ceased to be told once that conduct ceased. Public attention consequently waned, and the massacre disappeared from institutional memory as a lived experience, allowing texts of denial and doubt to creep in to fill the void. In a sense, Wiriyamu shared the fate of similar cases of precolonial, colonial, and postcolonial mass violence[61] in that they faded from public view once efforts ceased to sustain them. Recent developments to turn the death camps in Rwanda into a sustainable enterprise illustrate exactly this point,[62] as do testimonial works[63] and films[64] documenting with systematic frequency massacres in contemporary history. It is only by constant retelling, therefore, that these works can combat historical amnesia in the public sphere.

In the case of Wiriyamu, retelling it is all the more imperative given the scarcity of contemporaneous archives.[65] Resistance to memorial amnesia therefore may well rest with firsthand accounts of this massacre, and, unless these are read widely and frequently as a published primary document, knowledge of Wiriyamu and of similar cases of colonial mass violence in Africa will fall prey to knowledge erosion. And that is exactly what this book does—it seeks to prevent such erosion by hosting a selection of twenty-seven interviewees who tell us their side of the story of the Wiriyamu massacre with little or no interpolation.

[61]Kiernan, *Blood and Soil*; and René Lemarchand, ed., *Forgotten Genocides: Oblivion, Denial, and Memory* (Philadelphia: University of Pennsylvania Press, 2013).

[62]Ksenija Bilbija and Leigh A. Payne, eds., *Accounting for Violence: Marketing Memory in Latin America* (Durham: Duke University Press, 2011); "From the Editors: Genocide tourism—educational value or voyeurism?" *Journal of Genocide Research* 9, 4 (2007); Jean Comaroff and John L. Comaroff, "History on Trial: Memory, Evidence, and the Forensic Production of the Past," in *Theory from the South: Or, How Euro-America is Evolving Toward Africa* (Stanford: Stanford University Press, 2012); John Lennon and Malcolm Foley, *Dark Tourism: The Attraction of Death and Disaster* (London: Continuum, 2000); Tshepo Madlingozi, "On Transitional Justice Entrepreneurs and the Production of Victims," *Journal of Human Rights Practice* 2, 2 (2010): 208–28; Christopher Szabla, "Against the memory industry," *Maisonneuve*, January 6 (2012); and Marita Sturken, *Tourists of History, Memory, Kitsch and Consumerism from Oklahoma City to Ground Zero* (Durham: Duke University Press, 2007).

[63]Totten and Parsons, *Centuries of Genocide*.

[64]*The River Ran Red*, directed by Michael Hagopian; *The Devil Came on Horseback*, directed by Stern and Sundberg; Ponchaud, *Cambodia*; and *Shake Hands With The Devil*, directed by Peter Raymont.

[65]The only reference to Marosca is to be found in the Lisbon-based O Arquivo da Defesa Nacional (ADN, National Defense Archives), under ADN/GABMIN, SR. 7, 0035, 047, Ofício n° 3394/GB, Proc. PS-10-02, de 4 de Junho de 1973. The actual copy of the military commission of inquiry is missing from the folder.

1

THE COLONIAL WAR AND THE
WIRIYAMU TRIANGLE

Five informants form part of this first group of interviews on the colonial war. The first interview is on the nationalist insurgency in Mozambique. Authored by Lieutenant General António Hama Thai, a Frelimo commander leading the fight in Tete, it traces his induction into Frelimo, the logistical difficulties in sustaining the liberation front in Tete, the contribution of the missionaries in Tete's early mobilization effort among villagers to embrace Frelimo's liberation struggle, the strength of Frelimo's presence in the Wiriyamu triangle, and his role in leading the liberation forces to open up a new front below Tete's borders with the neighboring colonial district of Manica-e-Sofala.

Bulachu Pensadu Zambezi's interview follows next. It begins with the day he joined Frelimo. Zambezi reminisces about his life as a villager among goats and family illnesses, until the momentous arrival of Frelimo, momentous to him at any rate, and the impact that ultimately the two wars, colonial and civil, that followed the liberation struggle had on the lives of the people in the village. In the end, the wars brought nothing but suffering, he adds.

In contrast, Vasco Tenente Valeta's short interview memorializes village life before the massacre. Viewed as a trope, Wiriyamu is a bucolic cattle-rearing village, of big and small houses; of wives, children, and mothers; of football fields and goats; and of fat cattle buyers and their intermediaries and the animal sellers eager to do business with them. Pigs and machambas dot the landscape, while backyards and holding pens keep safe animals needing closer attention. Valeta's last two paragraphs end with a precise count of the people who died in the hut, from which he escaped before the grenade explosion, which flung open the side door.

Antonino Melo follows Zambezi's interview with a most powerful account as commander of Operation Marosca. It describes his life as a child, adulthood, military conscription, and training as an elite commando assigned to a unit, which he leads to launch Wiriyamu's erasure. The story turns dark, depicting burning huts and methods used to eliminate informants. Melo then delves into the night after the massacre and the unit's being ordered to return to bury the dead left exposed to the sun. Embedded in the story is his searingly felt compassion for a girl he ordered saved from a hut about to be set aflame. He ends on a set of two reflections, one on violence and war and the other on their impact on his family and their return to Portugal at the end of the colonial war.

Chico Kachavi, the man who led the interrogations during Marosca, was demonized by villagers in Wiriyamu and hated by his torture victims. Even outside the triangle, Chico elicited strong responses as an agent for Tete's secret police. His brother António Kachavi's interview paints a different picture—that of a family man, caring and lively, not at all cruel, he said. He concurs, however, with most people who knew Chico as a reckless womanizer, a fanatic football fan, a teetotaler, and an accomplished drummer. António denies any knowledge of his brother's use of torture, overwhelming evidence to the contrary notwithstanding. He ends with a lengthy description of Chico's death, as he lay wounded in the back seat of a Jeep heading to the local hospital.

Interviewee:
General Hama Thai
Date (yyyy mm dd):
1995 04 28; 1995 05 11
Duration (hh mm ss):
1h 26m 54s
Place:
Maputo
Language:
Portuguese
Interpreter:
None
Redactions:
Light

Tete's March to the South

My full name is António Hama Thai. I was given António as my Catholic name. Hama is a typical Ndau maternal name, and it means brother. My mother is Ndau. Thai is also my father's name who is from Mabote in southern Inhambane. He left there and got married in Mérica in Mutarara, Tete, where I was born.[1] I studied at the local Catholic mission school called Missão Sagrado Coração de Jesus near where I lived.[2] In 1965, I finished second grade and went to Beira. There I attended third, and then went on to do fourth grade at a Catholic school linked to the cathedral in Beira. I then took the entrance exams for the Liceu Peru de Anaia and I passed, but I was already fifteen—too old to enter the lyceum. The age limit was fourteen. I ended up applying to Escola Industrial e Comercial Freire de Andrade, which I attended from 1967 to 1969. My school schedule was from 7 a.m. to 1 p.m., although some days of the week it extended to 6 p.m. Soon thereafter, my father and mother divorced, so my brother joined me in Beira. That was in 1967. My mother did not have enough money to live on, so I had to work to support her. I worked from 10 p.m. to 2 a.m. at an office as a clerk handling announcements and advertisements for the local newspaper where I later met many journalists and politically active people. Because I worked less than eight hours a week, I worked also on Sundays from 7 a.m. to 7 p.m.

I joined Frelimo in 1969. In June of that year, after I had finished my exams, a Frelimo representative arrived in Beira on his way to Malawi to see his wife. About fourteen of

[1]Google Maps places the location at latitude −17. 0155556 / −17° 0' 56.0016" longitude 34. 8902778 / 34° 53' 25.0008".
[2]The mission is now located in Paróquia do Sagrado Coração de Jesus, Nova Mambone, Vilanculos.

us, including myself, went to see him, and after much talk we decided to leave Beira. We took the train from the central station and went to Mutarara, and at night we crossed the border and entered Malawi. There, we saw a friend of ours, the Frelimo representative, and stayed the night at his place. The next day we were too hungry to go on. Our representative and one other person went in search of food—neither of whom spoke English or Nhungwe, but that didn't pose a problem. They managed to meet several Malawians who invited us to join them to eat.

The problem was afterward. Once we finished eating, the local police arrived to question us and took us to the police station. When we got there, we were arrested for having crossed the border without a passport. They took our belongings and put us in a cell, the twelve of us—they placed the two women in our group in a different cell. The cell was a small cubicle. It had a cement floor. They gave us blankets and prison clothes. The food was terrible. It was June and very cold. We prayed for deliverance. Our representative asked the police to contact the Frelimo representative in Blantyre to let them know we were in Malawi and in jail.

We were in jail for four days, but we were not interrogated. On the fifth day, the police came and told us they were going to put us on a train back to Mozambique. And that is what they did. We got our belongings and were put on a train home. Of course, we knew that once we got back the Polícia Internacional e de Defesa do Estado (PIDE), International Police for the Defense of the State, would be waiting. We would have been tortured to death, of that I was sure; I thought of jumping off the train.

But as it happens we were lucky. When we arrived in Lamego, now in the Sofala province near Beira, the PIDE had a list that Jorge Jardim's men in Malawi had sent to PIDE agents working for him in Lamego, informing them of our arrival. When these agents approached us we told them that Frelimo had already intercepted the people they were looking for and had taken them away, and they bought the story. It appeared that they had not received full details of who we were from the Portuguese agents in Malawi—this is how we narrowly escaped detention. We then took the next train back to Malawi. This time a Frelimo representative was waiting for us. If I recall it was not General Gruveta; he was in jail in Malawi because he had lodged a protest against police brutality over the death of one of our comrades. When we were told of this, we went to the police station to persuade officers there to free Gruveta. We feared for his life. We knew that he could be killed by Portuguese agents in Malawi or sent back to Mozambique. The Malawi police were on the lookout for people suspected of crossing the border illegally from Mozambique. They had orders to deliver them to the Portuguese.

Upon freeing Gruveta we went to Nachingwea near Dar es Salaam. There we did our basic guerrilla training. We also received specialized training with Chinese instructors. After that, some of us went to Cabo Delgado. I was selected to go to Russia in 1970 as part of a group for training in military combat. I came back a year later and then in January of the following year I went to Bagamoyo, in Tanzania, again as part of a group. On February 2, I got my uniform, and my group and I received our marching orders for armed struggle.

Sixty percent of my group got sick almost immediately; only twenty of us survived to begin fighting right away. In December of 1970 I was told to return to Frelimo headquarters—and early the following year I went to Cabo Delgado with a new Frelimo group to develop our radio communication system. There was only one Frelimo radio on the border near Nachingwea.

Now you need to realize, the interior of Cabo Delgado where we operated was big, with many detachments and bases, and it needed a communication system for the commandos to talk to our headquarters in Nachingwea. Some of the Frelimo guerrillas thought radio communication with headquarters was dangerous because it attracted enemy planes—and that sort of thing. We had to explain to them that this was not necessarily the case. There was a proper way of using this communication system as part of our guerrilla strategy. One such strategy was to attract the Portuguese Air Force to our location, I said, which would give us a chance to shoot them down with anti-aircraft guns. After all, this was war. We explained to them that we should not use radio communication in heavily populated areas, because that would cause civilian casualties, nor should we operate the system near Frelimo bases. So, we instructed our forces to be far away from bases and away from heavily populated civilian villages. After I finished setting up this communication system and training our forces on how to use it, I was ordered to return to Nachingwea.

I was then sent to Tete. I was in Tete from June 1972 until April 1978. All the detachments of Frelimo's fourth sector were stationed there, including the eighth—which was created at the end of 1972. I was given two mission objectives for Tete: help with Frelimo's communication logistics there and develop operational strategies to advance south of Tete. When I arrived in June, the first thing I did was enter Cahora Bassa from the border to assess our logistic needs. I then went back across the border and then crossed the Zambezi River to supervise my artillery units south of Zambezi.

Cabo Delgado, Malawi, and the Tete Front

On June 25, 1962, our party had laid the foundation of our national freedom, which had resulted in the first Congress in September, at which the party felt it had only one alternative to seek independence—fight for it. The colonial government had refused to negotiate with us, with the result that we had no other choice; we had to fight.

Not everything went smoothly at first. As you know, Frelimo was a fusion of three political groups: Mozambique African National Union (MANU), União Africana de Moçambique Independente (UNAMI, National African Union of Independent Mozambique), and União Democrática Nacional de Moçambique (UDENAMO, the National Democratic Union of Mozambique). For one thing, Adelino Gwambe, who led UDENAMO, had refused to accept the leadership of Dr. Eduardo Mondlane and left to form Comité Revolucionário de Moçambique (COREMO, the Revolutionary Committee for Mozambique). COREMO was based in Lusaka, Zambia. The COREMO people knew we were about to start the fight in the north. They took this as an opportunity and immediately focused their attention and fighting activities in Tete. They sought help from Israel, which proved tremendously important to them at first. We knew this because we often saw their representatives in Cairo, where we had our representative office under the banner of the League of Arab Nations. Because of Israeli aid, they remained active for a while in Tete. But they could not sustain it for long because of internal divisions and lack of continuous external funding from other sources. By the time we established our presence in Zambia with General Mariano de Araújo Matsinhe as our representative, COREMO had virtually disappeared, until the Portuguese encouraged its revival a bit later under Kaúlza de Arriaga—but by then Frelimo had established itself as a national movement and with a clear goal: the total national liberation of Mozambique and not just the liberation of Tete.

Our headquarters was in Tanzania, which lent us much support in terms of armaments and aid. So, we decided in 1964 we would attack with two fronts at once, the north and Tete. There were three distinct groups that went to Cabo Delgado, Niassa, Tete, and Zambezi, all by way of Malawi. Zambia wasn't independent at this time; in fact, Zambia was at the height of its own fight for independence. Alberto Joaquim Chipande, who later became a general in the army, commanded the main group. He retired last year, 1994. He was the one who attacked the administrative post at Chai on September 25, 1964. After that attack, the other groups went on to fight in Niassa, Tete, and Zambezi.

But we had a problem here. Malawi obstructed our armed fighters heading for Tete and Zambezi, so we had to cease these two fronts. I myself traveled through Malawi to gather intelligence on Portuguese agents operating in Malawi, after the two fronts were stopped, and to free some of the guerrillas arrested. They had been arrested because of Jorge Jardim's diplomacy with the government of Malawi. It was because of this diplomacy that I was arrested, along with Bonifácio Massamba Gruveta. You know somewhere in the archives there must be documents that tell this story of Jardim and the deals he made with the government of Malawi to block us from operating from his territory. I was in prison for five days, along with Bonifácio. We were released with the help of Frelimo officials, but we concluded we could not use Malawi to penetrate Tete—not as easily as we could penetrate the north from Tanzania.

Our arrests proved President Banda and the Malawi government supported the colonial Portuguese presence in Mozambique, with Jorge Jardim leading Portuguese diplomacy as Consul of Portugal in Malawi. This position helped Jardim establish a deep friendship with President Banda, who in turn visited Beira to secure the import of goods much needed for Malawi. In return, Malawi collaborated with Portugal to capture Frelimo guerrillas heading to Tete from Malawi.

President Banda was very complicated. Like the Portuguese, the people of present-day Malawi were not the original owners of that land, he said. Therefore, he did not see any reason to oppose the Portuguese as occupiers. I think the real reason for Banda's support of the Portuguese was self-interest—to protect the Nacala and Sena railway lines carrying goods into Malawi, which was land-locked. Malawi's poor relations with Tanzania and Zambia created no alternatives but for President Kamuzu Banda to befriend the Portuguese. So, as I was saying, both the Nacala and the Sena railways, which linked Beira with the north, connected the Mozambique coast with the Malawi interior.

Once Kaúlza de Arriaga took control of the Portuguese colonial army in 1969, we knew we needed to reopen the Tete front. Kaúlza understood war in theory and intellectually, but he wasn't good in practice—at least that was the opinion we had among us, Frelimo's major commanders leading the war. You may remember he launched Operation Gordian Knot, in Cabo Delgado, with a force of over 30,000 troops. To do that he had to open up the region with roads, bridges, and landing strips, which was beneficial for the future of Mozambique. All this failed to achieve the military objectives he had imagined, because we were not a regular army. We were a guerrilla force, so we simply retreated; however, we suffered a lot of casualties during that operation. President Samora saw that operation as Portugal's giant failure. The giant is much more easily killed with an ant. No matter how many soldiers Kaúlza filled the bush with, we remained ants in the elephant's trunk. Once we were inside, the elephant would go on slamming its trunk, dying of self-inflicted wounds.

Since we didn't only have the objective of winning the war in Cabo Delgado, we took advantage of this offensive and began secretly preparing for the Tete front. For us, winning Cabo Delgado on its own meant nothing; however, for Kaúlza Cabo Delgado was everything. He thought it possible to liquidate all the guerrillas in Cabo Delgado and end the war in the north completely—that is why I and my fellow commanders thought him to be a poor strategist. His successor, General Tomás Basto Machado, was different! He was truly a worthy adversary, and he nearly succeeded in impeding our march to the south—not militarily but politically, by infiltrating our ranks. He was basically like António de Spínola; but before his tactic could take firm root, the situation in Portugal changed and its army felt the colonial war wasn't worth fighting, so they basically gave up.

Once Zambia gained independence, we reopened the Tete front in February or March 1968, if I remember correctly. The support from Zambians was important. Without them we could not penetrate the border and head to the south through Tete. Tete was very, very important because it secured a route for us to expand the armed struggle to the south of the country and put pressure on the colonial government to grant independence once we reached Maputo, which was Lourenço Marques at this time. You could say that the fight in Tete was simply a way to reach the south as fast as possible.

We viewed Tete as hikers viewed a hill—a goal to reach the summit. Actually, Samora Machel used to say, "Tete was the hump of a camel, a place from where we could march to the south." But initially it proved difficult to penetrate Tete. We first tried to get in through Marávia but failed. We then sought to enter it near the town of Fingoé, and that didn't work. Next, we tried near Lúrio in the northeast; that did not work either. We even tried to get in via Niassa. Niassa proved impossible since Operation Gordian Knot forced us to close our bases in that region. We finally got in—thanks largely because of Zambia, which came to our aid. Two years after we entered Tete, we crossed the Zambezi River. Once there we developed our route to transport arms to open a new front in Manica-e-Sofala.

Our first attack in Tete, if I am not mistaken, was in July 1972, which rattled the Portuguese colonial commandos. By the time they came to realize the threat we posed, we were already in Manica-e-Sofala, focusing on the colonial economy. As I've said, Kaúlza knew the reality of our presence in the region, and he and his forces knew that for us Tete was important—without it we did not have a strategy. I intimated as much to Frelimo leaders when I met them after I got to Tete. They had sent me to Tete to study carefully the Cahora Bassa project when designing our logistics strategy. We all had to study that project because the colonial Portuguese commandos thought the dam was going to make it impossible for us to cross the Zambezi River.

But they were wrong. There was a crossing near Boroma, where the river narrowed, and there we used mountain tracks we knew, and which we explored with the help of the local population. Some of these paths ran close to the dam but were hidden from the colonial forces. We did not view the dam as an obstruction against our strategy for the armed struggle in Tete and our march to the south; in fact, at least in my view, it was the opposite. Because of the flooding of the dam, which created a large lake, they had to use boats for their counterinsurgency. We came to have an advantage here as we used hidden paths in the mountains surrounding the river and the flood plains to attack Portuguese colonial commandos. So, for us the Portuguese committed a grave error in constructing the dam. They made the dam practically indefensible. Our aim, on the other hand, was not to destroy the dam—Samora Machel made that clear to us. We just wanted to slow down its construction and occupy the Portuguese commandos in a direct fight in Tete, while our forces built up logistics south of Tete to begin the front in Manica-e-Sofala.

As I said before, in the Tete Province we had nine operational detachments. They were mostly south of the Zambezi River. We called the first detachment Maconde. Across the river was the second detachment, headed by Pedro Magoé, which is not his actual name. Magoé coordinated with another detachment in Aluiro, and I cannot remember that base's guerrilla name, but it will come to me. Mariano Pinta Caetano was responsible for coordinating the Magoé detachment. Aha! I now remember the person who commanded the Aluiro detachment—he is still alive, and his nom de guerre was Salvador.

The third detachment was located in Mucumbura. There were various commandants in that detachment. The last commandant was Carlos Nunes Chissone, not his actual name, and he is here. He currently works in the fishing industry in Matola. The fourth detachment was around here—not here but here, here, and here—south of Wiriyamu, and was commanded at that time by Napalula, who is alive as far as I know. The fifth detachment was in Marara. Damião de Sanchez Danda, who is currently in Tete, commanded the sixth detachment in Chioco. The seventh detachment was in Changara, around the mountains, and was commanded by Zacarias Escabalca, who passed away during the war. The eighth detachment, which belonged to Raimundo Dalepa, was located near Tete, around the mountains toward Magoé. The ninth detachment was located further back. In addition to the detachments, we had two artillery units: one near Mucumbura. I cannot now remember the exact location of the second unit, I am sorry to say.

When we arrived in Mucumbura in November of 1972, we were greeted with open arms. I was actually amazed at how proud the people were of their culture and history, how happy they were to support us, and how important the war was for them to liberate our land, our country. Sometimes I thought they had a higher regard for us and what we were doing than their own children. It was extraordinary. I can say with confidence that sixty percent of young people in Mucumbura joined us in our armed struggle.

But what about Chief Buxo?

Buxo was not our friend. He supported the Portuguese and was sent packing. I mean killed. He was a traitor and an agent of colonialism. He had to go. The Portuguese troops did not help. Their threats frightened the population who then joined us in the freedom struggle.

There were many complications here in Mucumbura. This region was close to Rhodesia, with frequent migration of people, cultural exchanges, marriages, and family connections across the border. It was common for several family members belonging to Frelimo to live on both sides of the border. President Samora Machel knew this, and he also knew how important our fight was not only for us but also for the liberated future of Rhodesia and South Africa. That is why we formed an alliance with the Zimbabwe African People's Union (ZAPU) and the African National Congress (ANC), and we did this as early as 1964. They had offices in Tanzania, as we did, and we had great friendships, not just formal but personal and on many other fronts. When ZAPU changed its position to fight through negotiated settlement, we parted ways and realigned ourselves with the Zimbabwe African National Union (ZANU). We then worked exclusively with ZANU, and President Samora supported its leadership publicly, regionally, and internationally. I personally remember that, in 1972, we received many guerrillas from ZANU, and one group in particular located in this region crossed into Rhodesia at the time in October of 1972 to begin their offensive. The group was composed of twenty-five guerrillas. Other groups went south to cross the border near Manica. This group unfortunately was caught, but others that followed slipped across to begin their own struggle to liberate a future free Zimbabwe.

Of course, I could say the same thing too about Chaworha. This area was much like Mucumbura, with the same population mix from both sides of the border and highly politicized.

Political Mobilization and the Church

What about political mobilization?

Yes, it is very interesting that you ask this question about political mobilization. Frelimo consciously decided to mobilize the population using the traditional chiefs as a point of entry. Before 1968, our strategy was simple: identify traditional chiefs receptive to our message and use them to speed up our fight for national independence; and it worked! You could see that in hindsight, for on the whole, they played an important role in preparing the people for the armed struggle. They were our water, and we were their fish. Without them we would not have survived. This relationship between us and the people is what made our struggle possible. The traditional chiefs were a natural choice for us, as they and only they could lead the people below them to join us in the struggle.

In my way of thinking the Portuguese use of strategic villages was a grave mistake on their part. They concentrated people in one place, which simplified our recruitment to focus on them behind the barbed wires. Even though some chiefs and people supported the Portuguese, it was really impossible for them to control each and every one in these villages because, to survive, they had to leave these villages to tend to their *machambas*, look for wood, search for water, and even visit relatives in other places outside these fortified villages.

These villages were in reality big garrisons protected by a platoon of the Organização Provincial de Voluntários para Defesa Civil (OPVDC), Provincial Organization of Volunteers for Civil Defense, trained to conduct incursion against our detachments. The colonial government co-opted them to act on their behalf. You can say that they were honorary whites in black skins. Periodically, we would penetrate the villages to attack them—Marara and Cachembere come to mind as examples of this type of operation; however, there were lots of others that I cannot remember now. We did this to make two points: to tell the defense force that we were watching their every move, and to let the people in the fortified villages know we were fighting on their behalf. Every day the defense force would go out into the bush, capture people, and bring them back into these barbed wire villages. Sometimes we would go into the village and would find the people waiting with their belongings packed, ready to leave with us.

Not always, mind you. There were times when chiefs collaborated with the Portuguese Armed Forces and the defense militia. Other times they just upped and left everything behind and headed to the neighboring territories with their people. The Portuguese had great difficulty in controlling the borders, which were vast, and the people had families on both sides of the borders, and that made it all the more difficult. The chief of Buxo was perhaps the most notorious case; he was the last and only chief who was totally loyal to the Portuguese. Yes, we can say with confidence that by the time we got to Tete and laid out our logistics and other structures, the people were ready to receive us and support our struggle for national liberation. And they did that by helping our guerrillas with logistics, intelligence, food, and medical supplies from nearby missions.

Tete, and neighboring Zimbabwe, had many missionaries, mainly the Burgos Fathers. They were already doing our work—a conscious effort to develop our people socially, culturally, and professionally, particularly south of the Zambezi River. We had frequent contacts with the Burgos Fathers. In Mucumbura we had two priests who supported us. In Marara we have one priest. In fact, one father, Padre Vicente Berenguer, lives now in Maputo.[3] Then there was Padre Júlio Moure, who worked with Padre Berenguer. Other padres included Padre Luís Afonso da Costa who was a Comboni priest, and of course Padre Ferrão from Tete, who had worked closely with us since the beginning of our struggle in 1964. He was Dom Sebastião Resende's protégé. I must not forget Mateus Gwenjere and the other African priests—they were true patriots. They were on our

---

[3]Padre Berenguer has since retired and returned to his native Valencia in Spain.

side. In this respect the White Fathers at the Zóbuè Seminary were also important; they played an important role during the liberation war before they left—in 1972, if I am not mistaken? It was 1972, right? I can't remember the exact year.[4]

For us this triangle, this one here—no, not that one but this one, this, this, this, Wiriyamu, yes, Wiriyamu—was very important and I have already told you why. It was on our way to Manica-e-Sofala. The Portuguese, with their colonial mindset, thought they could obstruct our march south of Cahora Bassa by patrolling the Zambezi River; though, in a way they were right in the beginning. With so many troops, it was hard for us to use their roads. But then we switched our tactics. We chose to use bush tracks hidden away in the mountains and found places where the Zambezi narrowed for our arms carriers to cross the river on foot. It so happens that one such track was near Wiriyamu, just north of it.

Also, we knew we were in a race against time. We needed to establish our presence before they completely blocked us by flooding the south side of the dam, so we discovered one other crossing, also hard to detect. By the time the dam flooded the plains with water, we had secured our route to the south. This happened in early 1972, and one year later we had a firm supply line. From our point of view, the war was already won by us, but the Portuguese still fed into this theory that, once they flooded the region behind the dam, they would lock us out of Tete and therefore out of Mozambique. Well, they were wrong.

Of course, you have to also know that we could not have done all this without the help of Zambia, which I've mentioned once before during my earlier session with you. Our trucks would come loaded with fighters, arms, and ammunition from Nachingwea into Zambia, and, with the blessing of the Zambian leadership, we would cross the border and then head on foot using bush tracks to transport and distribute arms and ammunition in Tete and southern Manica-e-Sofala.

Also remember that the Portuguese colonial army was an occupying force of foreign troops relying on maps. Maps are beautiful, but you can't live in them. They do not give you the experience of mountains, rivers, the bush, trees, and animals. We lived the geography. They lived our land in barracks. We could be ten kilometers from their barracks, and they would not know we were looking at them. The garrisons to us were visible to the naked eye and vulnerable to attack; there was no way they could block us on our way to the south as we moved from village to village. It was almost impossible for them to know us, discover us, and defeat us. They tried to have an advantage by air, but in the end, we could hide or fight with anti-aircraft guns.

Our life as a guerrilla force was very different from theirs. Let me give you just one example: For us to go to the border, it took twelve days. We started walking at four in the morning, then rested at three in the afternoon to eat something. Right after, we started walking again, then rested at seven at night. We followed the same routine day after day after day. The population who lived near the border exported war material to

---

[4]The White Fathers left Mozambique in April 1971.

the next location, and the population from this next location exported to the next, and so on. This is how the war equipment would arrive at its intended location. Wherever there was no population, we would mobilize local cadres to transport the equipment. We were like ants—small, carrying heavy burdens, but too insignificant to be noticed by the enemy.

We kept confidential information to ourselves and did not share it with the people who helped us with logistics. We kept them away from this knowledge, in case they were caught. We wanted to be safe, and we wanted them to be safe too! We worked with colonially appointed chiefs where possible, not to attract Portuguese suspicion. But we also did put in place a structure for the future of a free Mozambique. Where chiefs opposed us, we eliminated them. We appointed a secretary of economic affairs, a secretary for public security, and secretary of administrative affairs. The secretary of economic affairs looked after the agricultural collective for Frelimo and food storage. When the guerrillas arrived and the population passed by, they were given food from the storage silos.

This food supply was very important for our guerrillas, and I'll tell you why. It took nearly two months for our people in Manica-e-Sofala to get to the border and then another couple of months to get back. They needed food supplies, which they got along the way from our food silos and storage units. We made sure the right people got the food, and we communicated with each other with relay messengers and sometimes radio. In Tete, we also had cipher machines to contact provincial commanders who then spoke with Nachingwea on the radio. Any major event, such as the massacre in Mucumbura, was communicated via radio, but, as I mentioned before, we used it in the bush a distance away from civilians and far away from our bases.

The Wiriyamu Triangle and Raimundo Dalepa

Yesterday, when we were looking at the Tete map on the floor in my office, I told you that the Luenha-Zambezi international road was very important for us. Wiriyamu was in that triangle, and Chief Gandar presided over that whole area. The population supported us in a number of ways: with food, with new recruits, and by staying put in their villages. Many refused to leave their homes for the fortified hamlets. I discovered all this a year after my arrival when I spoke to many of them. Some of them relocated and chose to be near our base, and that was very hard on them and us. We became most vulnerable to espionage. We understood their dilemma, and we tried to deal with it. Those that stayed put in their villages proved most helpful to us with food supplies, particularly those who lived near Frelimo's eighth detachment of guerrilla forces. Many of them also supported us logistically, particularly in the third operational zone by helping us cross into Manica-e-Sofala at Mandie. The most notable supporters here lived around our forces commanded by Raimundo Dalepa. The villagers here helped Dalepa's men cross the Luenha from the north side of the Zambezi—and, in this way, reinforced our military bases in Sofala. Yes, as I sit here and reminisce, I can say those were fun days.

Raimundo was a quick, efficient, and strategic thinker—by designing this route of transportation, he avoided Chioco, our other base, supplying the south directly. I came to know Raimundo well. He was thirty-something when we met. He was skinny and of medium height. We ultimately became very good friends. I remember I was in his detachment on April 20th or 21st, and I think it was 1973—I now forget. We had gone together to Tete, close to the slaughterhouse in the city, on a reconnaissance mission. When we got back to base, we were sitting on a table facing each other at around noon. It was almost lunchtime. We had been there for an hour or so, and people were preparing food for lunch. Two comrades, one was a colonel, joined us—I can't remember his name now—and the other was Frelimo's political commissar. Everybody knew him by his nickname, Nenhumfica. He had just returned on a similar reconnaissance mission from the southern front in Sofala. I was the most senior at the table, and I led the discussion on our findings and the best way to plan our strategies for Tete and the southern front.

Suddenly, we were discovered: Two helicopters whizzed by loaded with colonial troops. We estimated they would land three kilometers from us to unload Portuguese troops. The colonel and the commissar were "stumped." They were in shock. They didn't know what to do. After all, it was Raimundo's base. Raimundo studied the situation, including where the Portuguese soldiers were likely to land. Among us, he knew the area best, every hill surrounding the triangle; it was his backyard. With his help we determined they would land in a small clearing at the foot of the mountain close by. He ordered the immediate evacuation of the sick. We were ordered to leave with them, too. It was his operational theater and his base. The able-bodied were ordered to stay put and prepare to defend the base.

But before I could join the others, another helicopter flew over us, this time at low altitude. He ordered his guerrilla unit to fire, and they did. I joined in. The helicopter fell, very close to M'Phadwe, where the Portuguese had built a strategic hamlet. We saw the pilot bail out and, presumably, report his position and that he was hit. We knew then what would happen next: They would bomb the base. We left the base right away, but instead of taking to the hills nearby, Raimundo led the search for the colonial unit. Thirty minutes after the incident with the helicopter, two airplanes flew over us and began bombing the base, setting huts on fire, including huts that we had abandoned a long time ago. They spent the whole day bombarding while we were there watching from our hideouts in the nearby hills. They stopped in the afternoon around 18:00 hours. We came out from our hiding spots, and Raimundo ordered us to track the colonial troops. We walked and walked for two days and didn't find them. I think when they heard that helicopter shot down, they fled and went to Tete. They didn't stay in that zone.

Four days later, we searched for our group of the sick that had left with the colonel and the political commissar. We finally caught up with them and joined them for lunch. Raimundo then organized a party to look for the downed helicopter, and they searched for a while. Thereafter, I left Raimundo and his guerrilla units. I could not stay as I was headed for another mission.

This episode tells you how I remember Raimundo Dalepa—a courageous Maconde warrior sent to Tete by President Samora Machel in early 1971. His intelligence gathering of colonial troops and their movements was thorough and accurate. He was said to personally go disguised into Tete city to find out what was happening there. The main role of his detachment unit was logistical—to support our effort in opening and establishing a sustainable front in Manica-e-Sofala. So, he threatened the enemy troops outside the triangle for one reason: to keep the colonial troops engaged away from our efforts in Manica-e-Sofala. In that sense he was very, very focused and very clear.

Thereafter, Raimundo Dalepa and I talked, mainly over logistics and strategy. He always asked me how he and his unit could help us keep our logistic supply line intact into Sofala, and what were the prospects of reinforcing my troops with ammunition and guns from the north. He was aware of our work and our burden for the armed struggle in the southern theater. You see on this front, below Zambezi, we had nearly two hundred men and women split into four strategic units—one hundred of which were stationed at the main base. We also had one group near Manica and another north of Manica. Here, we had popular support, particularly from villagers living outside strategic hamlets.

Soon after that attack on his base, Dalepa got married to Rosa Maria, from Mucumbura. He and his close friend, Daniel dos Santos, went to her village to celebrate his wedding. You asked if he had children. The answer is yes, four—his first son had my first name, António. I do not know where he lives.

After the war, Raimundo Dalepa came to live in Beira. He was illiterate, you know; the first thing he did was to enroll in a secondary school. Periodically he would stop by or call. The last time he called was in 1989. He came to the military headquarters, and we talked. We talked a lot. He was worried about his children and their future and said he wanted to stop schooling and start a little project. I authorized his leave of absence from schooling and helped him with resources. We supplied documents and the necessary bank contacts, which helped him get a loan. With the loan, he bought a boat in Beira and took it to Cahora Bassa to open a fishing business. He came to me one more time asking to help him get a job in Tete to be near his business. But before anything could come of it, he died. According to Dalepa's widow, he died of gunshot wounds. He had come home to her, and they had fought over something, and both reached for the same gun. She got there first and shot him in, I think, self-defense. He died. One of his cousins came to see me and gave me the details. It was a marital dispute, and the matter was not investigated. This is truly an historical irony that such a great warrior should die like this. I was saddened by his death. It affected me deeply; I was paralyzed for a month or so. I could not get my head around it. Beyond being a commander of great repute, he was a friend, a comrade, and a partner in the liberation struggle. His death was needless.

The Manica-e-Sofala Front

Slow communication and the need for food supplies had its drawbacks.

Corruption?

Yes, you guessed right, corruption! Up to this point, we had been operating in Mucumbura where we had just finished a major operation a month earlier. Frelimo's provincial commissioner then arrived to assess the situation and called for a meeting of commanders and their guerrilla units in the region. We gathered near one of our bases— if I remember correctly it was Chioco. That meeting was at the end of June, maybe early July 1973. I cannot tell you the precise date, and I am sorry because I know you want things as precise as possible. We first discussed our organization and our operations. We also talked about party discipline, in particular the case of Zeca Caliate.

Zeca Caliate was the commander in the fourth sector. I came to know him when I was sent to Tete by President Samora Machel to do reconnaissance of Portuguese economic and military activities around Cahora Bassa and Estima—I think I mentioned this to you already. We formed part of a small group of three commanders who bonded together. First, I went to Estima and then headed south to open the Manica-e-Sofala front. Zeca was stationed around Changara first, and Matias, the third commander, went to operate in Mucumbura. Starting in June or July, we grew concerned about Zeca. He had committed, how shall I say it, irregularities. He was accused of several things: raping members of Frelimo's female units; embezzling funds recovered during operations in Changara and Mucumbura; and conducting unauthorized military operations in the region under his command. He neglected his guerrilla commandos, they said, forcing them to attack enemy positions, which resulted in failures he could not explain to us, and by this, I mean tell us why he was facing such mounting losses. We could not allow him to damage us. When we made inquiries, these accusations proved to be true.

In early June we had already talked to him about all these matters, because we really, really wanted him to succeed. We needed our forces to be happy and eager to face the Portuguese colonial army and defeat it in our armed struggle for liberation. During the guerrilla war we rigorously demanded respect of women. We insisted that their freedom could not be taken away; freedom was sacred. I remember telling my men that unwanted pregnancies were a security risk and must be avoided at all costs, and that included pregnancies among married guerrillas. Regarding this, Frelimo was very educated and vigorous in practicing this form of discipline. Frelimo dictated this on its armed men. The concept that the people see women as something sacred was honored—if we were going to talk to people in the villages and tell them what we thought of women and their rights to freedom equal to men, but not show this respect in practice, we would lose the war. The population would turn away from us and say we wanted the women and didn't care for independence from colonial rule. Our manners had to match our objective: independence. So, when the women were incorporated into Frelimo to form a parallel force of female units, the men were trained to respect their female comrades. This was made clear to everybody; if they violated this rule, they were severely punished. The discipline here was enforced with an iron fist.

During my first session with Zeca, he was told we were going to discuss his case at the meeting that was coming up. He did not want to face the party leadership and discuss his actions. He failed to appear at the meeting. We looked for him everywhere, and we sent our guerrillas after him. Before we could find him, he defected. He surrendered to the Portuguese authorities. I think that was in the first week of July 1973. At the time, I was in charge of that zone, as you know, so this case of corruption and the desertion that followed happened under my watch, and it was a source of great concern and irritation for me.

Dissent and the Final Attack

What happened next?

His leaving Frelimo had an impact on the morale of the guerrilla force under my command. Some of them were afraid to continue with the struggle because the whole region south of Zambezi offered little cover, and now that the Portuguese had Zeca, they knew of our strategy, probably, and our intelligence on their troops. Much of the region we were about to focus on in our next stage of the operation was in low-lying savanna with a few small mountains without trees to hide. It was difficult for our fighters to battle in an open field, and they felt really insecure and fearful to move forward.

On the other hand, I felt that we had to move fast to prevent the enemy from gaining an advantage over us. I gathered my forces. I took with me a highly experienced commander, an adjutant, and a communications specialist. On August 8, 1973, we mounted an ambush against the colonial army *com ferocidade*, with ferocity, at the foot of Mount Selinda, near the border with Zimbabwe, on a steep bend where it was difficult for the enemy to detect us as they approached their garrison. It was very early in the morning. We had a force of 200 guerrillas lying in ambush near that garrison, which had about 100 vehicles, according to our intelligence sources.

We took some mortars and a cannon with us.

Cannons?

Yes, cannons. I know it was not easy to carry them in the bush, but we did. We also took rocket-propelled grenades (RPGs). By two in the afternoon we were ready. We lay in wait spread around the curve. Some of my guerrillas were complaining. They felt exposed, and the sun was blazing hot—hahahahah! I told them we would be all right: "They are not expecting us." Why, you ask? Oh, this ambush was so bold and so outside the box of their thinking that they would least expect it. It was not normal. They were accustomed to Frelimo ambushes from undetected positions hidden deep in the bush. We aimed our ten-millimeter cannons at the middle of the curve toward the straight road to the north of us, then we waited.

At three in the afternoon, a Portuguese patrol traveling from Estima to Tete passed by. There were two full jeeps with about twelve soldiers. We didn't shoot at them because we didn't want them to alert the rest of the convoy following them; instead, we just let them enter the curve and pass through. I asked my guerrillas at the mouth of the curve to be ready to pull the trigger once they heard my pistol shot. Another small group of motor vehicles came behind them, and we let them go, too. When the last vehicle entered the beginning of the curve, they stopped for an unknown reason. That we did not expect. Thank God they suspected nothing. They had no clue that we were there, hidden along the curve. Once in the curve, they were trapped. I shot my pistol in the air to signal my guerrillas to begin shooting, and the ambush started. Normally, the mortar fire went first; however, this time we used the cannon on the vehicles. It blew them off the road. It was terrible. They didn't stand a chance. Whoever was in front still alive was hit with mortar shells, and those in the middle got the full blast of the cannon, again and again.

The cars were trapped. They had to move forward fast. They couldn't go back. They knew our guerrillas were lying in wait at the beginning of the curve. As the casualties mounted, we could see they were on the radio asking for help. By the time that help came, it was too late; we had packed ourselves up and gone.

This attack was a turning point for us. From thereafter, we had a whole new dynamic, and many soldiers noticed that even without the deep cover conditions offered by Tete, it was possible to fight the enemy without difficulty. We brought some of the soldiers there from different detachments, and chiefs of sections wanted to participate in that attack because they wanted to see how I would do it to march south of Tete. So, you can say that this attack was a new stage for our armed liberation, and it gave our armed guerrillas a new way to fight in this territory south of Mount Selinda. I just can't forget that day, August 8, 1973! It was carnage, total carnage.

Photo 4 Bulachu Pensadu Zambezi, Wiriyamu. Photo by Mustafah Dhada, © 1995.

Interviewee:
Bulachu Pensadu Zambezi
Date (yyyy mm dd):
1995 05 14–26
Duration (hh mm ss):
1h 57m 46s
Place:
Tete
Language:
Portuguese/Nhungwe Mix
Interpreter:
Abidu Karimu and Senhor Elídio
Redactions:
None

Frelimo's Arrival in the Triangle

My name is Bulachu Pensadu Zambezi. I am 1.70 meters tall. I am the son of Pensadu Zambezi and Antónia Panela. My identification card shows these details. I was born in the village of Wiriyamu on October 10, 1947. At twenty-one, I married Maria Luisa

Manteiga, and I have five children with her. Two year later I married again. My second wife was called Aesta Faluchepa. Yes, I have two wives. I can't write or read well. That is why I have not signed my identification card, as you can see. You see here, this is my thumbprint. I am a painter and live in M'Phadwe, near Tete. I speak Portuguese well now, though I didn't when Wiriyamu happened.

I was twenty-nine at the time of the massacre. We had no knowledge of the colonial war. We had no radio; not even the *mfumo*, the chief of Wiriyamu, had one. War had not come to us yet, but when it did, we got it two times: once when Frelimo came to us and we gained independence. Thereafter, we could go anywhere, from this village to that village. We also got poverty and famine, which is why people went far—from here to over there, to Malawi, and over there south of here to Zimbabwe. Some went even deeper south, to South Africa. Then came war number two. This war was more personal and punishing. Everyone suffered, and everyone was affected by it; even today, we feel the impact. As you can see, Wiriyamu is no more.

Before these wars, we lived here on this spot. We stayed home, in our village with our people, our community near and around our *machamba*. Yes, some people still went away to bring money, but not leave permanently—that is how outside money saved us from hunger and poverty.

Back then, before the wars, there were huts everywhere, right up to the road that leads to Luenha. You see those two boulders over there near that baobab: Homes, tamarind trees, and baobabs surrounded all this land, right up to that tree.

The house of the chief of Wiriyamu was here where I am standing. If you came from the main tarred road, you had to pass the village of Juawu; then you went up the hill, you passed those two boulders, then you passed my house, and the next house was his. It was right in the middle of the Wiriyamu village. He could see everyone and all the houses from the front yard of his house; he could see the homes and the people of Juawu. He could see homes and his people at the back of his house in Djemusse, behind that baobab tree—no, not that tree, this one. You see that dove making that sound. Yes, that tree. He even could peer down over my house into the houses in the Riachu that faced the village of Chaworha. The houses here were at the bottom of that dry creek separated by the dirt road that comes to this center of the Wiriyamu village.

Here, where I am pointing with my index finger, was my father's house, to the right of the house of Chief Wiriyamu. Right in front of his house was Tenente's home. His son had not arrived in this world yet, but he was coming. His house blocked the lower half of that baobab tree near the boulders, which held up the village from the Riachu below. I remember that tree well.

There were houses on the left of Wiriyamu's front yard, near where that monument is. Yes, that monument that has bones of those killed behind the small glass window. One house I forgot to mention was the house of that old man. His house was there, near where that monument is. After the massacre he went blind. He can see no daylight now. Others had their houses on both sides of the road to Luenha. There were houses all along the road. There could be more than one hundred houses around there. They were connected, with not much space in between them. And of course, there were also *machambas*, agricultural plots, spread around. It was a very busy community. Wiriyamu was the center.

Chief Wiriyamu had many brothers; Wiriyamu was the oldest, and the youngest was Pungusane, who had quite a few children. Chief Wiriyamu had countless goats and forty to fifty heads of cattle in a corral near the road leading out to Juawu. My father's corral of two hundred goats and thirty-one cows was on the other side, near the Riachu village. I also had a personal corral with goats, near my father's. I started with six of them, and I can't remember how many I ended up having. I did not have cattle, though. Among us, the richest man was Chief Wiriyamu, with the highest number of cattle, and goats. Then came his brother, with many domestic animals and *machambas*. Since he was rich and powerful, Wiriyamu had helpers, one of which was Tenente Valeta. Whenever there was a problem, Tenente would help fix it. He was that young man's father—not that one, this one I am pointing out there. Yes, there—he is called Vasco Tenente. His father passed away, not during the massacre, but recently. As I said, Tenente's house was close to that baobab tree, where the massacre happened; he lost his wife, kids, and one daughter-in-law in that massacre.

This area was known for raising cattle. It was normal for families to have goats, cows, and chickens. The cattle weren't used in wedding ceremonies; that is how we made our money, by selling livestock. We cultivated our own crops, but it was mainly for ourselves and we bought sugar from the shops to make *pombe* and *cachaço*, our alcoholic beverages.

Over there was the market for us to sell cattle and goats. People could arrange their methods of payment. The Portuguese veterinarian Gonçalves and the cattle buyer Mr. Aguiar would come to us from the main tarred road to buy cattle for their clients. The two of them knew their business well; they would always bargain us down every time they bought from us. They were well known for that.

Spiritual Life and Frelimo's Arrival

The Great Spirit, *mphondorho*, the power of the lion king, controlled our community; kept things balanced and helped us with our hardships, our need for rains; and made conflicts between us disappear. The *mphondorho* spoke by entering a person. Through that person it talked to us and told us what to do. We knew which person had received *mphondorho*. A person who had *mphondorho* in him always began by shouting and screaming, kind of like crazy. The spirit possessed him. If the spirit entered a person different from the person who had received *mphondorho* last time, a spokesman was appointed to sort out, though it did not happen often. The mediator was called *kabandazi*. Senhor Soda was the *mphondorho* receiver for our community. He was the last person to receive the Great Spirit. He died in M'Phadwe in 1992, two years ago.

He normally sat at the spirit place on a round mud platform over between my father's house and the village of Juawu. When he came to pronounce the oracle, he would come and sit on the platform leaning against his *thundo*, his bag. Through him, the *mphondorho* would normally ask first for a fresh pair of clothes and some tobacco. The tobacco was rubbed and rubbed and rubbed in the palm of his hand. Some would be spread all over the face, and the rest put in a tobacco jar. With this rubbing, the tobacco was inhaled so that everything travelled up to purify the head and the eyes. That way the person would feel, see, and talk clearly about what the *mphondorho* wanted from us.

Normally the *mphondorho* appeared to help us *com coisas de resolver*, with conflicts to resolve or things to sort out. We had to do what the *mphondorho* asked of us: sacrifices and visits to the sacred secret forest, for example. This way we were taken care of and the lion spirit stayed under control; otherwise the *mphondorho* would roam wild among us and harm the villages and its people. So that is how we lived here in the village of Wiriyamu. Remember, all this was Wiriyamu. Djemusse was Wiriyamu. Riachu was Wiriyamu. Juawu was Wiriyamu. All this was Wiriyamu. Chaworha, however, was not part of Wiriyamu. It was another village. Then one day Frelimo came.

Frelimo arrived in our village at 6:30 a.m. on October 9, 1972. I remember it well; I had just gotten up and finished stretching and yawning. The sun had not fully reached the village, and I stood leaning against the tamarind tree in my father's yard when I saw some movement behind that tree blocking the Tenentes' house. I then saw people. They were hidden behind the boulders until one of them came forward, followed by two others. They were not wearing uniforms. The others spread out—that is how I saw Frelimo the first time in my life. I later found out the names of the first three I saw: Armando Tivane,[5] Raimundo Dalepa, and Donai Nkume.

The person who entered first was small and skinny—I later found out he was Raimundo Dalepa. He came to me and said, "Good morning." I replied, "Good morning," but I was very scared. He was carrying a big gun. I thought I knew him but didn't know from where.

He then said, "Don't be afraid! We are Frelimo. Do Portuguese troops come here?"

I said, "No. We do not have Portuguese troops in this village."

He asked me where was Chief Wiriyamu's house, so I showed it to him. I actually took him there and was present when he approached the chief. The other two had already spread out to protect their friend who was now with the chief. He then started talking with the chief in Nhungwe.

"Look! We don't want to create problems for you. We are Frelimo. We have not come to kill you," he said. "We are fighting for everybody."

That was the reason they were there. He then invited the chief of Wiriyamu for a walk. His answer was, "Okay, let's go," because he wanted to hear what Frelimo had to say.

I was told to collect the people in the village and the surrounding area, so they could get to know each other better. At first Wiriyamu was scared; he did not know who Frelimo was, but some others in this village and in Juawu and Djemusse did. One of them was

---

[5]For his biographical details see Abel Mazuza and Xadreque Mate, *Vida e Obra de Armando Tivane, 1937–1973* (Maputo: ARPAC, Instituto de Investigação Sócio-Cultural, 2013).

George Nativo, and he knew them well. Nativo is alive and lives in Tete. He can tell you more. I know where he lives, and I can take you there.

Wiriyamu came back from his walk very worried, but what could he do? Frelimo had to leave the village soon because they could be discovered by the Portuguese patrol or by informants. Chief Wiriyamu sent word afterward to people in the village that there was going to be a meeting the next day, early in Machangazi, twenty to twenty-five minutes' walk from Wiriyamu, about three kilometers, at a house near the Luenha River.

I left early in the morning. Everybody was going to that house in Machangazi—there were people from Djemusse, people from Juawu, people from Wiriyamu, people from Riachu. Tenente's whole house was going, as was mine. I cannot remember how many people, but there were maybe twenty houses gathered there. The bush surrounding Wiriyamu was silent; not one person could be seen. That is how many people got there to hear Frelimo speak. Some people from Frelimo were wearing uniforms, others not.

Raimundo Dalepa and Tavane were present, but only Tavane spoke. He said they had come to us in the village, found us welcoming, and faced no problems. He said he felt protective of us and compared us to Frelimo citizens and children. They were there to fight and free our country, and with our help they could. His words of encouragement made us think about our suffering. They suffered as well, he said, and were ready to make a change. He said he had also left his family behind. Sometimes, he too didn't have enough to eat. Sometimes, he too starved, but he chose to fight to free us all. He asked us if we wanted to follow Frelimo to change for the better, because they were there to receive us and help us do that.

This meeting lasted about two hours. When it was about time to eat, Chief Wiriyamu organized a group to cook; they went back to the village to get food and then cooked it. We had *massa*, cornflour porridge. Everybody there ate together. Afterwards, Dalepa, Tavane, and the Frelimo soldiers left for a mountain called M'Chenga to speak to the people there, and Wiriyamu and the others, including myself, went back to the village. From this day forward, I can say that *mfumo* Wiriyamu had joined Frelimo; he did not go to the Portuguese when he got back to his village—he could have, but he did not.

The next day very early in the morning Tavane and Dalepa came to the village, and Chief Wiriyamu had sixteen people ready to join Frelimo: Luis Wiriyamu, son of Chief Wiriyamu, who is today the secretary of the party of the new Wiriyamu village; Fosse Wiriyamu; Cupitiwa Baute; David Xavier; Alverino Tenente; Verelino Maebeke, a nephew of Chief Wiriyamu; Seanane Matope, also a nephew of Chief Wiriyamu; Anhaidu Baulene; Cuzondiwa Baulene; José Baulene; Tomé Baulene; Muandezonda Lussekene; Luís Baulene; myself, Bulachu Pensadu Zambezi; Vinte Paganate; and Camulane António.

This was the first group from the Wiriyamu village—the October Group. Later, Armando Tavane and Raimundo Dalepa came back to meet us at Imphangarha with more recruits who joined us. The next day we said goodbye to our families and left on foot for Chioco, Frelimo's central base for the fifth operational zone under commander Zeca Caliate. It took us three days to reach Chioco. We were divided; some went directly to fight while others went for training. I went for training in Mucumbura by canoe. As soon as I arrived, I went to the border, to Cassende, where José Moiane was located. From there I went to Tanzania, where I stayed for about eight months in training. After that, I was given another training course for about one month. After finishing that I went to Cabo Delgado, where I stayed one month. I was taken to Niassa, where I stayed one month as well, and then my training came to an end.

I was then sent back to this area. Alverino Tenente, my comrade and friend, was already at the Kadembo base, as were the others from the October Group. Dalepa and Tavane chose us, the October Group, to open up the front in Manica-e-Sofala. Kadembo was Raimundo Dalepa's nickname. Of course, his real name was Raimundo Dalepa, but the people here saw the name as "bourgeois" and gave him an authentic name that suited him better—Kadembo. And it sounded better, too! Kadembo is an animal that smells.

A skunk?

Yes, a skunk; Dalepa was given that nickname because of the work he used to do there, and the population noticed it. I came to know him much better later on, of course. His base was in the M'Pharhamadwe area, an area that housed many bases of Frelimo's eighth detachment, although I cannot tell you how many bases there were in that zone; what I do know is that there were no Frelimo bases or guerrillas living in the villages of Juawu and Djemusse.

After the two-hour meeting, Kadembo lived up to his promise. He looked after us, and he attended to our needs and the population here like a father. He was a great spirit. He was very courageous and fought well—whoever fought him would lose. He lived among us. His troops began patrolling Wiriyamu regularly and gathered information on *as forças dos colonos*, the colonial army. The Frelimo patrol had at least ten people, depending on what they were doing, and they carried weapons at all times. I do not know where these troops were based, but they came from behind that monument near the Luenha River.

Wiriyamu and the End

November and December were hard on Wiriyamu. One day, and this happened well before the massacre, Chief Wiriyamu found his daughter, Nonica, waiting for him at his house. She had left her husband. Nonica was married to Thai Kongorhogondo, the son of Chief Kongorhogondo, who considered the people of Wiriyamu socially inferior. He and his family considered themselves more sophisticated, more genuine than the people in my village. Thai was a member of Grupos Especiais (GE), Special Forces of the colonial army. He had a brother, Johnny, who worked under Chico Kachavi. Both Johnny and Chico were PIDE agents. At that time, they were also called Direção-Geral de Segurança (DGS), General Directorate for Security.

Thai was violent and abusive; he and Nonica fought quite often, and he drank a lot. Nonica got tired of him and left. Her father said she could stay home until they sorted out what was what. One day, Thai came to the Wiriyamu village unannounced to take her back to Tete where they lived. As he approached Chief Wiriyamu's house, he saw Frelimo patrolling on this side of the Riachu—they were armed and transporting guns and things to the Frelimo base near the Luenha River.

He begged Nonica to come home. Nonica refused to go back with him. I also do not know for sure if Thai told his brother or the *forças colonias*, the colonial army's *Grupos Especiais*, Special Forces, what he saw at Wiriyamu. A few days later, *um misto*, a person of color, named Miranda was seen looking here and there, in and around Wiriyamu. He talked with the chief and became friends with him. I cannot say that he was a spy for DGS, but he came back again—and kept coming and going until he was caught by Frelimo soldiers, blindfolded, and taken to the base. They interrogated him at the base; he was stripped to his underwear and left to walk home with the threat that he would be killed if he told the Portuguese where the base was.

I do not know if Miranda told the Portuguese or not; however, I do know that soon thereafter, the colonial troops appeared, looking for Frelimo. Frelimo troops spotted them near the 18th parallel, crossing very early in the morning on December 15, and they launched an attack, killing several Portuguese soldiers. How many I cannot say *com certeza*, for sure.

On the day of the massacre, several people could not be found at Wiriyamu because they were at the sacred forest nearby, reserved for our ancestors. They had gone there perhaps a few days before accompanied by *chimbawas*—vestal virgins. December was usually a month of rain and seed planting, but this year the rains failed to arrive. The people were desperate—with little to eat and not much water. The creeks had dried up, and nearly all the hard-shelled fruits on the baobab trees had been picked. Virtually nothing was left. Chief Wiriyamu asked for the *mphondorho*, lion spirit, to be summoned. Senhor Soda was called, and he received the spirit, who asked the village to provide the ancestral spirits with sacrifices, including *pombe*. The old men in the village, Senhor Soda, Chief Wiriyamu, and the virgins went to the sacred forest to offer the sacrifices. They all stayed in that sacred forest until the first drops of rain fell on Wiriyamu.

That is where they were on the morning of December 16, 1972, when Wiriyamu happened. It was this same blind man over there that came to the village on the day of the massacre. He came running from the village of Chaworha—as I said, Chief Wiriyamu was not in his hut, so he ran to Senhor Tenente's house to warn him that they had to stay exactly where they were because the soldiers from Chaworha were coming this way. The soldier who asked the blind man to give the message was white—that is what the blind man told me, but I was not there, so I cannot tell you what I did not see.

Chief Wiriyamu, meanwhile, had returned from the sacred forest and was near his *machamba* when he found out what was happening in his village. He did not fight the Portuguese. He could not because they had weapons. Chief Wiriyamu didn't wait. He ran to escape, to save himself and his family. If he had stayed there, he would have died like the others in his village. Those that could, ran away; some went to the Frelimo base, some to the M'Phadwe *aldeamento* (strategic village), and some to a village near Gama. Kadembo did not know what was happening in Wiriyamu—he found out much later.

The Frelimo patrol found the chief *no mato* (in the bush), and took him to a small base called Richard. It was a sub-base attached to Kadembo's base. He was not allowed to go back to his village thereafter, so he stayed in a village near the Richard base until July 1973.

In that month the Portuguese colonial army discovered refugees from the Wiriyamu massacre who were taken to Tete and tortured—tortured and tortured—until they confessed. They told the Portuguese where the Richard base was, which was located near the margin of the M'Bewa River. Portuguese helicopters were then sent to land north of the base. They surrounded the base and the population near it.

Frelimo combatants were away; there was one unarmed man there, and there was no one to protect the villagers. The colonial army killed almost the entire population. Some escaped. That's where they found Chief Wiriyamu and his family; they killed his third wife and his children, but his first and second wives escaped. His eldest son, Laskene Wiriyamu, was not there—he too was saved this way.

Thereafter, Chief Wiriyamu's surviving family lived from base to base, except for Laskene, who stayed independent and free until April 1974. The colonial army found him, the chief, alone in the bush during an operation and killed him. Later in 1983, the first wife got sick from starvation and died; many people died of starvation in 1983. Nine years later, Senhor Soda passed away. The other wife, the second wife of Chief Wiriyamu, is still with us. She lives near Tete. That is how Wiriyamu came to an end.

All I said I saw with my own eyes.

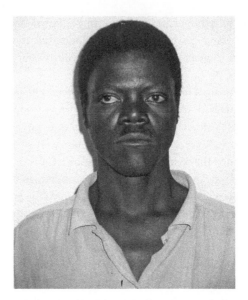

Photo 5 Vasco Tenente Valeta, Wiriyamu. Photo by Mustafah Dhada, © 1995.

Interviewee:
Vasco Tenente Valeta
Date (yyyy mm dd):
1995 05 25
Duration (hh mm ss):
1h 2m 13s
Place:
Wiriyamu
Language:
Portuguese/Nhungwe Mix
Interpreter:
Abidu Karimu
Redactions:
None

The Loss of Homes and Cattle

I am Vasco, son of Tenente Valeta and Foliana Kusai. I was born February 2, 1957. I am now married to Ernária Balo, and I am a peasant. I don't remember the number of people living in the village when Wiriyamu happened. There could have been ten, thirty, fifty houses and villages. Today, after so many years, I can identify some of the houses there. I knew Mr. Wiriyamu's house, his two brothers' places, and the homes of their children. In my family, we were six children. Three passed away, and three are alive. One is married; one is very young, and one lives in the new Wiriyamu village. There, in the new Wiriyamu village, I know two brothers of the old chief and some of his neighbors. Some people I know and can identify didn't come today to see you here but are in the new Wiriyamu, people like Chuva, Pungusane, Alegero, Cenceregue, Sinoia, Tenente, Naranguamene, Ningaebwe, and others whose names I don't recall.

There were a lot of *palhotas*, huts, in my village as I remember. In fact, there was a hut for each household. Chief Wiriyamu had three wives, so he had three huts. His kids also had their own huts since they were all married, so you see there were lots of huts everywhere. Many people had goats and cows, which they would sell in the market. When the massacre happened, they ran, leaving behind all these animals. Before the massacre, people would sell them to the Portuguese at the cattle market, near the football field. Mr. Gonçalves and Mr. Aguiar were two cattle buyers. They came to the village when they needed more—Yes. Just like that. Gonçalves was Portuguese, short, very fat, and had a long beard. He spoke directly with Chief Wiriyamu, who negotiated with Gonçalves the sale of animals.

Mr. Aguiar, though, did business in a different way. He spoke to sellers directly when he needed cattle, goats, and chickens—not pigs though, because pigs were not for sale. They helped keep the *quintal*, the yard, clean. We prepared the animals to be sold and delivered them to the buyers. Sometimes, Mr. Aguiar would contact Senhor Saize, Chief Wiriyamu's helper, who then arranged the animals to be loaded on Mr. Aguiar's truck. Mr. Aguiar did not wear a military uniform because he was a civilian. I do not remember Mr. Saize's details since he died when I was still very young. I also cannot tell you how much cattle and goats they bought from us.

Our life in Wiriyamu was simple. The men would wake up at 6 a.m. and go to their *machambas*, their agricultural plots. That was normal for most men. Some people would go a bit later at noon, and others even as late as 2 p.m. They would spend their entire day there. Those who went late would bring lunch to those who were there since early morning. They would eat lunch together at the *machamba*. When the sun was about to go down, at 7 p.m., they all returned home. They would herd their cattle and goats into corrals and go home to rest. Some had corrals attached to their houses, but most did not. If the animals were sick, needed tending, or needed to be ready for delivery the next day, they would be held in these overnight pens.

What about night life?

There wasn't nightlife as I recall. People would rest, eat dinner, and after a while go to bed—that was all I saw. We didn't have electricity. We had big cables carrying electricity on the other side of the village there, far away from Djemusse, the next village up.

I was a shepherd then. My life was normal. I usually got up in the morning and took the cattle near the village you passed on your way to M'Chenga. I usually left the cattle to graze there and went to play football with other kids my age. Everyone my age followed this routine, more or less.

Did you see any Frelimo bases near you?

No, I don't remember seeing any Frelimo bases in places I normally went—remember, I was very young. I do remember Portuguese commandos arriving in Wiriyamu in

December 1972. Some of them were Africans, and some were white; I remember most vividly that event.

On that day, December 16, I got up later than usual, took my animals and left, and came back before lunchtime. That is when I saw that blind man come from Juawu carrying a message from the white soldiers there. The road that starts from Wiriyamu splits halfway; one goes to Juawu, and the other goes to Chaworha. That blind man said nobody should leave their homes because the soldiers wanted to talk to us. He then went to Chief Wiriyamu's house, but he was not there because he was at his *machamba*. The blind man then left for Djemusse.

We were already gathered in the village because there was a party at Mr. Tenente's house. We did not expect anything bad to happen to us. We had no reason to suspect anything. Then two soldiers came, one African and one white—the African soldier spoke Nhungwe. They put me, my cousin, the son of this blind man, my three sisters-in-law, three nephews, my mama, my two young brothers, and some people I didn't recognize into this big hut owned by Mr. Tenente. There were twenty-two of us in total. The African soldier shoved us inside as the white soldier gave orders.[6] Unfortunately, I did not see how the grenade was unpinned and thrown in the hut. The door was already closed when I heard this noise inside the hut and I was near the back door, which had opened—Oh! The boom of the grenade must have done it. I ran, we, three people ran. The rest didn't get to escape, and they all died on that day. After that blast I do not know how the others died. We went and hid near M'pharamadwe and stayed there for three days. We ate *mbonde*, leaves from the baobab tree, and drank water out of the holes in the rocks. Then we decided to go to the city, to the M'Phadwe village. We arrived there two days later and have not moved since.

---

[6]The white soldier in question was Captain Antonino Melo.

Interviewee:
Antonino Melo
Date (yyyy mm dd):
1995 07 02–05
Duration (hh mm ss):
9h 10m 23s
Place:
Lisbon
Language:
Portuguese
Interpreter:
None
Redactions:
Light

Operation Marosca and the Aftermath

My name is Antonino Melo. I am an only child. I was born in Agueda, a small Portuguese village north of Lisbon on February 12, 1951. I have been married for nineteen years and have two children: an eighteen-year-old son, and a daughter who is eleven—about to turn twelve in August. I left Portugal to go to Mozambique very early in my life. I had an uncle on my father's side—my father's older brother; my father was one of five siblings—who went to Mozambique a long time ago, *estás ver*, you see! And some time after he got there, he called my father over, who was the youngest of the five siblings, and my father went to work on the railroads. He first worked in railway engine rooms in Beira. Eleven years later, he became a conductor. I did my primary education in Beira at the Maquinino school near the railway tracks close to the bridge over the river. I then went to trade school for over seven years. Thereafter I studied mechanical and electrical engineering. Meanwhile my father changed jobs. He became a factory worker.

I was then conscripted into the army. They called me to report myself at the army's instruction center in Boane, where I received military training for three months, and just as I was finishing this, a series of commando squads showed up from Montepuez to select a few of us to undergo commando training. We took several aptitude tests. I'm not exactly sure of this, but between seven hundred and eight hundred were chosen for commando training; however, only around 120 survived the training, and that is how the sixth company of commandos was formed, August 9, 1972. I was assigned to the first group of commandos of that company. Each group leader formed part of a larger company, which was headed by an army captain. After six months [the army captain] fell ill with hepatitis. He was hospitalized, and I was made commander of the company because I was next in line as the senior-most officer. [Furthermore] I had achieved a high score during training. My records indicate I went to Tete on November 17, 1972, to establish a commando base in Mavuzi. I had not been in Tete before. I had been assigned to a military base outside Tete. I could show you more or less on a sketch where I was in Tete. [Alas!] I don't remember now the name of the place—we could check it at home in my commando company's logbook of operations. All of the operations, or nearly all, are in that logbook. Anyway, I reached Mavuzi on November 17 to establish the military base there and on December 23 or 24, 1972, I left Tete. The day we finished burning the dead in a common grave in Wiriyamu we went to the airport to permanently leave Tete.

My job was to clean up an area as ordered by the high command. [In the case of Wiriyamu] we could not have known if the information they had received on Frelimo presence in that area was true or not. They got [this information] from the DGS. Superior orders were superior orders. When we got these we followed them. They were told of guerrilla bases, and when we were informed of this, we took off to clean the place up. Although we did various operations in this zone this way, we did not always find enemy presence. We would go into a place and essentially find ourselves in villages with huts—empty. They were not normal huts, though; they were different. Instead of being round, which would be normal, they were V-shaped, very small and covered with nearby foliage, and therefore they were temporary huts. You could tell that the place was an abandoned Frelimo base. Our information told us the zone was under Frelimo influence. We expected attacks by them, and often enough they did attack us.

Once we were ambushed—I cannot remember exactly when or where—a few days before Operation Marosca, I think. It was near one of these villages with temporary huts. One of our group was patrolling the area after an operation. So, we went to their rescue. The group contacted us on the radio. I went there in person with my men. We had many injured [and] needed to evacuate the wounded and get [the hell] out of the zone to a nearby location. There, everything was peaceful. What did we find? We found a village—a village with *machambas* and everyone there acting normal.

"Did you see anything?" Nothing, no response.

"Did you hear gun shots?" Nothing, no immediate response.

It was impossible for them not to have heard gunfire from the ambush nearby.

"No," they said, "We heard nothing."

This ambush happened very, very early in the morning, south of the Cruzamento Dezoito, near the fork off the road. We normally flew from Montepuez to a site in Tete, and we were there for three months. Now, I'm not sure when we were there, so let me grab the logbook of my unit because it will tell us when. It has [most of] the operations of our unit. This particular Marosca operation isn't recorded here—1974, 1973, 1973, 1973, September, October, October 1972, August, October—I am trying to locate myself in this history, so let me see, hmmmmmmmmmmm. The logbook says we left on October 20 and came back on November 7. We then came to this zone, near Luenha River . . . so, we came back on November 7 and left on January 20, 1973.

At this time there weren't any other compan[ies] of commandos in that area that I know of. We had five groups of twenty-five people. But since there would always be someone on vacation, sick, so on and so forth, it was more or less fifteen to twenty people in each group. So, six groups with an average of twenty people would make the entire commando company of around 120 people in total. The first group was the one that went to Wiriyamu. The third group and the sixth group left two or three days after, more or less. I'm still not sure about the days. They went by truck from here to this location, here, Cruzamento Dezoito. From there they went by foot more or less. They went early in the morning, after the briefing, which was done in the ZOT [Zona Operacional de Tete] building complex. When I got there, the zonal commandant was there. I don't remember his name now. I know that someone from the Portuguese Air Force was there. There were more people present, but I don't know who they were. Six people in total perhaps. In all sincerity, I cannot recall exactly the minute details. I know there were more people, but I don't recall who.

What I remember was discussing the planning of the operation. A major, whose name began with P, led the discussion. I met him a few months later in Nampula when I was ordered to be there for interrogation. I was in the bush at my military base when they called me to appear at ZOT. I got there in army fatigues. I was always in army camouflage—that green spotted uniform that commandos wear. There were others present in uniform from the air force, a commandant who was also in army fatigues, and two more people. I have the impression these two were dressed as civilians. The room was like a long room. The table wasn't big. It was narrow and long. I can't remember how many chairs. There was a [map] framed on the wall, those military area maps. When I entered, they were already there—waiting. I don't remember the words they said, but I know it was an explanation of the operation. Until then I did not know of the planned Operation Marosca. I was told about it at the briefing. That is when I first came to know. As I said, it was early in the morning, as these things generally are.

After the briefing, we went by truck to the airport and waited for helicopters to take us to the mission site in the bush. There were more than one helicopter waiting, perhaps five. We couldn't board yet. We had to wait until the Portuguese Air Force had finished bombing the area. After that was done, they gave us the orders to get in, where to exactly I cannot tell you, but the helicopter pilots knew where to drop us, me and my men of the first group. The third and the sixth group were already in the bush. It was planned that way. They went by truck in that zone to prevent the population from escaping. Well, not only the population but Frelimo elements mixed among them. That was how things were done. The logistics units would be sent to assume positions. We were next. We were heliported to the site ready to attack. The logistics units would lie in ambush waiting to capture escapees. The helicopters landed on site at 1200 hours, I believe, or just before.

After the operation we went back to the base that I indicated to you on the map. There wasn't any debriefing afterward. My men, the third and the sixth group, returned either the next day or after two days. So, let me clarify to you: My group was transported in five helicopters. We landed and we spread out. The moment we landed [pandemonium ensued]. People ran to escape from us.

But where did you land exactly?

I don't know precisely where we landed, but the helicopter pilot could tell you. I know it was in the middle of huts, though. There were rocks, I remember that. The helicopter landed. Usually, helicopters have two exits. I got out from one exit, right? If we divide twenty-five men in my unit into fives, I get five people in each helicopter. Right? There were no soldiers operating in the area aside from the two groups, my unit and the one that went ahead of us; not to my knowledge. We landed and hit the ground running. We could not afford to fart around. I got into one and sat in the front, I remember vaguely. I also vaguely remember the large boulders. And I remember we had to climb up to get to the village.

We got there. People were running helter-skelter. We surrounded them. This individual from the DGS was in the middle of all this.

You mean Chico?

Yes, him. He was busy asking questions. He was with me, us in the helicopter that brought us to the site. I think; I am not sure.

But wasn't this irregular?

Not really! Many of our operations were with individuals sent by the DGS to guide us to locate suspected Frelimo bases. It wasn't very often, but sometimes the DGS gave us informants that we did not know, to lead us to Frelimo bases, not only in Tete but also in Cabo Delgado's operational command zone. So, you got to a certain zone and took with you these informants, in fact, DGS prisoners. They had already been interrogated by the DGS, and their mission was to lead us to suspected bases, though most of the times, they would lead us to nothing.

So, Chico was already in the middle of all that. We tried to keep order and control the population. Generally, in such operations they would flee right away.

Were you on his right or left?

I do not remember if I was near Chico on his right or left when the interrogations began. It was not that simple. I wasn't in the middle of all this, standing and twiddling my thumbs. I was walking from one side to another, trying to control the population, because the area was big, and there was no telling what could happen next. We could be ambushed at a moment's notice. We couldn't be static. We had to be on the move, on the lookout. We were in that area until dusk. We landed on this site and went ahead. I don't know if we walked more than one kilometer; maybe not. Today it is hard for me to say if it was over one kilometer because I had no previous knowledge of the place. If I were there today, maybe I could say, "Look, we walked to there, from here."

The site I mentioned for the helicopters to land, [they] did not actually land. For that to happen, you had to have minimum clearance. It was not that easy to find that kind of clearance for helicopters to land. Where we landed wasn't very flat. I remember that. So, when we landed, my men and I hit the ground running; the helicopter took off, and another helicopter landed after us. So, I cannot tell you if we all landed on the same exact spot. This sort of details we didn't have to worry about. Normally in this type of operation, getting out of the helicopter fast was more important. This was normal. Not all helicopters would land at the same time because that would have been dangerous.

Did you send somebody to the villagers nearby, asking them to stay put until you got there?

I do not recall sending emissaries to other villages nearby to tell the people there to stay put. If you are talking about the group that was sent before us, it was there to set up traps to catch people who tried to run. They were well hidden. So, let me clarify. The people were not on lockdown before we arrived there, no. That is not how the operation went.

The operation started at noon and lasted until, say, 1730 hours, give or take. We were in that zone until then, you can say that, yes. Today, as I sit here with you, I feel the weight of some of the things we did perhaps more so than twenty years ago. These [intervening] years have softened my heart. At that time, we had been trained as commandos. The course of commandos we took, told us to keep our eyes on the target. Psychological action was essential, not only for combat action but also for survival, until we left the army. Every day was a battle for survival, day in and day out, as we killed in combat. There was no other option. Our sensitive side was asleep. And remember that the psychological readiness training was more important than military action. The enemy could eliminate us more easily with psychological action than with military action in the field. Therefore, this thing of going there to do a cleanup was just that. We were ordered to clean up, to kill, and we did it; we asked no questions. We cleaned. After all we were fighting a guerrilla war, and essentially, we could not afford survivors to testify. They could not be left behind because we were not in a conventional war. If survivors revealed what we did to them, we, my men and I, would be dead. And that was the brutal reality of the situation. Besides we did not know who was who in the population. We didn't know what to do with it. Chico did the interrogation; we cleaned, and clean up we did. That is when we shoved them in huts.

When this shoving into huts happened, I have an impression that we were here [pointing to a sketch quickly drawn on a fieldwork note pad]. There was a sort of a goat pen here. Well, the huts then caught fire, but we did not burn people. Yes, there was fire spreading everywhere, so people burned, and we burned them afterwards. Let me explain. Days after the operation we went back to burn everything—normally, we never did this. In this case we were ordered to return to burn bodies. Normally, whomever we killed, that's how they were left. We did not burn the huts. The huts were burned because of exploding grenades. True, quite a lot of people died, some burned in the huts, I imagine. I wish I could be there again to see for myself what we did. I am afraid I can't recall now if Juawu was the place we went to first or not. I think we landed and kept going from one place to another, so for us it was one whole operation. We kept moving, going from one place to another, with the DGS elements in tow. I did not interrogate. Chico did—it was the DGS's job. I moved from one place to another to keep the population contained. The population was already running away, naturally. The massacre of the people in the huts continued, naturally.

We moved on, as one single operation. We found a group of huts here and further down another group. To me, it was all part of one operation—it was only later that I came to know that these were several villages. But to us then it was one continuous area of villages, of separate clusters of huts with agricultural plots around them. So, the people were shoved into huts, and we threw a grenade with them inside, and we moved on.

I do not know if anyone in my group spoke Nhungwe. The majority of my unit was black. They were from all over Mozambique. I cannot guarantee you any of my men understood what Chico was saying. I was never supplied with that kind of information from the high command. But why do you ask this question?

Well, for operational efficiency. Knowing the language would have made it easier for you to know what is being said and pick up clues on which to act to keep your men safe. No?

I see now why you asked the question. There was one person in my company, a soldier whose family lived in Tete, but he was from Maputo, if I'm not mistaken. I am not sure if he was in this operation with me. I have the impression he was in the third group.

Well, let us now head to the center of the village of Wiriyamu, shall we?

Certain details are hard to remember now. I remember—let me say—I have a vague idea of constantly walking from one side to another in Wiriyamu, worried about the safety of my men. I also remember that I was almost never close to Chico. In fact, I was almost never near him, shall we say, because that wasn't my job; it was exclusively his. I didn't have anything to do with this line of work. He went with me to interrogate, to obtain information. That's why I didn't have to stay with him. Nor was I in charge of him. He was an independent operator answerable to the DGS. Essentially, my worry was not to get my men killed and keep moving; staying still, stopping for long periods in one place would have attracted attacks from Frelimo who could easily have detected our presence and launched mortars. You know what mortars are?

Yes, I do.

We lived by the maxim: False moves mean death in combat. Each mistake normally meant a death or several deaths. We couldn't take this risk. So, we moved on, and many times Chico was left behind, interrogating, probably; I cannot vouch that that was what he was doing. Many of the deaths in Wiriyamu were upon his orders. He came with us as an agent of the DGS, under their authority, and not under my command. I was told, "He is coming with you, and he is from the DGS." You know what the DGS did in the 1970s, right?

Yes.

Burning Huts and an Act of Compassion

During this operation, shoving people in huts and throwing grenades was a normal thing to do. Elsewhere, we used grenades to destroy empty bases. When we received intelligence regarding a certain base, we were dropped from a helicopter there, and we'd march forward and attack the base at dawn. Most of the time, though, we found nothing but abandoned bases. Sometimes, just as we entered their bases they would escape. Their observation posts would alert them just in time for them to pack up and flee into the bush. We found it very hard to remain undetected as we approached their bases. Normally we destroyed recently abandoned bases and observation posts—but not while at their base.

But why not?

Because they were watching us hidden from a distance, undetected, waiting to see the smoke from the burning huts to start mortaring their own base, hoping to kill us.

They knew we were there. So, what did we do? We'd all leave the base. Two or three were ordered to stay behind. They would throw grenades as they ran for cover to join us as we all fled the site. By the time the enemy mortars started, we would be far away from their base. It was a cat-and-mouse game. So that is how we used the grenades, to burn and destroy huts, silos, goat pens, animals, and other structures.

Animals too?

Yes, generally we destroyed domestic animals too, no exceptions. I remember this once—it was in one of the operations near Wiriyamu—we caught cows, but we took a few with us to eat. We had been airdropped in a remote area, full of tree trunks, with chopped trees everywhere. The helicopters could not land easily, and we had to jump and run. We detected a few small huts. You could see the place was a guerrilla base, with tiny A-frames for sleeping disguised under heavy foliage. While returning I remember going by a dry riverbank and finding there a half a dozen cows, or perhaps less. Since it was hard to find meat, I mean there was food but not a lot of it, we took advantage of these abandoned cows. We took them since we didn't have far to go; we were close to the main road. But these damn cows would not budge. They did not want to walk. We pushed, we pushed, and we pushed the cows. It was hard, and the commandos in my unit were no help; they were all city folk. In the end we gave up. We blew the base apart, cows included, and moved on.

Cows too?

Yes, we did, cows included. Look! We didn't take bullets for everyone. We took some. Normally, each one of us took between sixty—more or less sixty bullets. That is it. They were to be used in case of an ambush. We rarely engaged with the enemy. When we were sent on patrol it was to find the location of an enemy base and call for a backup. The bullets we carried were for emergencies.

So back to Wiriyamu, a complex village on a rocky outcrop past the river.

Let me tell you. The river was not really a river. It was dry, so it could not be called a river—more like a shallow depression, ideal for crossing and logistic transportation of arms, and if I remember correctly there were a tamarind and a baobab tree.

We communicated with our base. We had a radio, one of our soldiers did. If for some reason they needed to communicate with us, he would handle the message. Some of these details are now vague. I remember people fleeing from us. The sun was going down. And it was becoming dangerous for us to remain in the zone. Normally we would stop just before nightfall, so we could find a place for the night. It couldn't be near the site of the operation—that much I recall. This is a detail I don't remember. I know sometimes I say, "It would be good to recall," but I don't. They say hypnotism could be helpful to me here. They say people can recall details vividly, and I do, sometimes, only sometimes. I remember the girl who grabbed my leg. When we were shoving people in the hut, a little girl, about eight years old or less, grabbed my leg and started crying. She begged me not to kill her. I didn't have the courage to kill her and that way let her go off my leg. So, I let the girl and her mother go free; I remember that.

Look, for many years I was convinced that it was this girl or her mother who denounced the whole operation. I told this story to Felícia Cabrita the journalist in an interview she did with me.[7] Of course, now I'm sure it wasn't her. I know now that so many of the people that escaped spread the story of what had happened there. But I perfectly remember this child who grabbed my leg and started crying, begging me not to kill her. Really, that feeling, that crying, woke me up, and I couldn't overcome the feelings that that incident brought up in me. That is why I told my men to free her mom, and they were set free. Of course, all the others died by hand grenades. I saw this myself with my own eyes. What came off first is the roof. It lifted up. Then it came down, and the fire started. The walls of the huts do not normally collapse. The pressure escapes sideways, trapping fresh air inside. Normally the soldiers under my command would throw the grenade. I'd say, "You—so and so—go." We kept moving forward, and they would stay behind, throw the grenades, and join us. Normally that is what happened, I am sorry to say.

It is possible that people escaped from the burning huts in Wiriyamu. I know there were many that did. People opening doors and escaping—today I know, but not at that time. The grenade would explode, and the fire would start, so we kept going. There were times when people tried to escape in the beginning before the grenades were thrown, but they were beaten back. I do not remember some of these details; either that or I'm suffering from amnesia. I think after the cleanup we went to the bush to set up tents for the night. It was dark already, and the helicopters didn't come to get us that night. I think we went back the next day, headed toward the main road. Note that we did not walk at night. The army trucks came to pick us up. The third and the sixth groups stayed put and returned on the third day or so. They said nothing to us—absolutely nothing.

The Night after the Massacre and the Second Cleanup

After this operation of December 16, we slept in the bush. It was just us, a group of probably fifteen people or around that. We all slept in a circle turned outside, because the danger comes from outside, not from the inside, so you are turned outside so you can look around. The person keeping watch would neither stand nor sit to prevent casting shadows for the enemy to detect our position. The watchman lay as if dead with his gun by the side so the chances of his being detected were low to none. That is how we did things, and that night was no different. On that night we camped close to the operation, in a safe zone though. We then marched to the road the next day, as I mentioned before.

I don't remember the time we started marching the next day, but that region doesn't have a lot of vegetation, so we walked very quickly—I don't know what the place looks like today. It's easy to walk fast, and we walked very fast back then. Nowadays, I am

---

[7]Felícia Cabrita, "Os Mortos Não Sofrem," *Revista Expresso* (December 5, 1992); Felícia Cabrita, "Wiriyamu, Viagem ao Fundo do Terror," *Revista Expresso* (November 21, 1998); and, Felícia Cabrita, *Massacres em África* (Lisboa: A Esfera dos Livros, 2008).

much more sedentary. Then we could cover about six or seven kilometers per hour in the bush. In this instance though, I remember that we didn't walk much. I don't remember if it was one or two hours, however, though it shouldn't have been more than that. We weren't very far from Wiriyamu, though. By the time we left Wiriyamu it was dark, and we could not have gone very far because we rarely walked at night. Sometimes we had to, of course, to leave the zone where we were if we felt we were near a populated zone. We could not run the risk of an ambush from the enemy embedded among villagers.

We reached the tarmac road by the morning of the second day I think, but I'm not entirely sure that it was in the morning. Then we made a radio call, and the army sent a B Caç unit responsible for logistics with trucks to fetch us and take us to our base in Mavuzi.

I cannot tell you why we selected the first, the third, and the sixth groups of commandos and not the second, the fourth, and the fifth groups for this operation in the triangle—I don't know why. It all depended on operational needs. Sometimes the first group would be sent on sorties, and the others would stay put. When another operation came up, the second group would head out and so on. It was all based on rotation. It was by chance that the first and the third groups were on call to head into the triangle. The others had done their turn and were resting, so we had no choice. It was our turn, a roll of the dice.

Under my watch there were no irregularities in standard operating procedures in my unit—no, not under my watch. I was very surprised when I read in our Portuguese papers about the reports of sexual violence, children knifed, etc.[8] I wasn't there. Those named in the newspaper report were from the third and sixth group. I saw the names—did you read the article? Let me see here. These two people [names redacted] were in the sixth group, and for this operation they were integrated into other groups, and that is where some of the people fleeing from us probably were caught in their net. Their function was to wait and catch them. And that was a normal part of the cleanup operations, so they must have killed some of them. These two were from the third and the sixth group; they are still serving in the army—did you know that? They are captains today. They can't speak about this, though; Felícia Cabrita tried to talk to them, but the army didn't allow them. They are bound by the army's code of conduct and speak only if authorized, and that is not going to happen any time soon—but it would be good if they could.

Oh, in a way it does not matter. I am more interested in the where and the when, and details of the operation—more so than putting together a sensational story. You can see that from the questions I am asking you here. Mine is a forensic inquiry. I want to get to the bottom of this story and reconstruct what happened that day with as much depth and precision as I can. The three-day event after the massacre will have to wait until they are free to speak.

Yes. I agree with you. So, what I am getting at is that there are two aspects of the operation: what my unit did in Wiriyamu and what the others, the third and the sixth

---

[8]Felícia Cabrita, "Os Mortos Não Sofrem."

group, did in their manhunt for escapees. Later we were ordered to go there to clean up again, more than a week later. The bodies were already rotting. The ZOT contacted us this time—let me think—I'm not sure if it was the commandant, but I do know that the order came from ZOT to burn the bodies and clean up the rest of the site. The order was only to my group, so this time we were not that many. We were a little over ten. We were ordered to carry with us a gallon of gasoline and spades—to dig a communal grave for the bodies and then burn them. It was quicker this way, and we were not expected to be in the zone for long. Once we finished, we were told a helicopter would come and get us right here in the middle of this zone where the bodies were rotting.

When we arrived, there were burnt bodies—meaning that somebody had already gone there, probably the population, and had burned some of the rotting bodies. Normally we would not bury the dead, whatever we killed stayed as is. We never returned to the site of an operation. In this case they compelled us. We could not say no because we risked being court-martialed. So, I went and obeyed my orders. Can you imagine lifting the body with the shovels as tools, and the legs falling off? They were already fast decomposing, rendered putrid. I had to use a handkerchief with aftershave—I never used that aftershave afterward because that smell brought back images of the horrid smell of rotting flesh—the aftershave was Old Spice. My men and I left in the morning as this was what we usually did, never in the dark though because the helicopters did not operate that early. The operation was expected to take three or four hours according to ZOT officers. They expected us back by lunchtime, at least that is how they planned this follow-up—zip in, zap it, and zip out!

We were told to leave our guns behind. I was doing no such thing. We all took our guns.
Really?
Yes. We did. We took our guns.
It was insubordination, no?
Yes, we defied orders. We got there, and three hours later, the helicopter failed to pick us up. We could not call the pilots. We had not taken radios. They said it was not necessary—I was astounded when they said that. Two, three, four hours passed and nothing. I knew the area by now, so we walked toward the tarmac road. A little after we left the burial site, we were ambushed. It was a big ambush. Had we come without our guns, I wouldn't be sitting here today, telling you this story. The ambush occurred before mid-afternoon. We were ready to fight like we usually did, but we were desperate, too. There was a river with rocky outcrops on the south side of us, and that is where we were, among the trees. They were on higher ground—above us. We returned fire. We had limited ammunition and even less time. We wanted to reach the road before sunset, so when they stopped firing at us, we sprinted as fast as we could to the tarmac road. It took us some time to reach the road, but we did get there, eventually.

Once there, we waited and waited and waited for a car to drive by us. Finally, one came. He was a civilian and gave us a ride to the airport. I think he was Indian. The car had a truck box in the back. The truck was small, that much I remember. I don't remember if the driver of the truck had a mustache. I did not know him. We just stopped the first person that passed by, and because he was driving an empty truck, we asked him to give us a ride. That's it. He dropped us at the airport and left us. The color of the car was cream. I can't remember the brand. He dropped us at the Tete airport, in Moatize, because the day we did the operation was the same day my company of commandos was scheduled to leave for Montepuez. When we got there, they were waiting for us. The sixth and the third group had gone to the airport and were waiting for us to join them. They were not in on the whole helicopter fiasco.

When we arrived, the captain of the fourth company, I do not remember his name, was waiting for us at the airport. His expression told me he already knew what had happened to us. When I got off the truck, he didn't let go of me. My group was behind me. He said something had happened, and somebody forgot to send the helicopter; he tried to calm me down. The matter was never raised again, but I could not shake the feeling that we were sent there and left to fend for ourselves. Why else would the helicopters not pick us up? Why else order us to go there defenseless, not to take with us our guns? Someone had to be held accountable for this bungling. I have to tell you, I was not a happy camper.

Inquiry, Training, and Reflections on War

I continued to be in command of my unit in Tete until the following year, 1973, but not in that same place; we went to Songo a few months later. When the story broke out in London, I was in Cabo Delgado, Maconia. Do you know where Maconia is? I heard it on the radio, and I wasn't sure what it was, but I knew something was afoot. I got the full story a few days later. I was in the bush and very isolated from the rest of the world. The helicopters would bring us ammunition and water, and that was the only link we had with the outside world. We were camped outside the Maconia village. One day I was told to appear at the military headquarters in Nampula and—well, I had to obey orders. I showered and got into the awaiting helicopter. A lance corporal was waiting for me when I landed in Porto Amelia. I was escorted to board a Boeing, which was waiting for me, to take me to Nampula. I was not the only passenger, but the plane was probably ordered to wait for me.

When I arrived in Nampula, there was a jeep waiting to take me to the military headquarters. At the entrance, standing there, was the same major who had led the briefing in ZOT. He told me that he had already been interrogated and what he said to them, and told me what was going to happen to me during the interrogation and what they would probably ask me. He wanted to have our stories straight. I was not interrogated then. I went and spent the night on Mozambique Island with fellow commandos. The next day I was told to appear at the army headquarters. A person who'd come from Portugal—I don't know if he was a lieutenant colonel or a major—was waiting for me. He interrogated me. I think Felícia Cabrita wrote his name in that article. I am not clear about the details of this interrogation, though. In any event that is how my interrogation went. I was never interrogated again. I am sorry, I cannot remember any more details about this interrogation.

I never imagined that this operation, Operation Marosca, once revealed would become such a public relations nightmare for Portugal. The operation was to go with the DGS agents—they had reliable information, they said. Our job was to clean it up. But things in the field changed. We were unprepared to handle situations in which we found ourselves. There were some things that I saw, others that I did not see because I wasn't always present everywhere—some things escaped my notice; it was only natural. What I can tell you is I saw suspects being hit with rifle butts and shot dead at point-blank range.

Let us shift gears here and return to talk about the incident with the girl in Wiriyamu.

I remember that incident well. OK, so let me begin by saying this: We were trained to be stone-cold—to kill a person at that time was normal. We were trained for that purpose and prepared to be psychologically ready to kill. The psychological training we received as commandos shaped our minds and hearts. They were the enemy. We had to shoot them or else; it was either them or us. We did what needed to be done. We could not leave anything behind. You were told to clean up, and you did just that; therefore, killing a person was normal. There were no ifs, buts, or maybes. Back then killing the enemy and their collaborators was our mission. Now, though, I see that as abnormal. Life is nothing like that. In retrospect, I shudder at what we did, some of the people we killed—picturing them being shot and seeing the image of what one bullet could do to a human.

You know the shape of a bullet, right? We would cut the point off. The bullet then became unstable. On entry it would leave a small hole. Then it would twist inside the body, and when it exited it went like this: It opened the innards, ripping your stomach, spilling your guts out. Most companies of commandos shaved the tips of their bullets because then we would be sure to kill our targets. A regular bullet could hurt somebody but leave him alive. This is what we were taught during our commando training. It was passed down from instructor to commando trainees. I saw people dying with a shot to the back of the head. When it exited it took away with it the brains and everything. A shot to the forehead would rip off the entire back of the skull; the exit wasn't a little hole; the entire back of the head flew off. When I remember this today, it hurts me to think—that's one picture that doesn't leave you; it stays there, like a bullet inside me refusing to leave me. But at the time I was, we were, trained to be emotionless and cold.

You asked about grenades, but we didn't use many grenades. We took them with us, of course, but we didn't use them usually. There were exceptions. This Operation Marosca was one such exception; it wasn't a normal operation. Our kind of operation was going into the bush to a region where, according to the PIDE, Frelimo fighters had been spotted, and setting up an ambush. And we'd be there for days. Usually nothing showed up, and we'd leave. We'd go to another region, and we would set up another ambush—that is what we usually did. When we were ambushed, we used bullets—the same ones I talked to you about. Sometimes, we were asked to mount raids on a Frelimo base following reliable intelligence. We were dropped from a helicopter several kilometers away, and we would walk on foot early morning because we, as commandos, would normally strike when everyone was asleep. Even here everyone came to the raid with a gun; we hardly used grenades. Grenades were used to set abandoned huts on fire after people had either died or fled, or to destroy installations, underground shelters, observation posts, and anything else that helped Frelimo operate in the region. I don't remember ever using grenades to kill people. Our war was a guerrilla war, completely different from these sorts of grenade-throwing operations.

I wish I could actually remember some of the stuff that appeared in the papers. Maybe it is my subconscious—who knows—but I can't remember using grenades instead of bullets to kill people. I have no reason, at this time or in any of the previous years, to deny anything because I have been open about everything.[9] I admitted to you, "Yes sir! We launched grenades into tents," so it wouldn't be hard to say I saw stabbings, but honestly, I didn't. I don't remember seeing children pounded. If that happened it was behind my back. When I left, something like that might have happened, but in my presence, I don't remember seeing Chico or even one of our soldiers stab a child.

It was normal for a commando to move around from place to place, and as I said I didn't follow Chico Kachavi all the time. There was no exchange of information between me and Chico. This was the first time I saw him, and I never saw him again. It was impossible to just stand still near him and watch him interrogate. He did that without my supervision. Some of my soldiers stayed behind as I moved on. They threw grenades to destroy homes and domestic animals, and they could have engaged in things I did not see or was not made aware of because there were soldiers just slightly ahead and others just slightly behind. Sometimes I would order some of my men to throw grenades, as the rest of us moved on. They did that and caught up with us. It is possible that there were instances when grenades were launched into a practically empty hut with one or two people to kill them—but that was an exception. The usual thing in this place was to concentrate a large amount of people in the huts and then throw the grenade in there and walk away.

In retrospect, this was a useless war—utterly useless. A stupid, useless war that did nothing but ruin the lives of those who fought it on both sides [of the equation]. Nobody gained anything from this—except perhaps the top military brass. They'd go to war without risking their lives like we did in the bush because they didn't leave their offices; they gave out their orders from safe sanctuaries, and when their two years were up, or when they tired of war, they'd return to Portugal and get promoted with accolades and a secure career in the ranks. In the meantime, we continued, in the trenches. We weren't beneficiaries of this war. We were a conscripted militia. I was a militia captain, not a career military. I was a passerby. Of course, had I stayed in the military after my mandatory army service, I would have benefited from the army as they had done. We were mere pawns, forced and conscripted into this senseless war.

My company of commandos, the sixth, was dissolved on August 9, 1974. On that day we threw a farewell party for the commando groups of the company in Montepuez. All the members of my company left the next day, but I stayed for two more months to resolve

---

[9]Melo is clearly contradicting here since he does admit to using grenades as a way to save bullets.

all outstanding issues with the company. I had to visit every barrack in Mozambique from Nacala to Mueda, Porto Amelia, Nampula, Beira, and Lourenço Marques to see if there were any unresolved issues related to my company and get their final seal of approval to disband the unit. Once I got all the exit permits stamped and sealed, the company was decommissioned, and I was allowed to return to civilian life in October of 1974. The archives of the company stayed behind. Everything was in Montepuez and probably came to Lisbon.

Of course, I remember my unit and socialized with members of my company. One that I know had family in Tete, because I met his family when in Tete. They were holding a party, and he said, "Hey, come to the party," and so I went and stayed there in the city of Tete for a while. One of those houses with a ground floor only and no stories. It was in town, in the center—well, not in the center itself, but near the center. He wasn't actually African. He was—how do I say this—he wasn't Indian, and he wasn't African. He was a person of mixed heritage. His skin was a bit darker, yes, but not Indian—he was Afro-Indian, let us say that. I don't remember his name anymore. I think it was a big party. Someone's birthday probably, because there were a lot of guests. There was plenty of music and drinks, including whiskey. I was dressed casually. He is the only one I socialized [with] during my stint with the army.

Of the people I knew in the company, two men are at this moment in the Portuguese army as captains. I do not know of others. Usually we had four companies of commandos a year, two in formation and two in active duty. The regular training program lasted four years, but in Mozambique, we did it in two. There were commando companies trained in Portugal, too, but I don't know if there was any difference in quality. Those trained in Portugal would train commando units in formation in Mozambique, and this tradition continued. At some point we in Mozambique had enough of us to be training our own units, which is what happened in the end. The curriculum was the same, rigorous and very exacting, because the methods of instruction and the course contents were very much set in stone: the combat techniques, the sort of weapons we learned to handle, the sorts of traps we learned to set, the mines we learned to activate, and the nursing basics they taught us. When we went into the bush, we didn't take a nurse. It was one of us that did it. If necessary, we would give each other injections.

I remember, for example, when a member of my group stepped on a mine, it was past four in the afternoon. We had to wait until the next morning for the helicopter, because they wouldn't fly out in the afternoon; the air force guys were a privileged class, so after four in the afternoon, there were no flights for anyone, not even for people in mortal danger—they just wouldn't fly after dark. I remember at that time we had to apply a tourniquet to his wound, give him a shot of morphine, and wait until the next day to evacuate him. I was the only one allowed to carry morphine and other sensitive medication until help arrived. We were taught these procedures during our training, and this is what our training entailed to fight in a guerrilla war: how to walk around the bush, how to set up ambushes, how to jump off a vehicle, how to jump off a helicopter. All of these techniques that they taught us had to be followed very strictly.

Violence on Girls and Informants

That girl crying touched me in so many ways. I can't explain it, though. Here is the [abject] reality of where I was then: Before we became commandos, we were schoolkids. In just six months they managed to change us psychologically, turning us into something completely different. Today, and I say this for the sake of the good in us, I feel different. I would give the shirt off my back to someone I felt deserving. When I go to Lisbon it makes me so sad to see people begging in the streets, with nothing to eat; that touches me. Something changes inside me. My thoughts go toward my family: "What if something were to happen to my family, my kids, what would I do?" I am now able to think and talk about what I did then, and face the demons of my past. We were transformed, and it was momentous. We were taught to kill or be killed; it was either them or us—there was no half way, no middle ground. We were their targets, and we went in to hunt them as targets.

I remember once this, it wasn't near Tete; it was somewhere else. We had set up an ambush. It was nighttime, and we were on high ground. Our operation lit the sky. The next morning, we went to see what we had killed. I saw two kids, in the middle of this bush among the dead. We could not leave them there, could we? At the same time, we could not take them with us. They could not keep up with us. We usually walked for hours on end. There was only one option left. It was to shoot them; either them or us—no choice, no compromise. To this day they haunt me. But we faced an impossible dilemma, and we found no other way to deal with the situation. To this day I cannot think how we could have avoided doing what we did. If you think we could have, please tell me. I say this with complete sincerity—if one day someone comes up to me and says, "Hey Melo! You could have done this and this and not kill the two kids," I will gladly hear what they had to propose as an alternative, a secure alternative, one that didn't threaten the lives of my men. Until then, I do not think I had much of a choice but to act the way my men and I did.

Come to think of it, there was one exception that I recall. We once caught this young woman, a young girl in fact, perhaps sixteen to eighteen years old. We were a day or two away from the base. We tended to walk in a single file on these long marches and leave a wide gap between us to give us enough space to maneuver in case of enemy attack. She was near me with all the [attendant] risks that this implied to both her and me. When night fell, she stayed with us, [and] I gave orders to my men to leave her alone. I even threatened retaliation in case they attempted to violate her. Perhaps my men would have respected my authority more had I turned a blind eye to what they wanted to do to the girl. Who knows? At the time though, I strongly felt I had to protect her from predators. Perhaps I was wrong in doing what I did, bringing her with us and in this way placing my men in the line of potential fire; it is in situations like these that I now think in retrospect I risked the safety of my men. The next day, we let the girl go, once we felt she was safely near her people. I can't tell you if she got to see her people or was caught by a different group of Portuguese commandos. I hope not the latter. I did my very best to save her.

It is quite possible that the third and the sixth company of commandos caught her before she reached her people. They may well have; the *Expresso* article suggested as much. It reported that members of the third or sixth group did violate a woman. Felícia Cabrita took the statement from one of them saying this very thing. One of them surely knows who raped her or some other girl and if so where. The commanders are still serving in the army. They won't speak out, though. The Portuguese soldiers interviewed by Felícia Cabrita did speak out because they are civilians and free to talk; the ones in the military cannot. They are prohibited from talking to the public on such sensitive matters.

I once watched a PIDE interrogation from afar. On the first operation that we went on after the company was created, we went to a region of Tete that was unfamiliar to me because I had not been there for so long. After a while I had to walk away; I wasn't used to seeing so much violence. They were beating for the sake of beating rather than getting him to talk, to cough up Frelimo's whereabouts. You would think the DGS would know better than to beat up on suspects to get to the truth, wouldn't you? Most of the time the guides the DGS gave us to track down enemy bases yielded nothing, no enemy bases to speak of. In most cases our orders were simple: "If he doesn't lead you to a base, he does not come back." You understand what this meant, right?

To a point, but help me understand this better.

When we saw that we were going around in circles, going nowhere, I would order my men to double back. The last commando was now leading the file. The first commando, now the last, would then shoot him and join the line as the last commando. Yes, the PIDE were violent and had the authority to do anything. A piece of intelligence from the DGS could send me or any soldier to jail. We had no authority to do what any member of the DGS could. They were the mighty lords. They could destroy your life in seconds. As a state security force, they could arrest anybody without due process and do whatever they wanted. Even more so in this case of the Wiriyamu [triangle]. The fact that Chico went with me and I had no say in refusing [to have] a civilian accompany our ranks tells you the power of the DGS. Yes, of course I had my orders to clean the place up. His were interrogations. He had the authority to work independently from us—even when his actions threatened the security of my men. What is interesting is that as a commanding officer of the operation I was completely in the dark concerning his orders. The truth was, he was a law unto himself.

I think that he was murdered, right?

Yes.

Maybe he got in bed with some woman . . . From what you tell me it sounds as if his killing was premeditated—perhaps to avenge a killing or stealing someone's woman, who knows?

My Family and Their Return to Portugal

Did you remain in touch with your family while serving in the army?

Yes, I wrote letters to my parents while in the army. It's only natural, man! Yes, I did, but I don't know if they kept them—that was something I never asked. I don't know if my mother has kept my letters because I've never asked her about the letters I wrote. Letters that I wrote to my wife, at the time my girlfriend—when we were dating before I went to the army—she kept them. I wrote to her often. I never spoke of the war to my parents, so for them, everything was all right. When I wrote to my parents, I never spoke of what I did because we knew that often the letters were intercepted; some letters never reached my parents. I told them normal things about going for walks, something on the Island of Mozambique, or that the weather was nice, and that I was allright and they should not be worried about me or my health and safety. We were all terrified of saying something about what we did, in case we ourselves were interrogated and jailed. Telling my girlfriend about fighting and the actual war—it would have been suicide, so I didn't tell her.

My parents were naturally concerned about losing a son in the colonial war. The news that they got from the war was that there was no news. Because war was in the north of Mozambique, people in the south weren't aware that there was a war raging in the north. They were in Beira, and there news was scarce on the colonial war, nor could they see publicly the effects of the war. The wounded went unreported and stayed in Nampula. You almost never heard about the war in the north. My mother used to say be careful—those regular motherly concerns. "Be careful." That was how she expressed her concerns. After the war was over, we did talk about it, and when the article in the *Expresso* came out my father was a bit upset with me for having done that, for speaking out. He was worried that the article would attract needless attention and threaten the life of his only son. My wife shared my father's concern. Not me—I mean, I was convinced there would be no consequences because all of this was in the past. It had happened so long ago.

I met my future wife in Beira, when we were in Mocidade Portuguesa, our equivalent of the Boy Scouts, sort of. I don't know if you remember the Church of Our Lady of Fatima, do you?

Yes, I do.

I lived next to the cemetery. Here's the road; there's the church on the other side of the street. Twenty or thirty meters away from the house was the church where every Saturday there was a Scouts meeting for boys and girls alike. I belonged to the Scouts there, and my wife started going there, too. And that was where we met. After we met a day came, and it happened; there was love. I was seventeen or eighteen—no, I was eighteen years old, and she was fourteen. We were in love—well, we started dating. Love back then was not like now. Back then we talked, and talked, and talked, but not now—today it is different. We could hardly even kiss back then! We spent time together, that is all. I think it was better then. Now there is freedom in excess. People jump into the sack and later on end up not knowing each other, questioning, "Who is this person by my side?"—and as time goes by they become estranged from each other. Then each person goes their separate way.

Even after the war, we continued to date while she went to school. She graduated [from] high school and went on to night school, started working by day and studying by night, and I left the army and found a job. Meanwhile her parents decided to leave and come to Portugal. The two of us were left with two options: Either she joined her parents, or she'd stay behind; and she could not stay behind as a single woman. So, we got married. We married in March 1975. A month later I got a job with a Portuguese airline.

My parents returned to Portugal, but they had nothing to their name. In Mozambique they had worked all their lives and lived off their salaries. In Portugal they had to find jobs. We had to start from scratch. But you know how difficult that can be, don't you? Today my dad is an unemployed factory worker. My mother still works at the local clothing manufacturer to pay the bills. And they get by. It is just the two of them. I also don't have much.

Well, we have been talking solidly since four in the afternoon—and it is now around six in the morning. Feel free to contact me any time you need to clarify things. You can write to me or phone me, whichever you like. You have my address, right? Here it is; and here you go. This is our home line. Oh, and tell me, when are you leaving?

In a few days; I am heading to interview Father Adrian Hastings in Leeds. Any last words before I close the interview?

I honestly feel such sorrow for the things I did, things I did not think, and things I did not feel twenty years ago. I now get very emotional when I remember the past. I constantly ask myself a myriad of questions. "Why did this happen to me?" "Was it because I wanted to?" I didn't join the army willingly, you know. I was conscripted. They molded me to be a killing machine, and I did things that I thought I had to and was taught to do. What else can I now say to you or to mankind? That they forgive me? Forgive me what?

Photo 6 Chico Kachavi, Tete. Identity card photo, public domain. Used with permission from a family member.

Interviewee:
António Kachavi
Date (yyyy mm dd):
1995 05 20
Duration (hh mm ss):
1h 2m 22s
Place:
Tete
Language:
Nhungwe
Interpreter:
Abidu Karimu and Senhor Elídio
Redactions:
None

Chico, the Secret Agent, and His Death

My name is António Kachavi. Chico was my brother. My brother was strong and tall. I do not know how much he weighed. We were two brothers from the same mother. He was older than I and the eldest; we had seven other brothers and sisters from another mother and one brother from a woman that my father had married. In total we were ten. He and I did not play together because of our age difference. Besides, he was already a man by the time I came into this world. He went to school here in Tete, not at Missão São Pedro school but the government school, Escola Rudimentar, Rudimentary School. He did not finish his elementary schooling. According to my father Chico played truant, and that is why he did not finish his fourth grade education. In fact, he barely learned to sign his name. I do not know if later in his life he learned other things such as reading and writing, but he spoke Nhungwe well.

He treated his women well.[10] He provided for them well. The first woman he lived with was Dona Noria of Nhampha. He had children with her, but only one stayed with them, a girl. He divorced Noria after a while. She eventually passed away. He married again, this time to Rita Fatu, who was originally from Nhantambarha. They had three children, and one was a boy. Two died, and the boy was alive until last year—he died in the hospital. His wife caught him fooling around with a girl here in town. She hit him in the head with a stone, wounding him in the back of the head. The wound healed, but he kept up his fooling around with the same girl. After a while he started complaining of headaches. Eventually, he was sent to the hospital. There he got worse. He stayed in the hospital for two days where he died. He was twenty-one.

Chico then married Medalia Joaquim. This marriage lasted for a while. There were many other women in his life, though; Didegwe was one. He had two children with her, one boy and a girl. They are both alive. Then came another woman with three children, Avelia Caetano, who lived in Moatize. He separated from this woman because she was always ill. He then had [a string] of others, too many to recall their names. One thing is for sure. I do not recall him having a woman called Zubeta Latifu, as some people claim in this city.

When he left school, he came to live in this neighborhood, not in the house where I was, but on the same piece of land that had belonged to my father, which he inherited from him. When my father died, my mother came here in this section of town to build a house for herself. The original house where Chico lived, not far from here, is no longer there. It was pulled down because no one wanted to live in it after my brother's death.

My brother was lively and fond of his family. He was a feeling and caring man. It is a pity I do not have a photograph of him, except for a small one from his identity card. Yes, here it is. Here you can see for yourself what I mean when I say he was lively and kind. Yes, you can take a picture of his identity card. He is dead now anyway. I remember, after my father's death I had to get a job to feed the family. I could no longer go to school. I got a job working on the bridge and learned a trade—welding. My family arranged for me to marry, and my brother helped me pay for the wedding. He also bought football boots for me and generally looked after the family.

He did not play football but supported it. He bought football gear to help out the kids in the neighborhood. We would go with him to play football in Boroma and around Tete. I never saw him as an evil man, not where he lived. I did not know what he did at work. He was not a religious man. Usually on Saturdays and Sundays, when he was not at work, he would play the drums, sometimes until early hours of the morning. If he had money, he would buy *pombe* for people to drink as he played the drums, but he himself

---

[10]Independent accounts suggest otherwise. See testimonies by Bulachu Pensadu Zambezi and António Chuva Culher.

never drank. I don't know why. I don't know what he did outside the family and the neighborhood or at his workplace in town. I never knew what kind of work he did out of town. This much I know: He never drank, and many people knew about this. He only drank Pepsi-Cola and Fanta, soft drinks only.

He related well with people. He had many childhood friends with whom he would play and accompany on trips into the bush. Many went to Zimbabwe while others left the area. Since he played the drums, he was very popular. His nickname was "Chico Kangoma Kabodzi," Chico the Drummer. He played the drums very well. He played with people in this area and went around the area to play.

I cannot remember very well what his first job was; however, I think that when he left school he went into the army. I was very small then—in fact when he returned, I remember that it was then that I realized he was my brother. He was in the army well before the troubles started here. When he returned from the army, he went to work in the canteen of the technical school. It was then that he was taken to work for the Organização Provincial de Voluntários (OPV), Provincial Organization of Volunteers. I cannot remember how long he stayed with the OPV or how they got him to work with the DGS and when. I cannot tell you if he was worried about his DGS work. He would go to work and sometimes come back here to sleep or go there to sleep. At other times, he would go into the bush for a month, a week, or a day or two, and then would return. He never spoke about his work to me. I never came to know of Wiriyamu because he never talked about it.

How He Went

At the time of his death I worked as a foreman in Tete's metallurgic company. By this time, I was already married. I had a house and a wife. He was killed on August 16, 1973. I was at work on that day; we usually clocked in at 07:00 in the morning until noon. Then at 14:00 hours we clocked in again until 17:30. On that day, I was working a bit late. I was welding steel joists for the Cahora Bassa dam. Well, it was 18:30 when I left work with my workmates on my bicycle. As we headed home, I heard a boom. We stopped.

"But where is this sound coming from?" I said. When I got near home, it was 19:00. I saw my family gathered in his yard, crying. I got off my bicycle and ran to ask, "What is happening?"

They said, "We only heard a shot fired."

"Where?"

"Your brother was taking a bath there . . . and we do not know what happened then."

I went into the house to get some light. Then I went into the bathroom. I saw him there. He had been hit just below the nape. I do not know if it was a grenade. All I saw was a hole. He was about to take a bath when it happened, I was told. He was crouched. I could hear his lungs' breath through the back hole. I tried to move him by the arms but couldn't. He was too strong for me.

"Shall I take him to the hospital? I may not get a car to get him there. Perhaps his place of work will have a car?"

I left him there. I went to the DGS on my bicycle to inform them of Chico's condition. I got there twenty minutes later and spoke to the guard on duty. He went inside to inform someone. I then got back on my bike and got to my brother's home before they did. My brother was still breathing. I waited. They came in a cream Land Rover driven by Santo António, a DGS agent, to get him to the hospital. It was well past 20:00. I could still hear him breathe through the hole. I held him by the legs, and the driver and another white DGS agent held him by the arms and head, and we got him into the back seat of the Land Rover. We got to the hospital, but by then he was already dead.

We left him in the hospital that night. From there I returned home in the DGS car. On the following day, we went to the hospital. We got a casket. On the afternoon of August 17, we went to the cemetery near here to bury him. The family attended the funeral, as did people from his work, the DGS. He is still there, buried in the cemetery.

2

THE ANATOMY OF THE MASSACRES

Six accounts populate this second group of interviews, which focuses on the massacre. As texts of survival, they are tough to read, and tougher to absorb in one sitting, in part because each of the six accounts is a lived experience, and not a massacre story painted with death tolls. António Mixone's text on the Chaworha massacre, the first of the five in the triangle, begins with the role a failed marriage played in triggering the first shot in Chaworha. Mixone then addresses his escape from the funerary pyre, his encounters with priests and journalists, his penultimate journey into protective custody with Frelimo, and his final return to his village. In essence Mixone's narrative adds flesh to the casualty figures Padre Ferrão recorded in his massacre report for the Church.

Kalifornia Kaniveti's account of the massacre at Juawu is brief but dramatic. His story of escape from Juawu before its erasure is rancor-free and recognizes a Portuguese pilot's act of compassion amidst carnage. Kaniveti ends with a sad note: In the face of so much destruction, "[he] did not want to stay there for long." "I don't want to remember more," he told me as he signalled to stop there.

Three eyewitnesses reveal the anatomy of the Wiriyamu village and the massacre of its inhabitants. António Chuva Culher's testimony describes a soulfully tragic happening. It begins with his family background and the events of the morning before the massacre. Chico and the commandos arrive and were treated with utmost deference as colonial representatives. This deference fails to placate them from their mission to clean up the area. Soon thereafter matters turn violent. They are shoved into a hut about to be set on fire with an exploding grenade. Culher identifies some of the people packed in the hut nearest to him before the grenade explosion flings open a side door. He then escapes. In so doing, he is wounded in the palm of his hand. He reaches Raimundo Dalepa's base, but twenty-four members of his family do not. They perish in the hut now engulfed in flames. Culher seeks an herbalist to treat his wound. He ends his testimony with, "We wailed and cried at the loss of so many young sons and daughters. We stayed in the bush thereafter . . . This is my voice on Wiriyamu."

The testimony of João Xavier, also known as João António Chuva Xavier, paints a vivid picture of a vibrant village. He views Wiriyamu life as protected by the spirit of the great lion, a cosmic force for the greater good, as long as this force is invoked periodically by village sorcerers during complex rituals in the sacred forests nearby. Village life with the world outside was equally rich in his view. It was based on buying and selling cattle, with Portuguese cattle traders and their locally established agents interacting frequently with Wiriyamu cattle sellers. One such agent warns his elders of perils to come—which Xavier wishes they had not ignored, but they did, given the agent's reputation as a "bit unhinged."

What follows next is a detailed anatomy of death as Xavier escapes to reach Frelimo base in Luenha.

Enéria Tenente's testimony confirms Xavier's narrative of life before the massacre and the deaths during Wiriyamu's demise. Enéria's morning begins with a visit to her parents in Wiriyamu, and before she knows it, she is caught in Chico's interrogation and thrown in the largest hut, which was packed with people like sardines in a can, she remarks. She escapes from the same side door Xavier used and looks back and sees a "bullet [catch Xavier] in the palm of his hand." Her dash to alert the people in her village near the Luenha River saved many lives as the village was burned to a crisp during the manhunt that followed the massacre that afternoon. She relocated afterward. "I would never want to go back to Wiriyamu. Every time Wiriyamu is mentioned, I see my mother. Then my eyes don't shut; every blink brings her alive. She stands in front of me parada—motionless."

The chapter ends with a recollection of Djemusse's demise. Authored by four survivors, Kudangirana, Magaissa, Baera, and Djemusse, their story is given here as a collective. The text is relatively short, the sequence of events distressingly familiar, the reading hard to stomach. The colonial forces descend and corral the villagers into the largest yard they could find to begin the interrogations and the final kill, which bears not repeating here for fear of spoiling the primacy of the narrative they provide for us to read about the events firsthand. Their testimony, though, when read with care, is the clearest evidence we have of the colonial army's lack of moral restraint in this counterinsurgency operation.

Photo 7 António Mixone, Chaworha. Photo by Mustafah Dhada, © 1995.

Interviewee:
António Mixone
Date (yyyy mm dd):
1995 05 15 and 24
Duration (hh mm ss):
3h 17m 46s
Place:
Chaworha
Language:
Portuguese/Nhungwe Mix
Interpreter:
Abidu Karimu
Redactions:
None

Chaworha's Demise

I am António Mixone, son of Mixone Cimente. My mother was Azois da Maguina. I was born in 1955 in Chaworha, about three kilometers from Wiriyamu. I was single when Chaworha happened. I am now married to Eminita, daughter of Bigausse. I married her in 1990, one year after I returned to Tete. This is my first and only marriage. I am a peasant, and so is my wife. We have two children: a son, Mateus António, and a daughter, Maria António. My son was born in 1992, and he is about three years old. The girl was born this year, and she is nearly six months. I live in Chaworha, New Chaworha, as I have since 1989. New Chaworha is about one kilometer from the old village where I lived as a child.

Chaworha was a big village then. The most important person in the village was Chief Chaworha, my grandfather. His house was the biggest, right in the middle of the village near a shady tree. He had built a courtyard forty by sixty meters with three gates and had the door of his house facing it. The courtyard could hold lots of people and was used for the business of the village. One of the entrances to the courtyard was near his cow pen, which faced the Inhamungo River.

His son Mixone, my father, lived next door to him. His house was to the left as you faced Chief Chaworha's front door. My mother, my father, and nine children—two daughters and seven sons—lived in my father's house, including me and my younger brother, Zeca. Other families whose names I recall were the Xaviers, the Irhisones, the Marizanes, and the Mantrujares, all of whom had several grown-up children with families of their own. The Marizane children included Cunsembere, who had the most contact with the outside world as his wife was from M'Phadwe. My village was two and a half kilometers from Wiriyamu, across the Inhamungo River and around a sharp bend. The village was isolated. Frelimo had not visited our village as they had Wiriyamu. We in the village did not know Frelimo soldiers or Raimundo Dalepa Kadembo. I came to know them after the massacre.

On Saturday, December 16 [1972, I was seventeen], I got up early in the morning at six and opened the cow pen. My brother was with me. He usually took care of our forty-five goats. We both took the animals across the river to graze. My brother did not stay long because one of our goats was about to give birth. So he walked back, holding her in his arms for her to give birth at home. He got home, he later told me, and my mother said to him, "Come and eat."

My brother replied, "I am not hungry. I don't want food."

Just then the village elders, including my mother, saw a Portuguese red flag rising on a *Ngozi* tree outside the village. We later found out they were markers for the Portuguese planes, to signal where they were to attack around Chaworha. But since we didn't know [about] war, we expected nothing would happen to us. As I said we did not know Frelimo, and they did not know any of us in the village. My mother noticed the flag and pointed it out to my brother:

"Look, look! There is a flag going up there. Do you know why? I wonder what it means."

He said, "I don't know."

Just then they saw helicopters, and they both panicked—they had never seen a helicopter so close to the village.

"Do you see those helicopters?" my mother said to my brother.

"Yes, I see them, Mama."

Why were the Portuguese here—so close to the village?

"This does not look good," said my mother.

My brother said, "Mama, let us get out of here."

Mama said, "You go ahead. I am going to get my clothes and other things inside."

My brother grabbed his blanket and ran out. My mother did not manage to escape.

We Gathered to Clap

It was eleven when I left the riverbank to head home. On my way home, I saw two jets coming from the direction of Tete, going to Wiriyamu. I also saw two helicopters going there. When I reached home, I sat on the porch waiting for my mother and my brother. I got up to look for them, and through the door I saw troops coming. They were mostly white, with two blacks, fifteen in all. I was shocked—How [had] they got here? I wondered to myself. I did not see how they could have come from the riverfront, the main entrance to the village, because that was the road I took to come home. They must have left their trucks at Nkhuiyo in Nharhkune, seven to ten kilometers from here, and snuck into the village from the back route, not by the riverfront. I realized that they had surrounded Chaworha. They were calling everyone to gather at Chief Chaworha's place. I went back inside the house instead.

It was twelve o'clock. I was in the house when I saw this black man standing at the door with a machine gun. He was in a commando's uniform, not a black uniform worn by the DGS [Direção-Geral de Segurança], and had a red beret on. He had a red scarf tied around his neck. He spoke fluent Nhungwe. You could see he was silent and angry, very angry deep inside. I did not know who he was at first, but I followed his orders. I was asked to join the others in a line, and that is when I saw my mother. I did not know she had tried to escape.

We all fell in line as told. I was in front, and my mother and my father were right behind me. He followed behind us, with his gun pointed, and directed us to the center of the village near Chief Chaworha's front yard. He looked very familiar, and yet I could not quite place him. He appeared to know the village well—and my grandfather's, Chief Chaworha's, central courtyard. It was then that I recognized him. It was Johnny Kongorhogondo.

Johnny was from our area. His father was the village chief of Kongorhogondo five kilometers from here. Johnny, his son, had married his first wife who was from the area outside Chaworha. She lived in M'Phadwe. He married her there and brought her to Chaworha where they both lived. His other brother married Nonica, the daughter of Chief Wiriyamu. I do not know what happened between Johnny and his wife, but one day he threw her out. She went back to her parents in M'Phadwe, and they divorced soon thereafter. Cunsembere, the son of Marizane, who lived close to us here in Chaworha, got to know her when she lived in Chaworha, and the friendship continued when she moved to M'Phadwe. After a while they got together, and he brought her back to Chaworha— she had been happy in Chaworha and was happy to return—and married her.

When Johnny heard this, he said, "Cunsembere! Cunsembere! Cunsembere of all people." He was angry, real angry. I mean real, real angry. Everyone in the village knew Johnny. When he was angry, he was silent. He became *uma pedra*, a rock. His face froze *como mascara*, like a mask, living in the middle of a dark storm. He was cold, *sem sangre no corpo*, as if his body was without blood. After he lost her like this, he never spoke to us again—as if we had caused this to happen to him. Before he would call Chief Chaworha *avô*, grandpa—that is how close he was to this village.

When we got to Chief Chaworha's courtyard, several village elders and their families were already there. I watched another line of people come out of Cunsembere's house;

the Cunsembere family was our neighbor. A group of soldiers ordered that line to join us, but Cunsembere was not there. There was a big area of shade near old man Chaworha's yard, which was connected to our yard through a big door. I can't remember whether it was a tree or a veranda that gave the shade. I saw Cunsembere walking by himself through that door connecting the two houses. He was coming toward the shade where Johnny was. Chico Kachavi was standing beside Johnny. Johnny saw Cunsembere and recognized who he was. Johnny shot him with his machine gun. Cunsembere fell. We watched. No one spoke. We knew [we] could be next. Yes, I saw Cunsembere killed. I was standing here, and he was there, perhaps fifteen feet from me near that tree.

While we stood, groups of soldiers searched from house to house. They looked into grain silos, goat pens, and hideouts. After a while we were all brought to the courtyard— the courtyard had three main gates, as I said before—and the Portuguese soliders blocked all of the three gates. Johnny stood with his legs apart at one of the gates. They were fifteen in total; we were surrounded. We could not escape, and those that could were already far from Chaworha—and safe.

"Why have you not moved to M'Phadwe? You have been asked to do that again and again, but you refuse to go. Why? Why? Tell us why," Chico said. He was standing near Johnny. Chico spoke fluent Nhungwe, and he did most of the talking. Johnny kept a watchful eye on us, but he was silent. The soldiers, the fifteen of them, had formed a semicircle with guns ready to fire in case of attempted escapes. They stood watching Chico and Johnny do the talking and the interrogation. The two of them appeared to be fully in charge of this operation.

"But we have been waiting for your orders! Once you give us some compensation for moving, we will go," said Chief Chaworha, who spoke on behalf of the elders in the village.

"Very well then. You all, form lines here." He pointed, with his back to Chief Chaworha's front door, facing his goat pen. We did as we were told. We formed four lines of nearly sixty-five people. We thought they were about to help us move to M'Phadwe. All the lines now faced Chief Chaworha's house with his goat pen behind us. The first line had mostly our fathers, including Chief Chaworha, my father, Mixone, and the family elders: Xavier, Marco, Peter, Haguimo, Briefe, Wirhisone, Batista, N'deka (who was also known as Supinho), N'chenga, Alberto, Luis, Djeepe, Mauricio, and Chamambaica. There were others there that I do not recall.

The second line was for our mothers. My mother was in this line. I am sorry, I cannot recall all the names now. Then there was a line for us boys; I was in that line. The last line was for smaller children. Rita Mixone, my young sister of twelve, was in that line, but standing next to me on my left. On my right stood Muambe, son of Haguimo Chaworha, Chief Chaworha's brother.

Chico said in Nhungwe, "Clap your hands and say goodbye."

Johnny added, "Today is the last day for you, you little macaques."

We clapped our hands. They shot us. Chico fired first. Others followed him. I fell on the floor, and the others fell on top, almost all dead. I lay there almost unconscious. I gave my list of the dead to Padre Domingo Ferrão.

When I Woke Up

They stopped firing, and I heard them throwing grenades. I also smelled burning; some soldiers were burning our huts and the dead. They used [roofing] straw as kindling. The village was choking with smoke. The soldiers could not breathe. They ran back and waited at a distance to see if there were any survivors in the pile. The heat from the fire over me woke me up. I was in the middle of dead bodies. I must have lain there for twenty minutes or so. I managed to get out from under the pile, and others not dead followed. Nearly ten people got out this way.

I ran. The Portuguese soldiers saw me get out of the burning pile and started firing in my direction. One bullet hit me, but I kept running. They telephoned the army base. I could hear the radio noise as I escaped, asking for a helicopter to search for me. When I saw the helicopter, I hid under boulders. The helicopter went around and around but did not see me. I got out of Chaworha at once and went to Mkumbi, *mfumu* Thaurhu's village, an hour's walk from old Chaworha. The *mfumo* here was family, and I felt I would be safe there. Also, it was easier to get to Tete from his village; the tracks were easier on your feet. I took the back route to avoid the soldiers. I got to Mkumbi after nearly an hour. When I got there, they saw me bleeding and asked me how I was wounded. I told them—I said the whole family was dead, but I got out and was shot, and that is how I got hurt. The *mfumo*, Mkumbi, and his people in this region heard what had happened to me and our village.

At around three o'clock, I saw Zeca, my brother, arrive at Chief Mkumbi's place. Zeca asked me about father and mother. I said father died. Mother also died. We are the only two left. Zeca cried and said he wanted to wash away bad luck. He left for the local *poço*, water well, owned by the *mfumo* Mkumbi's second wife, some distance from Chief Mkumbi's village. I was in pain, very bad pain. I needed medical attention at the hospital in Tete. But *mfumo* Mkumbi feared taking me to the Tete hospital. He said he could get caught helping me, then questioned and tortured. What could I do? I boiled some water and washed my wounds. I took some gauze and bandaged the area. I waited for Zeca. I could not wait for him any longer. I told the *mfumo*'s people to tell Zeca that I went to the hospital and not to worry because I would be all right. I could not stay in *mfumo* Mkumbi's village. The Portuguese could sneak into the village at any time—besides, the people of Mkumbi were leaving to escape the Portuguese themselves. No one stayed home. They headed toward M'Phadwe. When I left Mkumbi[, the village] was like a corpse, empty [of] life.

I walked to Tete. When night fell, I could not walk any longer. I got to M'Phadwe. I slept in the house of Mr. Djasse, who was not a family relative, but someone who took pity on me. My brother was told where I had gone, and he went to the house of the *mfumo*'s other wife, far away from the Mkumbi village.

The second day, on Sunday, Luis Djasse—whom I called father and who was a nurse— came to see me on his bicycle at six in the morning to find out if his family in Chaworha [had made it out alive]. I rode to Tete hospital on the back seat of his bicycle. I felt safe with him. He was an OVP [Organização Provincial de Voluntários], and he was in full uniform. The Portuguese would not bother one of their own. When we got to the hospital, Luis explained to the emergency nurse, a black woman who was also a sister, that I was not a *turra*, a terrorist, but his own son and needed attention.

The nurses asked me, "How did you get this wound? Are you a terrorist?"

I said, "No, I am not terrorist; I am a person. I do not know terrorists."

They said, "No way you could receive this type of wound. Tell us, are you a terrorist?"

There were other people there from families I knew, and they defended me:

"No, he is not a terrorist. We know him. He is António, Chief Chaworha's grandson."

In the end they agreed to examine my wound. They saw that a bullet had pierced the back of my left shoulder and had cut through the back meat and come out through the front of the left arm. I was stitched up, given painkillers, and put on bed rest that very morning. Djasse left after this. Nurses began to ask me questions. I said what happened. They had already heard from similar victims coming to the hospital for similar medical attention.

Deliverance

The following day was a Monday. After breakfast, the same nurse who treated me—she was a black sister—asked me to go with her to see Padre Domingo Ferrão. Padre Ferrão asked me a lot of questions and took notes. After seeing Padre Ferrão that morning, I returned to the hospital to go to bed. My bandages were taken off on Tuesday morning, after which I was taken to see Padre Ferrão again. Padre Ferrão gave me a new set of clothes to wear. The nuns and the sisters in the hospital treated me well. They gave me food and presents. Padre Domingo Ferrão visited me four times during my stay in the hospital. It was during this stay on that Friday, December 22, I met and then got to know Padre Castro. He was large and had a big beard and *olhos como água azul*, eyes like clear blue water.

I left the hospital on my own one day after Christmas at around nine in the morning. It was a Tuesday. I told Padre Domingo Ferrão that I was leaving the hospital and going to M'Phadwe. I took the back route—not the one that runs along the Missão São Pedro where Padre Ferrão lived. On my way I passed that white man Gonçalves' cow pen. He bought cattle from us when he would come to Wiriyamu, and we would bring our cows for him to see and buy on cattle market days. He was there, but he did not recognize me. I recognized his house immediately because I saw some of the cows we had sold to him.

I got to M'Phadwe and stayed with Gizado Xavier and his brother, Fulucano Gizado. They were both from Chaworha and had survived the massacre. There were other families from Chaworha there, too, but I do not recall their names and details now. We lived under a big baobab tree. There was nothing there. We prepared to build a mud home—we did not have hay for the thatched roof yet. We were going to find and collect the hay after building the walls.

On December 28, a Thursday, Padre Castro came to M'Phadwe in his white Land Rover. I was with the Xaviers staying under a baobab tree. It was early, around seven in the morning, and before breakfast. He could not find me. He went to the local school instead where he found Zeca, my brother, attending class. He asked him, "António Mixone? Where is he?"

Zeca took him to the baobab tree where we were staying. I was not there, they said. He has gone to the river, he was told. He drove to the river. The Zambezi River where I was, was empty of much water. I had to be right in the middle of the river to be waist deep in water. I was with others. We saw a car coming to where we were. "Why is that car coming to us?" We got concerned. As the car got closer, we recognized it as Padre Castro's car.

He got out of the car and called me. When I got to him, he said, "Get in. We are going to Boroma."

There was no one else in the car. It was me and Padre Castro. I was in the back behind him, but I was not hiding. We left M'Phadwe at seven-thirty and first went to Missão São Pedro—I don't know why we went there first. Padre Castro never explained that to me. He went in for a few minutes. I stayed in the car. We then went in the direction of Songo, using the old route. We reached Boroma at around nine o'clock. When we got to Boroma I met four white men—one was tall and very, very thin. They were Burgos Fathers: [Among them were] Miguel Del Bosque and Padre Vicente Berenguer.

They explained to me why I was there and [about] the massacres elsewhere. I was then asked lots and lots of questions. They asked me how the massacre of Chaworha happened, and I told the story of how it happened. Then one tall father, with a white man's hair and blue eyes, photographed me. They photographed me two times: The first time I had no shirt on, to show the bullet wound; and the second time, they asked me to put the shirt on and took my full picture. We had lunch. They cooked rice and fish—and just before leaving they gave me an orange and a banana. We left Boroma at two in the afternoon. I got into the car, and we went back first to Missão São Pedro, where they took more photographs. After that I was brought back to M'Phadwe. It was already evening when we got home. The sun had already gone to the other side of the world. Padre Castro then went back to Missão São Pedro—Padre Castro is not alive today. I heard he died, perhaps his car overturned, though I don't know, just that he died. All this happened before Padre Sangalo came to take me away for good.

Into Exile and Back

In 1973—I cannot remember exactly which month—it was a Sunday, and it was early in the morning, at nine or so and after breakfast, when Padre Castro came again to see me. This time there was an English visitor at Missão Sao Pedro who wanted to see me and talk to me. Padre Ferrão was there waiting. He translated my Nhungwe for me. The English visitor [Peter Pringle] took photographs of my bullet wounds and of me. The Englishman's eyes were red. He asked me in great detail how the massacre happened. I was with them for an hour. At around ten-thirty, they asked me to wait near Padre Ferrão's car, so I did. They came out with Padre Castro leading the way. They took another photograph with me standing near the car with Missão São Pedro in the background. I returned to M'Phadwe. Padre Castro brought me back.

By this time, [foreign journalists had arrived in Mozambique and were reporting their findings to their newspapers]. The PIDE [Polícia Internacional e de Defesa do Estado] now knew of the documents that Padre Ferrão and the Burgos Fathers had put together. They had heard from radio broadcasts as well that there is this child who survived the massacre at Chaworha. He still lives and is talking. The PIDE started looking for me. Padre Ferrão, Padre Castro, and the others grew concerned. My life was in danger, they thought. I could be discovered and killed, and there would be one less eyewitness alive to tell what happened. They decided to send me away before the PIDE could get hold of me. That day came. I was taken away—never to return to M'Phadwe—until after the war. A Burgos padre took me to Marara Mission, which was then part of the Boroma Mission but a bit further than Boroma. I cannot remember the padre who saw me in Marara. He was Spanish, though—ah! Yes. I now remember. It was Padre Sangalo, the Burgos Father.

One night I met with the commander of Frelimo halfway between the Marara Mission and the Boroma Mission. They did not tell me the name of the Frelimo commander I was to meet. Padre Sangalo handed me over to Frelimo. They sent me to their central regional base in Chioco, which was commanded by Zeca Caliate. There I also met António Hama Thai, who became a general in the Frelimo army and someone big in the government today. I stayed at the base for a month. From there I went to Lusaka, Zambia, where Frelimo selected me to return to Mozambique to study at their school in Fingoé, near Tete. I was there to study but could not. I could not concentrate because of hunger, and I was not the only one. There was a group of us, but not much food in Fingoé. We knew that if we stayed like this, we would all die of hunger.

One day we ran away. We walked for two days to reach the border town of Chifombo in Zambia. From Chifombo we got a lift to Lusaka. The school found out where we were going. When we got to Lusaka we were met by this man, whose name I forget. He was fat, had a big stomach, and went about in a Land Rover like Padre Castro. He was from Frelimo. I was once again in the hands of Frelimo.

We were asked, "Why did you run away?"

We said, "There is so much hunger there. We are not able to study."

They did not then send me back to school. I stayed in Frelimo headquarters. I was fed well and lodged there. A week later a Mercedes-Benz covered truck came and took me and thirty others for military training to Nachingwea—we avoided going through Malawi. We reached Nachingwea and were there for two months of military training. At the end of that training I was called to Dar es Salaam—at first, I did not understand why I was being called, but I suspected it had to do with the massacre at Chaworha.

Then, one Monday at noon, I saw a white, fully covered Land Rover arrive at the base. Samora Machel had an office at this base—but he was not there. He was in Tanzania. A man got out and went into Samora Machel's office. I later found out the man was Samora Machel's right-hand man, Joaquim Chissano. I was then called [into Samora Machel's office].

Joaquim Chissano asked, "Are you António Mixone?"

I said, "Yes, I am, sir."

He then said, "You need to get ready. We are going to go to Tanzania to report on the massacre."

He then called the chief of supplies depot. I was dressed in military uniform. When he came back, I was asked to accompany him to choose a spare set of decent civilian clothes.

Chissano then went to have lunch, but not with me. After lunch we departed in his car, Chissano, the driver, and myself. It was late afternoon, and we drove for three hours to reach Mtwara. During the journey, Chissano was silent. He sat beside the driver, and I was behind them. We reached Mtwara at six o'clock that night, and we slept there in Mtwara. In Mtwara, there was a big Frelimo hospital about fifteen minutes from the airport, and I went to the hospital to spend the night. The next day, Tuesday, we went to the airport. We got there at seven in the morning and boarded a civilian plane, a Boeing, for Dar es Salaam. We flew for two hours more or less, and still Chissano did not speak with me. We got into Dar es Salaam at nine in the morning. When I got there, five members of Frelimo asked me questions about the massacres. Then I understood that Frelimo was also investigating what happened to my village and at Wiriyamu. I began telling them about it. I only spoke to Frelimo, who wanted concrete proof of the massacres, not just what was given and reported to foreign journalists before and upon their arrival in Tete. They wanted to hear of other massacres, so I told them what I knew. I stayed with Frelimo until the end of the war.

Today

After the war I came back to this area and established myself at the new part of Chaworha. Here I have built a church, and I tend to my flock. I visit Padre Ferrão regularly and ask his help with the church when I need it. No, I do not visit old Chaworha. It is gone. I do not want to wake up memories that need sleep and rest.

Interviewee:
Kalifornia Kaniveti
Date (yyyy mm dd):
1995 05 14–26
Duration (hh mm ss):
0h 57m 10s
Place:
Juawu
Language:
Nhungwe
Interpreter:
Abidu Karimu
Redactions:
None

Juawu's Killing Fields

My name is Kalifornia Kaniveti. I am a peasant. I was in Juawu when they came on that Saturday at twelve noon. I was sitting outside my two houses, with my two wives and children, waiting to eat. At that moment a little airplane passed over us, and I looked up. A few minutes later, two more planes flew by. They were Fiat airplanes—Fiat combat airplanes are Italian, and the Portuguese used them here. They flew over us and starting bombing *machambas* nearby. When I saw that, we knew we had to run away. Next to my house was the house belonging to the chief of the village, not Chief Wiriyamu but one below him. He had been relaxing. We all were, but especially him as he had been drinking. He advised me not to run because, as he said, white people did not like [it] when you ran. It would invite them to shoot you, he said. Just then five helicopters arrived—four of which went in Wiriyamu's direction. I did not see where they landed, but someone told me that two landed in the Wiriyamu village and two in Djemusse. One of the five helicopters came to us in Juawu.

I only saw the one that landed in Juawu. It did not land completely; it only got close enough for the troops to jump off. As soon as they jumped off, they started running and shooting. A lot of people died right there. Many escaped once they saw what was happening. They took their children and ran, many to the main road near Cruzamento Dezoito. I was one of them; I took a goat on my neck and my children in each arm. The helicopters chased after us. The pilot circled over us and nearly dropped on me. I could see what they wanted. They pointed me and the others to go not to the main road. I understood the sign and did what they wanted. The helicopter then got higher but continued to follow us, right up to the river near M'Phadwe. We stopped because I was thirsty. We drank water. They stopped above us and waited—I could hear them hovering. Once we finished drinking water, the pilot signed me to keep going to M'Phadwe. The helicopter left me when I got there. That is how I was saved—that pilot saved my life. He and the others could have easily killed us, but they did not. I stayed in M'Phadwe for a week.

After a week, we ran out of food, and people were starving. I had nothing to eat, so I was forced to go back to the house to see if I could find something to eat. I was sad when I got there to see all those burned homes, dogs and pigs eating people spread all over the place. I found nothing I could take with me to eat. I saw skeletons in some of the houses. I kept looking for something alive to take with me. I lost everything, my cattle, and my homes. After a while, I saw two goats I could take to M'Phadwe. There was nothing I could do there. I knew then I would have to stay in M'Phadwe. I was afraid to be there. The place was completely empty, not a single soul alive. Instead of people, there were dogs and pigs roaming around among the dead. I did not want to stay there for long. That is all I have to say, I want to say. I don't want to remember more.

Interviewee:
João Xavier
Date (yyyy mm dd):
1995 05 14–26
Duration (hh mm ss):
1h 25m 22s
Place:
Wiriyamu
Language:
Portuguese/Nhungwe Mix
Interpreter:
Abidu Karimu
Redactions:
None

The Premonitions That Went Unheeded

I am João Xavier. Actually, my real name is Mário João, but everyone calls me João Xavier. I am unemployed at present. I am married to Rita Manvel, and together we have two kids, both of whom are boys. One is called Wengai João Mário, and the other is named Dafadta Mário João. I was fourteen when our homes were burned and people were killed. At the time I was a cowherd, and I lived with my father and his children. My family was close to *mfumo* Wiriyamu. They were not like Tenente's family. Tenente was *mfumo* Wiriyamu's go-to person, his problem solver; he made conflicts disappear. My father was outgoing and made good *pombe*. We lived under the shade and protection of the Great Lion King. The Great Lion King was a spirit, a *mphondorho*. He didn't just live in Wiriyamu—he lived all over this area right up to the Luenha River, and in the north and south. Senhor Soda had the power to receive *mphondorho*. Pirhoti, who lived near the Luenha River, also had that power. Gama had two people with the spirit: Shingambo, who lived near Gama in Ghutta, and Chinzongha. There were two sacred forests for *mphondorho* ceremonies. One forest was on a little hill on the way to Djemusse in between the two Massigo hills and close to the Juauw village. It was a big place; it fitted everybody for huge ceremonies to petition for rain. Chief Wiriyamu owned the place. He and the village elders usually stopped by the forest before returning home to Wiriyamu.

The four *mphondorho*s used this sacred forest, but Senhor Soda did more than the others. He came regularly to Wiriyamu during October, November, and December to make rain happen. The last time he used the forest was in December, but I did not participate in that ceremony—I should have, but I did not. He also came if there was supposed to be rain during other months of the year and there wasn't any. They would ask for him. During harvest, if there were insects eating sorghum [corn], they would call him to summon the spirits to come down to Earth and help us get rid of pests in our *machambas* and grain silos. If people were thirsty, they could ask him to have a ceremony and petition for water. There was another place for *mphondorho* ceremonies near the thick neck of the Luenha River. The ceremony in that place was intended to *incarnar* (incarnate) the lion spirit—the *mphondorho*. He would actually enter the body of a chief, a village elder, or a certain person and allow that person to control the spirit. The lion spirit then became a good person when it lived this way.

Normally, it was usual for *mphondorho* to give orders to the chief of the village. If there was no chief, then the spirit would give orders to all. People usually obeyed the spirit, and it was very important for us to do what it asked of us. The spirit authorized us to go to the agricultural plot, and when not to go. If there was anybody disobeying orders, the spirit would do something to that person. For example, this same spirit could actually become the lion and scare the disobeyers in the agricultural plot. Now when [they were] running away from the lion, the spirit would appear and ask them, "Why are you running? What did you see there? Didn't I tell you not to go there today?"

The *mphondorho* advised people if asked to help. Some people needed to change themselves, their circumstances, and their attitudes; others needed to be happier with their lives or wanted help with keeping things the way they were. The spirit would help them. One thing the great lion spirit did not do: It did not tell your fortune or the future, like what was going to happen that Saturday. Those signs of the future, we smelled in the air, the wind, the way people said and did things, the way unexpected conflicts happened, and [how these conflicts affected] the entire mood of the village.

Signposts to War

I remember four white cattle buyers in all: Senhor Miranda, Senhor Aguiar, and Senhor Monteiro. Gonçalves was the fourth cattle buyer. Gonçalves was very tall, fat, and married. He had a big belly. He had a Bedford truck, with [an extended] bed. He came to us twice a week. Senhor Miranda and Gonçalves would come in different cars, but usually on the same days. Some would buy a cow for 250 escudos. Others would buy for 350, even 450. At that time, money was valuable, and somebody could refuse to sell to Gonçalves but sell to Miranda. If they refused to sell to Miranda, they could sell to Senhor Aguiar. If they didn't sell to Aguiar, they sold to Senhor Monteiro. As sellers, we could choose the white buyers to whom we sold cattle. Like the others, Senhor Miranda used to come to Wiriyamu on Wednesdays and Fridays. He spoke Nhungwe. He didn't need a translator. He would come by truck and leave it at a walking distance from the cattle market near the Juawu village.

One day he came in his truck to see *mfumo* Wiriyamu. They were talking to each other near a tamarind tree, opposite the chief's house, when he saw an armed Frelimo convoy of fifteen soldiers transporting guns on the margins of the dry creek running alongside the village, leading to the cattle market. Frelimo soldiers took him to their base. There they talked. He was asked to meet them again and bring them food. They let him go, barefoot. This way, he had to walk to the car from the base, drive to Tete, remember where the base was, and then lead the Portuguese army to them—by then, the base would be gone, moved somewhere else safer.

Miranda was very embarrassed to have to walk barefoot. It was difficult for him. The day was very sunny and very, very hot. He had to walk very slow and use shade. He finally reached Chief Wiriyamu's house. There, he rested and waited for the sun to go down. That is how he met Frelimo the first time. I cannot tell you if Miranda told the Portuguese army what had happened to him. What I can say is that he [and a Portuguese soldier] returned with food for Frelimo. By doing that they hoped to gain Frelimo's trust. When they came in our area, they went one more time to where he had met them. Miranda honked, but Frelimo failed to respond. Miranda waited a little for an answer but didn't get any. He went back.

On his way out, Miranda asked the people around if they knew or had seen any Frelimo soldiers: "Those people, who have guns and knives, they who took me to '*la fora no mato*—out there in the bush.'"

"No," they said.

He kept asking for details from people to see if anyone knew. Although some knew from which direction they came, they were afraid to say so. Frelimo didn't show their bases to anyone. We didn't know where they were. In fact, they would show up unexpectedly, like worms coming out of the ground. They were everywhere. Nobody knew their fixed whereabouts. Perhaps the chief of Chaworha may have known or the chief of Gandar, but I couldn't say for sure. Anyone among us then could have been a Frelimo soldier. We had to be careful. They would usually come from the bush, but they didn't know exactly from where. Therefore, if anybody knew, they refused to say.

Miranda said, "Tell Frelimo that *m'zungo* [white man] who brought you food waited and left."

He left with the Portuguese soldier. Before he got into his truck, we heard a shot fired. Perhaps it was the Portuguese soldier who did it, but I don't know. I did not see this with my own eyes. Perhaps Senhor Miranda and his comrade wanted Frelimo to know they had come and gone.

After this incident, we noticed changes in the wind. We had a big wind, and that meant some people had not died and were visiting us to tell us something. Among Nhungwe, people usually knew that to be a sign of things to happen. But we did not feel deep enough to see it. Even Gonçalves changed his greetings. His goodbyes in Nhungwe had a different ring and became heavier. I felt he was saying goodbye for real, as if any day now we would see, as we say in Nhungwe, *afafa sarhasarha* (who dies, dies; who stays is saved). Maybe the way Gonçalves said his goodbyes of late was truly an omen—war was coming. He was not the only one with signs. Mirhos too began acting strangely.

Mirhos was Nhungwe—a black man who lived with us here, right here, in Wiriyamu. But we would see him only on Wednesdays and Fridays in the afternoon during cattle-buying time. The other days he worked with the *m'zungos* [whites] in Tete.

"Someday, you will see, something will happen here. Who knows?" he whispered to some of us:

There will be fire here, perhaps. Parents will leave their children and run. Some will carry them and their things like rocks on their backs and run like dogs. Some will leave children behind. *Tudo isto aqui vai queimar* (all this will burn). You will see. Then you will say Mirhos was right. That is what I see. That is all I can say.

When I first heard him speak like this, I had said to myself, "That is Mirhos for you." He works with the whites, and he may have picked up bits of conversation among them about doing something to Wiriyamu and is now filling in the blanks. Mirhos is like that, too much imagination and a bit *parvo e loco* (mad, unhinged). "This something could mean anything," some of us said. "But attacks and destruction of home, no!" We did not take his blathering to be a warning. In any case we said, "He did not say tomorrow. He said perhaps someday," and that is how we left it. We ignored Mirhos. I wish we had not.

The Ending Begins

That morning the colonial army helicopters came, landed far from the village, and dropped the colonial troops, who then snuck into Wiriyamu. We did not notice them at first. The helicopters followed the troops, flying low and with caution—and we saw that. The troops marked their territory; they hung flags—I think they were red—in Chaworha, Djemusse, and Juawu, and close to that hill between us and Juawu. I thought they had come to plan for a meeting with the people for later. I never knew they were posting signs along the village perimeter to signal Portuguese jets to bomb. I found that out a bit later.

As I said, I was a cowherd and had to take care of my animals. So, I led my cows and goats near the main road to our village. At around midday, I heard shooting and gunfire. I got scared, really scared—very afraid. I abandoned my cows, left everything behind, and ran to my father's *machamba*. I knew I would find him there. He was with my mother, my uncles and aunts, the chief of Wiriyamu, my father's five kids (three boys and two girls), and one girl who had just married a man from Djemusse. They were talking and drinking. The children were playing around nearby. Chief Wiriyamu's second wife was in her own *machamba*.

In the meantime, Chief Wiriyamu's neighbor had been sent by a white soldier from Chaworha to ask him to play the drums and call everyone to the village for a meeting. But the *mfumo* was not at home. So they sent the *mfumo*'s little girl, Anirva, to get her father from the *machamba*. She ran to get him. The first person she met on the way was Wiriyamu's second wife, Luíza.

"Where is my father? Is he there?"

"Yes, he is at the *machamba* with João Xavier."

João Xavier, my father, not me—also not the João Xavier from Chaworha! Our *machambas* were close to each other. My father had the *pombe* and was hosting. I saw Anirva running, calling for her father. She saw him—I was standing nearby. I heard the conversation between father and daughter. She said that he must play the drums and call the people to a village meeting.

The daughter added, "The colonials want you to do that. They are on their way here from Chaworha and are already in Juawu and were heading this way."

She said the troops had guns and wore uniforms.

Mfumo Wiriyamu said, "In my entire life and that of my father and family, I have never seen troops, wearing uniforms and carrying guns, come to the village to hold a meeting."

He [then] asked his daughter to run and get her mother and his other children and take them to a safe place near his own *machamba*.

The chief didn't go back to his house. He did not play the drums. I don't know why. Maybe the *mphondorho* spirit told him not to play. I know the *mfumo* believed in the *mphondorho* spirit as we did—and was perhaps guided by it. Had he played the drum the Portuguese army would have killed us all at once. The massacre would have happened right there and been quick. Everybody would have obeyed once they heard the drums— they'd have come right away. This *mfumo* was well respected, and he was an example to everyone.

Seeing Is Believing

My father and my oldest brother went to Wiriyamu to check. My father wanted to see what was happening with his own eyes and advised the rest of us to stay out of sight in the *machamba*. When they got there, they saw more helicopters land, troops running here and there, and gathering people in front of Wiriyamu's house.

Soon, other helicopters came and bombed our *machamba*. Some of the cattle near the baobab tree fled; others were killed. I knew [then] that war had come to us. I went up [to get a closer look at] what was happening. I saw weapons and heard shots. I had never seen that before. We didn't know what a war looked like. It was happening at a walking distance from me. I couldn't watch everything that was happening, though. I was very afraid. I did see the helicopters land, though. When the troops arrived, they chose the men, confiscated their belongings, and beat them up. Some even died. Chief Wiriyamu's three wives didn't die because they were already safe in the *machambas*.

Other people ran away at just the right time. Some white soldiers, I noticed by their gestures, felt pity on the people.

They said, "If you know the way, escape. Go, go!"

That is how Wiriyamu's daughter escaped and came back to tell her mother that their hut was gone and everybody inside had died. One child, Manungo, who had gone to play in the village was in the hut and did not survive.

I saw women with children in their arms being dragged and interrogated,

"Where are *os turras* (the terrorists), Frelimo soldiers? So how come they knew their way to escape into the *mato* (the bush)?"

Both men and women were beaten. Some could not take the extreme pain and told [the soldiers] what they wanted to hear:

"Yes, yes. I know where they are and where they have a base."

"How many *turras* does that base have? Do they have heavy weapons? When did you see them?"

The troops got out an aerial [map] of the zone to pinpoint the locations they were given. More interrogations followed. I hugged the earth tight. I did not want to be caught.

Then suddenly, I heard more helicopters and jet airplanes attack the fields near us. My father saw the helicopters coming, but he couldn't even tell us where to go because they came so fast. There wasn't time, and everybody just spread out. My father didn't get a chance to speak with the chief of Wiriyamu. I got separated from my father, my brothers, and my family. I didn't know where they went. I kept running faster and faster away from the helicopters and the jets until I got to Luenha. As soon as I got there, I told people we were running away from the war. The village I went to was called Nhacambiza. It took us about two hours to get there. The chief of Wiriyamu and his family saved themselves, but I did not see them until much later. I later found out that some houses had people in them as they burned from the blast of the grenades. What happened in Wiriyamu happened also in Chaworha, Juawu, and Djemusse. People were pushed together into huts and burned with exploding grenades, and those that escaped from burning huts were killed.

My Escape

I escaped the massacre because I ran fast when I saw the troops coming my way—other people escaped, too; I met them at the margins of the Luenha River. They were afraid of war. From the Luenha River, we passed through Sirhenga and realized we couldn't just stay there. We could be discovered. We went deeper into the bush and stayed there for about four days. We found some people there, but we didn't really talk much about the massacre. We were afraid—everybody was. People we met mentioned there were refugees in the villages in and around Gama. We were scared to go there. We had seen and heard of the Portuguese killings. They killed people, and we thought we were going to die as well. So, we went with our group to the village nearby and stayed there for about a month. I didn't even know where my parents were.

When Frelimo found out where we were, they were suspicious at first. They were only collecting people from Wiriyamu and placing them under their protection. They took the adults first. They left the children—perhaps because children were less informed and therefore dangerous to Frelimo and less useful to the Portuguese than adults. Perhaps people would leave the children alone, and they would find their parents in the end. I do not know, but that is how my parents were taken into Frelimo custody. My father had run into the bush and was found by a Frelimo patrol. Even Chief Wiriyamu was taken under Frelimo protection.

Frelimo was suspicious of people who went from place to place, particularly to places near their base. They thought people like that were Portuguese agents collecting information. They had caught one such person called Capricórnio who became well known afterward as a Portuguese collaborator. Frelimo usually told people to either stay in the villages where they lived or to come and stay under Frelimo protection—not both. Because we moved from place to place, we were questioned. How did we escape? Where were we before they found us? Did we come in contact with the Portuguese? Did we see anyone, a stranger among us? After many questions and answers, we were allowed to stay where we were. A group of soldiers protected us there. After staying there for a while, we were moved to another site, near a small base—Frelimo operated several such small bases in the area. In addition to the ones we were moved to, I remember two such bases: One was in Marangwe, and the other was somewhere I can't remember, elsewhere. This base was commanded by Raphael, a Frelimo officer. Near the main base, there were people living that Frelimo had caught in the bush.

The first soldier who stayed to protect us was Azevedo. If I am not mistaken, Azevedo was moved, and then Danga came; he was also moved. Then Ricardo came, stayed for a while, and was moved as well. All of these small bases operated under the command of Raimundo Dalepa Kadembo, whom I eventually met during the moves Frelimo made for us from place to place. In the end my mother got tired of moving. She was afraid to be near a Frelimo base. We could be bombed any day, at any time, as we had been at Wiriyamu. We lived in the area with very few Frelimo troops to keep us safe. She took me to a village with relatives who were not protected by Frelimo. When we got there, we heard people saying what we had done was dangerous because we had escaped this time from a Frelimo village. They were saying, "Everybody knows what Frelimo does. They find you and kill you. Perhaps, tonight you will be dead." We were afraid of not being wanted in the village and of being left alone in the bush. So we moved to a village called Ndewa, which was near a small Frelimo base. That is where we found Chief Wiriyamu living with his two wives, the second and the third. His first wife had been in the village and was killed.

That is my story.

Interviewee:
António Chuva Culher
Date (yyyy mm dd):
1995 05 26
Duration (hh mm ss):
2h 28m 2s
Place:
Wiriyamu
Language:
Portuguese/Nhungwe Mix
Interpreter:
Abidu Karimu
Redactions:
None

I Ran from the Wiriyamu Fires

I am António Chuva Culher. I was born in Wiriyamu on June 5, 1967—actually, this is not my real birth date. I have this date recorded on official documents because of schooling opportunities. At the time of the massacre I should have been eleven years old. Our houses in Wiriyamu were at the very bottom of where the village starts, very near the boulders just before Pensadu's house, near a tamarind tree. I lived there with my stepmother, Ameria, my birth mother, Luiza Dique Calenço, and my father, Chuva Culher—and all his other children. My father had many wives, so there were many brothers and sisters. My mother herself had several children. Her first daughter was called Aqueria; then came my brother Jaime Rosário—who just goes by Jaime now and lives in Maputo. Jamie, at the time of the massacre, was away looking after our domestic animals. I, António, came next, and another child came after me. Today I have one more sibling, a small sister named Cinema, who lives with my mother in Chimoyo. From a different mother, there were just as many: my older brother, Jorge Chuva; another brother named Cantorho Chuva; Sodista, my sister; and finally, one more sibling— whose name I cannot recall—who was breastfeeding at the time of the massacre.

We had four houses. One belonged to my stepmother, and my birth mother and her children lived in another one. I cannot remember how many animals we had— though my father had many, many goats. He had no cattle, but he had many, many pigs; there could have been over ten pigs. We also had chickens. Our four homes had no walled yard, unlike that of the Tenentes, and was approximately 800 meters away from Wiriyamu's gathering place—the place where village business was conducted, where forced labor was recruited, and where cattle were bought and sold. We had *machambas*. Ours was near M'Thane, and an hour-and-a-half walk from our village in a place called Shiússaquala—named after the Saquala River, which meant "rags." At one point [the river] may have been used by rag traders going to the city north of here. Wiriyamu village had frequent contact with city folk who came to us to buy cattle, goats, chickens, and firewood. Around the 1970s, Frelimo too came to the village. They had arrived to mobilize the population.

In the Morning before the Massacre

On the day of the said massacre I was with my sister, Aqueria, and my brothers. We had left the house at six in the morning because we had been asked by my mother to take the goats to graze near the *machamba*. My mother had just given birth to Cinema a week earlier. Cinema was not well, and on that day my mother was going with my father and Cinema to see a *curendeiro* (an herbalist) in Kabvumbo who specialized in treating children. They left very early; it ought to have been around four in the morning because Kabvumbo was farther than M'Thane, where we had our *machamba*. We left for the *machamba* with the goats and food for the day. When we got near the *machamba*, perhaps a meter or so, and were very close to the tarred road, we were greeted with shots. It was an ambush by Frelimo.

This was at seven in the morning—maybe a little bit later than seven. Frelimo had already mined the road, not the tarred road but the old road, near the windmill. We heard the mines explode as a Portuguese army vehicle crossed it. We froze. We were terrified. We left the goats, the food, and whatever else we had and ran to our village. We got home. My stepmother was not home. She had gone to fetch water from the creek that's halfway between here and Chaworha. We found the people in the village drinking, relaxing. There was much to drink in the village, *pombe*, *cachaço*, and a lot of happiness. Tenente's house, which was near Fuguete's, had the most people and much to drink.

I felt something was bound to happen because of this ambush. Soon, some close friends of mine appeared, and we decided to get out of the village. We left. We went to Pensadu's *machamba*, halfway between our house and our *machamba* in M'Thane, but still far from the village. There were four of us: myself; Aqueria, my sister; another sister; and Cantorho. We got there and stayed there under the care of an old woman whose name I cannot recall. A little later, perhaps around two in the afternoon, my stepmother, Ameria, appeared. She had returned home from the creek and was told we had gone out to come here. She followed us to the *machamba*.

When she saw us, she said, "What are you doing here? Let us go home. It is lunchtime, don't you know? Let us go. Are you not hungry? I have cooked a vegetable curry especially for you."

We were little and could not say what we felt. If we had been adults, we would have known what to say.

The Massacre as It Happened

We left with her and headed home. We could not have been more than a kilometer from the village when we saw jets in the air. They began dropping bombs around the village.

How many helicopters? How many soldiers?

Then three to four helicopters arrived and dropped soldiers in the middle of the village. I cannot tell you if the helicopters landed or just hovered to let the soldiers out. I cannot tell you how many soldiers landed, nor if the helicopters were armed with guns. I was too small to notice such things. All I know is that there were more black soldiers than white, and the three or four helicopters were very near the boulders where we played often, near a tree, which has since disappeared, that provided shade to the houses we had at the bottom of the village, near the public tracks leading away from Wiriyamu.

As we got into the village, near our house, we found three black soldiers ordering us to go to Tenente's yard. They took us there, hitting my stepmother on the way. They hit her very badly. I was behind her, crying. My sister, Aqueria, and Cantorho were with me. We entered Tenente's yard from the front and found Chico Kachavi there. He was resting on a chair that he had been given by a member of Tenente's family, which had been placed for him under the shade of a young tamarind tree near where we were about to be ordered to sit, along[side] Tenente's goat- and pigpens. I saw three white soldiers on that day. They sat under the shade of the same tree but on the other side with their back to the front yard facing the three houses that Tenente had. One of these white soldiers was young and looked like a commanding officer. He too had been provided with a chair to rest while his soldiers gathered more people. As they came out of the houses, the soldiers set them on fire. More people were brought to the area where we were. I cannot recall the names of the people that arrived after us—except for one, my sister, Sodista. They had gone to her husband's house, on the other side of the dry creek along the boulders facing the main tarred road, only to find her alone. Her husband, Fucane, and her father-in-law, Aljero, were not there.

We sat there as the houses around us burned. Men, women, and children had gathered beside the goat- and pigpens, close to Chico. Neither pens had any animals in them. I cannot tell you how many there were. The truth is there were many. I was there. I do not know where Vasco Tenente or his sister were. I was near my sister. My sister, Sodista, was on the other side of me, as was my stepmother, Cantorho, and my other brothers. I also do not know why they chose Tenente's house to gather us—perhaps because many people were already gathered there to drink *pombe*, or perhaps Tenente's yard was easy to secure as it had a well-constructed, walled yard, making escape difficult. I don't know. All I know is that mothers, sons, and daughters, old and young, were crying, watching houses being burned. Just then a woman entered the yard crying with her child wailing [inconsolably]. The child would not stop. Chico bellowed out, "Kill this child. Get rid of it. Pound him to death, I don't care." He motioned the mother and child toward a mortar and pestle in the yard. The child was pounded to death.[1]

Throughout this, Chico remained seated. The white soldiers looked on. He then motioned a twelve- or thirteen-year-old girl that he found beautiful to come to him.

---

[1] The evidence António provides here could not be corroborated with eyewitness accounts.

She went to him. She was a fully developed girl. She was not yet a woman and was not married. I cannot recall her name now, but she was the daughter of Aljero, whose son had married my sister from my stepmother, Ameria. She stood beside him, but isolated from the rest of us. Aside from this incident, I did not see her violated. I did not see, with my own eyes, women being violated at Wiriyamu. I did hear that a pregnant woman at Wiriyamu had her belly cut open to show her the sex of her child because she said she did not know when asked.

Chico then ordered his men to take old women and young children to Fuguete's cattle pen next door. The soldiers took them there and stayed to guard them. My stepmother was among them. I cannot recall how many soldiers were involved in this. I was—in the meantime—trembling with fear as I was left with the other men and young women to face the rest of the soldiers.

I then heard my stepmother run in our direction, perhaps attempting escape, crying out loud, "I have forgotten my son. I want my son, Cantorho. Oh! My God, they are going to kill us, burn us alive. Where is Cantorho, my son?"

The soldiers beat her and brought her back to the pen.

She continued to scream and cry out loud, "They are going to kill us today!"

Moments thereafter, we saw the cow pen on fire. They must have thrown a grenade. They died. I do not know of survivors from that cow pen. This is how my stepmother died.

Then Chico led us into Tenente's big, round house, slammed the door shut and locked it, and gave orders to his men, "*Aphani Wense!* Kill the lot." They launched grenades into the house. The first grenade landed but failed to explode. The second grenade failed to set the house on fire. With the third, the house began burning. They stood on guard at the door. I don't know if the white commander was still there because by then I was inside of the house. We were there trembling, crying, watching the thatched roof. The fire was eating [the roof] and the doorframes.

The Escape from the Fire

I was crouched on the floor near the door, which had burst open as the grenade had exploded, leaving an opening—but the soldiers stood there, on guard. I saw a black soldier knifing a child as it was thrown into the burning hut. I saw Chinteya and Nharhuo die this way. As did Cantorho, the son of Ameria, who perished in Fuguete's cow pen.

Did you see with your own eyes children thrown against trees?

I did not see where they were knifed. Nor did I see any children being hit against trees. All I saw was these children like Chinteya with blood dripping. Chinteya was the daughter of the man who had offered chairs to Chico and the commander to sit as the soldiers gathered the people around. Children were thrown into the burning hut. People were burning, dying, crying. It was hell.

"I need to get out of here, soldiers or no soldiers," I said to myself.

I dashed out. I saw from the corner of my eye two soldiers guarding the door, but I kept running. They fired. I caught a bullet in the palm of my left hand but did not stop to look. I ran to Djemusse to hide in the dry creek that separates Wiriyamu and Djemusse, called Kabwiri. I was not the only one to escape. Vasco Tenente and his sister also escaped, but they did so before me.

I lay hidden and [kept still and] quiet when I saw someone running toward me. It was another fugitive. As it turned out it was someone I knew, someone older, and someone who proved to be perhaps more experienced than me. He is called Zegue now, but also went by the name Marti in the past. Marti was the son of this Aljero I mentioned earlier, and therefore the brother of Fucane, who was the husband of my sister, Sodista, and also brother of the girl that Chico chose for himself.

Marti was with me in the burning hut. He had hidden in the cellar of the house, which caught fire and burnt his face. I was burnt here and here, the sides of my arms, chest and neck.

When he saw me, he said, "Ah! Brother-in-law, you here?"

"Yes, I managed to escape," I replied.

"Let us get out of here. The soldiers are about to close in on us." I got up to go.

He said, "Let us go now. I know where the Frelimo base is."

We left there together.

Do you remember what time was that?

I cannot tell you, precisely, what time of the day it was. It could well have been four-thirty or five in the afternoon. The sun had not set. There was still sunlight.

I was bleeding, and I could do nothing until we reached the base. I managed to bandage it tightly with rags that I found on the way near a creek where I also washed the blood off my palm. We slept the night in the bush. We heard no shots, no movement of soldiers, and no helicopter sounds where we were on that night. We reached the base in the morning the next day, Sunday, at around eight. In total we had walked for six hours to reach the base. I later found out that Raimundo Dalepa Kadembo commanded the base.

An End of Sorts

At the base we found many from my village.

How many?

I cannot exactly tell you how many they were or who they were. I did find my brother-in-law's family. I was also told that my parents were in Magwirhimba, an area near another Frelimo base. Someone volunteered to go and call them to come to this base. In the meantime, a woman herbalist applied flour paste with crushed leaves over my wounds. I went to see family members at the base. On my father's side, twenty-four members perished that day. We wailed and cried at the loss of so many young sons and daughters. We stayed in the bush thereafter and treated my wounds at the base. This is my voice on Wiriyamu.

Interviewee:
Enéria Tenente
Date (yyyy mm dd):
1995 05 25
Duration (hh mm ss):
0h 50m 0s
Place:
Wiriyamu/Riachu
Language:
Nhungwe
Interpreter:
Abidu Karimu
Redactions:
None

The Flames of War and the Spirit of My Tears

My name is Enéria. I am the daughter of Tenente "*O Grande*"—The Senior. At the time of the massacre, I was married and had several children. I had lived with my husband at his house in Machico, some distance away from Wiriyamu, near the Luenha River. My parents lived opposite *mfumo* Wiriyamu. My father's house was big. It could accommodate lots of people. It had two doors and a big round balcony and was near a big tree on the edge of the village. Below on the other side was the creek with big boulders. I knew very little about the *mfumo* and his family except that he was rich and powerful. He had lots of cattle and goats. He had *machambas* too. I had my own *machamba*, which I shared with my husband and his two wives—I was his third wife.

That morning, I was visiting my mother. They were having a social get-together. I had left my children with their father back in Machico. When I got to the village, I passed by the *mfumo*'s house to get to my parents. I saw the *mfumo* was not there. He had gone to the main road for cattle business and then to visit the sacred forest for ceremonies before going to his *machamba*. It was usual for him to pass by the sacred forest when returning home. When I got to my parents' home, I found lots of people, mostly women, mostly married. There were some men there. Their children and the village kids were playing nearby. They were mostly young girls. The boys were elsewhere, though I don't know where.

How many people in total, do you remember?

I can't tell you how many people there were—perhaps other survivors can. I can't tell you where most of the other men were. Quite a few were in the *machambas* doing the same thing as us, I think. I can't say for sure.

The Loud "Woorh . . . Woorh . . . Woorh . . ."

It was before lunchtime. It was nice to be home with my mother and to visit with the neighbors. We were drinking *pombe*. Everybody was. I did not drink a lot; if I had, I would not have escaped the fires. Then I saw helicopters with big blades fly, making a loud, "woorh woorh woorh" noise. I had never seen such a thing before. I had seen passenger airplanes fly over us, but way, way up there. They made a humming noise like Senhor Miranda's cattle truck on a good day. Almost immediately, I heard jets bombarding. I was scared—really scared. I had never heard the exploding sounds of bombs dropping. I never knew war. When the troops arrived, everybody was gathered in the backyard of my father's house. The Portuguese soldiers pushed me through the main door. I was inside. They pushed and shoved more people into this big house, women, children, and my mother. We were packed *como sardinhas*—like sardines. I cannot tell you how many there were. I did not count. I was [terror-stricken]. I was [pushed] at the back [of the house] and got farther and farther back.

A black soldier was ordered to close the door.

Do you remember how many soldiers you saw?

I cannot tell you how many soldiers there were or who gave the orders to throw the grenades. I did not stop to look. He closed the door. I did not see who threw the grenade because I was in the back. The whole roof lifted up. They forgot that the house had a back door. I escaped. I ran and stopped at that baobab tree and looked back. I saw and heard another big explosion. João António Chuva Xavier was running to escape the fire. They shot him but missed. The bullet caught him in the palm of his hand, and he survived. Today he is a principal of a school in M'Phadwe. Oh yes, now I remember, there were two others whom I saw survive that fire—Vasco Tenente and José Inácio. The rest of the people I watched burn with the house.

I ran home to save my family. I got to my husband's house in Machico on one of the margins of the Luenha River and told him how I escaped and what I saw. People gathered at my husband's house to listen. My husband and the others in the village could see smoke in the distance and the fires burning. We knew that sooner or later the soldiers would come this way and do the same to us here if we stayed behind. We gathered the family and ran from the village. Others joined us. Machico practically emptied—except for cattle, goats, and other animals, which we left behind. We stayed the night in the forest and the next day headed to M'Phadwe. We had heard that that was where most people had gone. We got there and found people like us.

We could not stay in M'Phadwe for long. There was no food, no family, and no support for us. That night we talked. Where could we go? We did not know any of the Frelimo-protected villages. We thought it would be dangerous to be in one. The Portuguese soldiers could easily bomb us there, too, so who knows?

"But we know Chief Gozinho. We could go to his village, M'Chenga," I said.

That night we decided we would go there. Early morning before the sun could see us, we walked to M'Chenga. We took the back roads. Night fell, and we spent it right there in the *mato*, the bush.

The next day my husband got up early and told no one where he was going. He left for Machico to rescue his livestock. He got closer and closer to the village. They had burned Machico. Some of the houses were still smoldering. He looked around for his animals. Just as he found one, he was discovered by Portuguese troops who ran after him. He escaped before they could grab him. After making sure he was not being followed, he returned to us without his animals.

We were waiting for him, not knowing where he was. When he arrived, he said he had gone to rescue his animals so we could eat. But then he said soldiers saw him, and we all got worried. We packed [up our things] and hurried to reach Chief M'Chenga's village. We got there and stayed [put]. In the end, we did not want to overstay our welcome [in that village]. We moved to M'Phadwe when it got less crowded with people displaced by war. Some of my children died within two years of the massacre. Others died of cholera in M'Phadwe. I have new young ones now. That is where we are today.

The Spirit of My Tears

I would never want to go back to Wiriyamu. Every time Wiriyamu is mentioned, I see my mother. Then my eyes don't shut; every blink brings her alive. She stands in front of me *parada*—motionless. Memories of death and of dying women and children still haunt me. I cannot wipe away the memory of how the heat of guns and burning grenades lit up the roofs of our homes. I cry but cannot close my eyes. If I do, I see flames; I see moving arms, stretched high, screaming for the sky to help. That day and the days that followed, the *mphondorho* was loose among us. No, I will not go to Wiriyamu. It is bad enough that I survived the fire. I do not want to give that fire more *lenha* (kindling).

Can I take this sardine and bread home?

Yes, of course, you can; and that is how the interview ended.

Interviewees:
Kudangirana, Magaissa, Baera, and Djemusse
Date (yyyy mm dd):
1995 05 26
Duration (hh mm ss):
1h 32m 55s
Place:
Djemusse
Language:
Nhungwe
Interpreter:
Abidu Karimu
Redactions:
None

Djemusse's Lengthy Erasure

We will talk together to help each other remember and tell you what we know. I am Horário Kudangirana, and I was one person that escaped the massacre. Here is Magaissa. Baera is over there, and that man you see there is Djemusse. So, this is what we remember the most on that Saturday at noon. We were gathered. There were many people here in the village, some from here, some from other places such as Juawu and Wiriyamu, and a few visitors from the city of Tete. They had come to socialize. Some had come to drink, some to spend the weekend with us. Most people were in my house, which had a lot of booze. The other place that had a lot of booze belonged to Armando Dausse. Djemusse was the chief of our village. He ruled us as a subchief of the chief of Wiriyamu. So that meant we were part of the village of Wiriyamu to the left of us. [That day the] women and the children were gathered along with the men. We were all waiting for lunch to start. We had not started drinking. Then it happened. The Portuguese soldiers landed by helicopter in a huge yard near Djemusse's house.

How many soldiers do you remember?

We can't tell you how many soldiers there were. And we cannot tell you how many helicopters brought the soldiers. But we can tell you there were many soldiers. A lot of them were Africans. A few were Portuguese. Their leader had a walkie-talkie to speak to other Portuguese soldiers and their bosses, that much we can tell. We later found out there were soldiers also on the main road [on the other side of] our village. You know, the road that you can reach from the village of Juawu.

Did you notice any red flags?

We did not notice any red flags or anything like that. If we did, we cannot remember now. When they landed, they immediately started burning our homes on one side of us, between them and us. That way we could not run, and we were stuck between them and the burning huts. They started collecting us. They shoved us all in Chief Djemusse's yard—it was the biggest yard in our village—and they blocked the entrance with soldiers. It took them a long time. There were many people gathered. Some had already escaped. They were trying to make sure no one else escaped. By the time they got us all in one place, it was maybe two o'clock or later. Those who attempted to escape were shot. Then they asked us to form a line. The women and children had been together with men until this point. When we were asked to form a line, we did. We started walking behind each other. The Portuguese soldiers fell in line alongside us. Portuguese soldiers spoke to their leader in the group. We did not hear what they were saying because they were talking secretly amongst themselves. They were mostly black. They collected the women and the children in a group. Three soldiers were put in charge of them so they would not run away. Our women and children watched us form the line and could see everything.

Where did the line start?

The line started here, where we are standing. You see that man there. He was third in front of the line, and the line went on until where that truck is parked—let us show you where. Here, you see. There were many people in that line. On the other side of the line was the military. They were also forming a line, exactly where that baobab tree is. Behind them were the huts they had set on fire to prevent us from escaping. Our line was seventy-six steps long right up to that truck over there.

Abidu, can you confirm that?

"Yes, he is right more or less," said Abidu.

There was no tree here, and we could see the people in the line. At the end were houses. They were on one side of the line. We were all packed in that line, quite a few people. By this time, as we said, the women and children were separated from us, and they were sitting to one side, watching. Three soldiers were guarding them. Some people in the houses near the dirt track had managed to escape already, once the houses there caught fire. The fire then got bigger and bigger. The sky became darker, full of smoke, and that is why they were able to escape. The Portuguese soldiers were walking around, here and there, controlling the operation via radio. Their leader was leaning against that baobab tree. The rest of the soldiers were watching and waiting.

Then they started interrogating us. We said nothing. We said we knew nothing. They beat us. Some people even fainted, but they kept beating. This happened before Chico Kachavi arrived. They didn't beat up women, though. The black soldiers would ask questions in the dialect from Tete, Nhungwe. They started again beating—they had already started beating us before we made the line, but now they did it more. They used sticks that they had gotten from a construction work site. The sticks were very thick and heavy. If the stick broke, they'd get another one. Even the man who fainted and fell was not spared. They continued beating him.

"Where are the terrorists?" they kept asking.

We said we did not know. Nobody knew that Frelimo had been in Wiriyamu a few months before. Baera could not take it anymore. He was the one who finally answered: he knew. He said he had seen them once when he was walking his dog. They asked for a helicopter to come and get him. It landed, and Baera was taken to the main road to be interrogated. Baera was brought back to where we were. He was bleeding.

Where?

It was hard to see where he got hurt because his head was covered in blood. [Then] Chico came with Johnny Kongorhogondo. There was another agent with them [this time], Galiciano Nhungwe. The three of them came walking toward us.

They started interrogating us, "Where are the *turras* (terrorists)?"

Baera was about eight and a half to nine paces from the helicopter that had brought him back to us. The Portuguese commander was leaning against the baobab tree, twenty-six paces from the helicopter.

They continued asking Baera where the *turras* were. He said he did not know. They beat him, and beat him, and continued beating him. In fact, many people were killed right there from having their heads stepped on and smashed. This is what happened to Baera's younger brother, Tinta Kudangirana—in fact, Tinta and another man were beaten to death. The other man had just arrived from Tete, and they both had brought with them their work permit identification cards, used for manual labor. The Portuguese soldiers thought they were there as Frelimo activists to connect with the Frelimo base. They were called up, and one was shot in the head and killed. Tinta tried to escape, but they shot him as well. The shooting was done near the women. The women saw this. The soldier who shot Tinta was black, and he was standing near the women. Tinta's wife and two kids saw his killing. Then, we were asked to sit down. After ordering us to sit down, Chico left us to speak to the group of Portuguese soldiers.

Do you recall what they discussed?

We do not know what they said. I could not hear them talk, but we were told to get up, one by one, and keep moving; we were going to be running.

We did what they told us. The soldiers started shooting, and one man fell down, dead. And so three soldiers in front of our line started discussing. One said he had shot the man dead. The other soldiers said no. He claimed he had shot him dead because "you see, I have no bullets left." They agreed the second soldier would fire at the next man running from the line. So that second man was ordered to run.

"*Pita!* Go," they yelled.

It was the second soldier's turn to fire, and he did. The second man fell down dead.

The soldiers then shouted again, "*Pita!*" to Chico Chipica, who was the next person in line.

He was five paces away from one of the three soldiers. He ran, but not into the burning huts in front of him—he ran toward the soldiers, who did not see this coming. They fired but missed him. He hid behind another set of burning houses behind the soldiers. They were full of smoke. He did not go through the houses, but the smoke around the houses saved his life, he said to us later.

Chico Chipica is alive today. He lives in Chimoyo. Baera was behind Chico Chipica, and he also ran. Another person we remember who survived, though is not alive today, is Jeepi Sangurhane. He escaped from the line but was shot in the head and died. The others we do not recall their names. We are sorry that we can't help you. It is now painful.

Kudangirana escaped after Luis Mancajo ran. He was about twenty-four paces from Kudangirana, roughly. We saw two more people ahead of us who fell and died. We did not see exactly how they fell—they were shot perhaps, but we did not see the bullets that killed them. When we saw Luis Mancajo and three others run, Kudangirana and the others panicked and knew they had to run to escape. Some of us did just that. We did not run ahead of us, but we ran to the side. This side, on the right side of us, away from the Portuguese soldiers on the left of us. Then they started shooting at us. This time we ran toward the huts near the dirt road. The smoke from the huts protected us. They could not see us well, and we could escape. Kudangirana was one of the first to run into the huts, and he escaped. We remember one other person who escaped that way, Cachiche Juawu, but his escape was sad. He got shot in the arm, and he lost it. He was so afraid to go to the hospital in Tete because of the white people there. The whites led the massacre, so going to Tete was like committing suicide. By not going to the hospital, he passed away. He died on that same day, at night, because he lost a lot of blood and his arm was hanging from his body.

After escaping, we went to M'Phadwe. We settled there. We did not go back to Djemusse. In M'Phadwe, we searched for others from our village but could not find many. We knew then that they had passed away. Some of us returned once more to collect the bones where the women had gathered, and we placed them in the monument there—which you can see when you get to the main village of Wiriyamu.

3
GATHERING AND SURVEYING THE EVIDENCE

Three authors govern this third group of three interviews, which is on evidence gathering and aerial surveillance of the killing fields. Domingo Kansande leads off this group with his encounters with survivors on the day of the massacre as he heads from Tete to visit his family south of the triangle. His presence of mind and sense of the historical moment kick in, giving birth to Wiriyamu as a fact-based narrative just as Wiriyamu faces the three-day manhunt for survivors. While Berenguer heads off to Tete to brief himself on the events, Kansande pens the first list of the dead, which he subsequently offers to Padre Ferrão upon his return to Tete days later. Kansande returns to the triangle repeatedly to help Padre Ferrão cross-check the data collected, for which he pays the ultimate price: torture at the hands of the secret police. Kansande ends his recollections by adding he never returned to his ancestral village M'Chenga after that, electing to settle in Changara, near Berenguer's mission complex.

Padre Ferrão's testimony neatly expands on Kansande's text on data collection. It begins with a brief personal and professional introduction before launching into Chaworha survivors and their stories collected for the report he compiles with Kansande's help. The remainder of the testimony is split among Kansande's torture; Mixone's protection and escape to Frelimo as an eyewitness; and the coercion the secret police and colonial administrators exercised on him in the face of journalists seeking his transparent input in the affair.

Irmã Lúcia's narrative, the third in this group of testimonies, is unique among eyewitness accounts, none of which gives us a visual overview of the killing fields. Her account does, describing what she saw from the air, during a visit she paid soon after Operation Marosca: a visit that subsequently leads the army to send its men to clean up the site. The remainder of her testimony recollects her first encounter with Mixone, her military interrogation, and her efforts to avoid speaking to journalists.

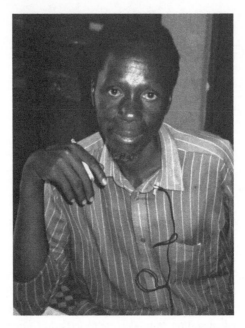

Photo 8 Domingo Kansande, Cantina Raul, Tete. Photo by Mustafah Dhada, © 1995.

Interviewee:
Domingo Kansande
Date (yyyy mm dd):
1995 05 17
Duration (hh mm ss):
0h 46m 3s
Place:
Changara
Language:
Portuguese
Interpreter:
None
Redactions:
None

Family Life, Data Collection, and Torture

I was born on December 25, 1948, in M'Chenga in the same house that my parents occupied before they left for the city. I was not given a Nhungwe name but was named Domingo because I was born on a Sunday. I had three sisters, who are all married now, but at the time they were not yet of school age. I had a younger brother. He was in the military—Frelimo military, that is. He died during the colonial war of liberation, after the cease-fire. Not all of my sisters and brothers had the same mother. Three of us are of one mother. Our family was spread out in this area, including Inhangoma, Wiriyamu, M'Chenga, and Mazoe.

Originally, my parents were from M'Chenga. I had an uncle who lived here in Mazoe—I used to live with my uncle until the second grade. At that time there were no teachers available to take third-grade students in Mazoe. Then I came to talk to Padre Vicente Berenguer to get into the Changara boarding school. Padre Vicente accepted me. I stayed for a year, in Changara, and then asked him to let me go to the Missão São Pedro School. Padre Berenguer helped me to get into São Pedro boarding school because the day school was too far for me to commute from the house.

I interrupted my schooling at the Missão São Pedro once my parents left the village to come to town. They had no means to survive, so I had to abandon my studies and look for a job in the city to support my parents. I was in the fifth grade in the old colonial system. Since then I have not returned to school. I am now married with nine children, [ranging from] nineteen to two years old. Padre Ferrão married me in 1977 at the Missão São Pedro. I live in Changara and work for the provincial school board.

Wiriyamu—Near Escapes

On December 16, 1972, I was in Imphangarha visiting friends in the village and friends from the mission when it happened. After the helicopters left some military on the ground, the jets appeared and started to bomb the area right in the middle of the population. I had to run away if I wanted to stay alive. In fact, everyone ran in different directions looking for safety. I ran away from Tete toward M'Chenga, twenty kilometers from Wiriyamu and where I had family and relatives. My father lived there at the time. It took me three hours to reach M'Chenga. I got to Mr. Raul's retail shop in M'Chenga at approximately six-thirty. I saw a lot of people enveloped by fear. Some were seated on the dirt floor. All had gathered at the veranda of Mr. Raul's shop, including my father and my mother. Many had been accused of crimes and were tied with ropes by the DGS [Direção-Geral de Segurança]. There I also found Johnny Kongorhogondo, accompanied by elements from the DGS. He was in the middle of the crowd with his back to the shop's main door, dressed in uniform.

I arrived really very tired. Johnny Kongorhogondo looked me straight in the eye and asked me, in perfect Nhungwe, "Where did you come from?" I lied. I said from Tete city. I did not tell him I had come from the Wiriyamu area. I was not about to tell him the truth. Had I done so, I would have been dead. Then I added, "I have relatives here, and that is why I am here." "Well, today you shall see, all your relatives and fellow brothers in that village there that you see from here are going to die. You are all nothing but a bunch of terrorists." This was Johnny Kongorhogondo's remark at Mr. Raul's retail shop, and he then continued hitting people in the crowd with sticks and a *sjambok* [whip].

Thereafter, he left Raul's shop with prisoners, people suspected of having given aid to the terrorists, Frelimo.

Do you recall the names of Johnny's victims?

Now I cannot remember the names or identities of the people that were taken by the DGS. All I can say is that all were male, [both] young and old, and some were recently married men. Johnny Kongorhogondo led the way, with the prisoners sandwiched between DGS agents. By now, it was dark. They marched on foot toward the Wiriyamu area to be transported to the DGS headquarters in Tete city.

I then left the shop with my parents to go to our house, which was approximately one kilometer away, behind Mr. Raul's shop. My father and my mother had not been accused of any crimes. We got home at around six-thirty—then I told my parents what had happened—but we did not sleep in the house. In fact, many of us around M'Chenga, Wiriyamu, and Imphangarha did not. We slept outside, though none of us could actually sleep, given what happened. I cannot remember if it was a moonlit or a moonless night. We were afraid they would come back. The whole night, the conversations held in whispers were filled with tears and terror of what had happened late into the night. In fact, it was three in the morning when we went to sleep. On the following day, December 17, 1972, at around two in the afternoon I went back to that area. I was worried because we had relatives in the Wiriyamu village. Later, I found out one of those relatives had been killed in the massacre. Accompanying me were others, many of whom also had relatives in the area.

We got to the Mpharamadwe near Raimundo Dalepa's base at around five-thirty in the afternoon but did not go into Wiriyamu proper as we feared the military might still be there. We approached a neighboring area to meet anyone from the Wiriyamu village proper. We were lucky. We met some eight refugees, five men and three women, who had witnessed the massacres. They did not give their names, and I did not ask for fear that they might think of me as an informant. They then began telling us who had survived and who was killed. I was told which of my family members were killed.

I made a preliminary list with details of the people I was told had died. I remember I only had a small brown pencil with an eraser on top. We had no paper, except brown wrappers for rolling tobacco. I asked for whatever they had and was given four such bits and pieces of wrapping paper to jot down my list of names. I looked for a stone on which to sit with my back to a big tree. They sat around me. The place was deserted, in the middle of nowhere, deep in the bush.

It got dark. I could not see what I was doing. Someone, I remember it was a man, left for a nearby *machamba* to get kindling while others gathered wood to prepare the fire. A small fire was made near where I sat; with that light, I continued with my list. All the while we feared the Portuguese would find us, but I felt it was very important to make the list, because what had really happened at Wiriyamu was inhumane. Everybody was affected by the massacre. I was old enough to feel that—I knew the importance of the list; I knew that I needed to have concrete, provable, statistical figures of what had happened.

Silence reigned Wiriyamu. Even the surrounding areas were silent, because the Portuguese soldiers had gone as far as Imphangarha, which is where we were. The whole area was crying. I deeply felt the pain. Who else could tell what had happened? The government? The government could not give the report of the dead. It is the people who had suffered the massacre who could tell the truth. I made the preliminary list to hand it over to the priests in the hope that the priests would understand the situation out of humanity. I do not remember at what time I finished the report. I remember having recorded fifty-three or fifty-five dead. After finishing the report, we left the place and spread out to avoid detection. I went to M'Chenga with my list. I got to my father's house. I found my mother had been crying the whole day. She felt we ought not to remain in the area, let alone me return to Wiriyamu the very next day—but as a man, I felt I needed to go find the whereabouts of my family. I ate something, not much, but something, and before going off to bed I said goodbye to my parents. I told them I was going to the city the next day to see what could be arranged to move to the city. They did not know of the list.

On December 18, 1972, at three in the morning, I got up. It was still dark. I put my list in my right trouser pocket, and off I went to Tete. It was too early for the Portuguese to be up and about to search the area for survivors, so I was [relatively] safe. I took the back route, via Mkumbi and M'Phadwe and from there to Tete. It was Monday, and I was due to attend school at the mission. I got to the mission at eight in the morning. When I got to the mission, I found out Padre Ferrão was not there. He was gone. The first person I met at the mission was Padre Castro, whom I had known for some time. I started telling him this and this had happened in that area. He listened. He said that he had already heard of the massacre on the day that it had happened and that everybody at the mission was deeply worried about it. In fact, Padre Castro revealed that they had already talked to the bishop. I did not tell Padre Castro that I had with me a list of the dead. I don't know why—perhaps it was just that I felt more comfortable with Padre Ferrão.

I waited for Padre Ferrão outside his office. Thirty minutes later, Padre Ferrão appeared on his motorbike. He parked the bike opposite to his office and walked into the office. I followed him. "Excuse me," I said. He motioned me to come in and asked me to sit on a nearby chair. I walked in, sat down—now, I cannot remember what my first words were exactly. I told him what had happened and what I had done. He repeated what Padre Castro had told me, that they had talked with the bishop of Tete and that they were worried about the situation in Wiriyamu. Then I handed him the list. He took the list and transferred the data on white sheets of stationery. He said he was, again, going to talk to the bishop about the situation and on how to proceed. It was then that I told him which of my family members had been killed.

"This is the situation of my family. I need help. I want to get my family out of there so we can be here in Tete," I said. I then left the office and went to have my lunch. The following day, December 19, I went to my classes until Friday. On Saturday, December 23, I left the mission at two in the morning to go back to my village in M'Chenga. Padre Ferrão had asked me to collect more names. According to the information Padre Ferrão had received from others, the massacre and the killings had continued the following day, Sunday. There were more killed, and the names of those who had been killed had been left out of my report.

As always, I took the back route. I got to M'Chenga at five in the morning. I did not find my parents at home. I got worried. I went to Raimundo Dalepa's base. I walked some twenty-five kilometers to reach the village near Raimundo Dalepa's base. I walked up to a woman who was fetching water near a well and asked if she had seen my parents and family. She said that she did not know my family but that all the people from the M'Chenga area were gathered, "there," she said, pointing in the direction of Raimundo Dalepa's base.

I headed toward the base. I got near the base at around three in the afternoon. Several soldiers standing guard ordered me to stop. I stopped.

They asked me, "Where [are] you coming from?"

I said, "From the city."

"Ah! Yes. What are you doing here?" they asked.

"I am looking for my family. I have come to know of the massacre and have come to find how my family is doing."

I was afraid they were going to shoot me. Instead, they took me to see Commander Raimundo. He was not there, so they went to fetch him. Since I had never seen him, I was really afraid of what was going to happen to me next. He came. He was of medium height but strong—it was only after the war that he really became fat with a round belly. He stood there in full uniform, pistol in holster, and asked where I had come from and what I was doing there. I explained as before. He asked details of my family, and I told him these. He said he already knew some of my sisters. He sent someone to inform them that I was here.

He then took me to my family a distance from the base.

He then asked my family, "Do you know this man?"

They said, "Yes, he is our brother."

"Oh! Okay, then," he said.

I was allowed to greet my family and be with them. I was then taken back to the base. I had lunch with Commander Raimundo and his adjutant, Alexandro dos Santos, a large man who spoke Nhungwe. I was served rice and meat, and we drank tea. Frelimo military personnel served the food from the officers' mess—they had two messes, one for officers and one for the soldiers.

The soldiers at the base were all dressed differently. Some were in uniform, while others wore shirts. Others had shoes on, and some were shoeless. There was lots of food for everyone. There was rice, sugar, beef from stray cattle Frelimo had caught in the area. They also had shrimp, salt, and sometimes bread. [The impression I got is that they] had many contacts in the outside world through intermediaries. I stayed with them for three days, including Christmas morning. They did not celebrate Christmas day, of course. During my stay, I slept in a hut in the officers' quarters.

How many huts?

I do not remember how many huts there were in the base. In fact, it was not possible to count; it would have raised suspicion. The hut had a bed for me made from tree branches. I did not sleep alone, though; an officer slept in the hut with me.

On the following day, Sunday, I was given breakfast of tapas, but no tea. I went to see Commander Raimundo about collecting the names of the people killed in Wiriyamu. He took me to where my parents were and invited the village elders including survivors to gather around him. They came and sat on the floor. He, his adjutants, and others were also present. They chose to sit on boulders. He explained to those present why it was important that the statistical data be collected and given to me to be taken to the city—but remember, I had no paper. He took out a notebook from his stationery supplies and the people began to talk. It was nine in the morning. One said, "I have lost my brother." Another said, "I have lost my parents." Someone in the back recounted how he had lost everything. I took notes, but I only recorded the names of forty-three people that had died in the massacre. Some names were repeats from my earlier report. I did not take notes of how the massacre happened. I was not asked to do that.

The massacre happened on December 16, 1972, [precisely] when I was at a village south of Wiriyamu near the main road called Imphangarha. First, a group of soldiers got there on foot. Trucks may have dropped them off some distance away. Some soldiers appeared to be DGS types led by Chico Kachavi. He was dressed in military uniform. He always appeared as the commander of the DGS group. The survivors told me they could only recognize two members of this group: Chico Kachavi and Johnny Kongorhogondo. They were both from Tete.

They started gathering people. After a while, jets bombarded the area before helicopters dropped more soldiers. They said they could not remember the total number of soldiers that were there. Soon thereafter, they forced people into huts. They hit children against trees and sometimes forced mothers to place children into pestles to pound. This happened, I was told. Not only that, but on one occasion a pregnant woman was asked if she knew what she was carrying, a boy or a girl. The mother replied she did not know. "You will know soon." They bayoneted her. "Look, now you know the answer." This did happen, I was told. These were white, black, and mixed-race soldiers.

Chico Kachavi then said, "We cannot leave people alive. We have to kill them all. No witnesses are to be found. Otherwise, they are going to denounce us."

Some escaped and ran into the nearby ravines. The survivors did not indicate which tree in the village they had seen being used to hit children. Then they set fire to the huts, and the people inside died one by one. As the huts burned, shots were fired into the crowd—near where the memorial is today. Other soldiers grabbed women to take outside the village, to "join with them."

What do you mean?

Rape them. They were then killed.

The session ended at eleven in the morning. It was this second list of names, in Commander Raimundo's notebook, that I took to Padre Ferrão. After this meeting [the commander] took me back to the base, where I was given lunch. After lunch we rested and talked for a bit. I asked Commander Raimundo to let me say goodbye to my parents. He invited me to stay at the base and offered to send me for military training. I said I had already lost three days of schooling and wanted to get back to the mission to catch up with my studies. I was taken to where my parents were by a Frelimo soldier. I said goodbye to them and returned to the base.

Commander Raimundo then asked me about Padre Ferrão. I don't know how he knew Padre Ferrão.

I said, "Yes, I know Padre Ferrão because I am also at the mission."

Then he wrote [a letter for me to take to] Padre Ferrão, but I can't tell you the contents because I do not know. He gave me two letters, one to give to Padre Ferrão and one to post, which was addressed to someone—his relative in Zimbabwe. He gave me money for postage stamps. On Monday morning, Christmas, if I am not mistaken, I got up at two in the morning. Yes, it was Christmas morning. I remember, I celebrated Christmas at the mission. I recall having made my contribution for the festivities to be held at the student lounge at the mission. Besides, that day was my birthday.

Commander Raimundo selected five Frelimo military personnel to accompany me. They stayed with me for some thirty-five kilometers before they went back. I continued, heading toward the city. I got in Tete at eight-thirty. Once at the mission, I headed for the boarding house and the refectory to get some breakfast, and from there I waited for Padre Ferrão. At ten, I went to see him in his office. He asked me if the people of M'Chenga were still where they had lived. I said no, they were near Raimundo's base. He asked me about water availability and the level of water in the river nearby—now, I forget the name of the river. Then I gave him the letter from Raimundo Dalepa and the second and last report. He was really sad. He had already spoken to the bishop, but nothing had come of it. Eventually I took the other letter to the post office and posted it.

Rescue and the Tortures

It is kind of Padre Ferrão to say I was critical in collecting the information for him to write the report that was eventually submitted to others. Padre Ferrão also collected information from other sources, including Cebola, a classmate of mine, who was in the Temangau region. I do not remember who else he used to collect the information on the massacres. The actual deaths were over 400, but I only succeeded in collecting a portion of these in the two lists I made for Padre Ferrão.

In the meantime, I wanted to go back to the base to bring my parents to the city, but I could not. One day, three weeks after my last trip to M'Chenga, Padre Ferrão came to see me to ask if I could escort a student in the technical school to Raimundo's base because he wanted to join Frelimo. The boy did not know the back routes to reach the base.

I said, "I would be happy to take him, but he has to be someone I could trust."

Padre Ferrão invited him to come to the mission to meet me. The three of us met and talked.

He said, "[I swear to] secrecy not to reveal the route."

I was satisfied. We planned to head for the base a week later. Just before leaving, I went to Padre Ferrão to say goodbye. He had prepared a parcel of medical supplies, a camera, and film rolls for me to take to Raimundo. I took these things, and the student and I left at two in the morning—which was the usual time for me to leave Tete. When I got to the base, I gave the things to Commander Raimundo, who was very pleased to get them. I believe he is now dead, after having risen to a very high post in the provincial government here in Tete. This time I stayed at the base for two days and returned to the city once again. That was my last visit to Raimundo's base.

Then one day in the month of February, 1973, my parents appeared in the city, found the mission, and asked for me. A bit later, we went to the place where we now have the house—the mission gave me the place to build a house. Two weeks later, my father built a house on that small piece of land. This is how we came to live in the city. To this day, I still have that house where I stay when I go there.

Perhaps one month after I had taken that student to the base, during I think the month of February, a Land Rover from the PIDE [Polícia Internacional e de Defesa do Estado] came to my house. I was arrested, accused of collaborating with Padre Ferrão and of taking young people to Commander Raimundo's base. I still don't know how they came to know of this. I do have my suspicions, but I cannot say and let this be placed on record since I do not have concrete facts to prove it. I do know that on the day before my departure to the base to take that student, I had revealed to some of my classmates that I was going to the base with a student. Perhaps someone from within the Missão of São Pedro betrayed us.

Anyway, the PIDE tortured me right there and continued [to do so] after they took me to their headquarters. They put me in a small cell and interrogated me time and again, but I did not reveal the whereabouts of the base. [I said to myself, I would rather die] than reveal what I had done. They asked me if Padre Ferrão gave me things to take to the base.

I said, "No, he gave me nothing to take, and I do not know anything about a Frelimo base."

They had a water tank outside the cells, which they used to torture prisoners. I was taken to that water tank three times. They tortured me again and again. I still have scars from it.

Where? Can you show me?

You can see them, here and here. I suffered at their hands for forty-five days. Then they released me. I went to see Padre Ferrão and told him what had happened to me at the PIDE headquarters. Thereafter nothing happened to them or me. After this I never returned to M'Chenga.

After the war I moved to Changara and got this job in the provincial directorate of education and have lived here ever since.

Photo 9 Padre Domingo Ferrão, Tete. Photo by Mustafah Dhada, © 1995.

Interviewee:
Padre Domingo Ferrão
Date (yyyy mm dd):
1995 05 16
Duration (hh mm ss):
2h 25m 43s
Place:
Tete
Language:
Portuguese
Interpreter:
None
Redactions:
Moderate

Evidence Gathering, Cover-Up, and Coercion

I am Padre Domingo Ferrão, and this is my story. I came to Tete in 1969, a year after my prison sentence in Maputo, which I spent in the Machava penitentiary. I went to Missão São Pedro as a priest working under Bishop Félix Niza Ribeiro. Shortly after Niza Ribeiro left, Dom Augusto César Alves Ferreira da Silva became bishop. After Wiriyamu, he was appointed bishop of diocese de Portalegre-Castelo Branco in Portugal.

The massacre at Chaworha happened twenty-two years ago. It was December 16, 1972, and I was here at the mission on the other side of the valley in Tete—which is a big city now. It wasn't so big then. It was after lunch. In fact, since young I never took a siesta but rested. After lunch, my colleagues would go take siestas until two o'clock. I would grab a book and go to a tree and sit on a stone, or take a notebook in which to write. In those days, it was all bush and outcrops surrounding the Missão São Pedro. There were no mud huts and houses surrounding the mission. At two or two-thirty I would return, have a wash, and get back to work. It was during this period of rest that I saw them. I would say it was noontime or thereabouts.

Was that the exact time?

I did not look at my watch to see precisely what time it was. I saw helicopters pass over the mission coming from the air force base nearby and heading over there behind the mountains. It made quite a noise—with a bunch of helicopters coming and going!

How many helicopters?

I can't recall how many there were. It could have been half a dozen or perhaps a dozen. The sun was really hot that day, I remember that.

Chaworha Survivors and Their Stories

Then, late in the afternoon around five, I heard something had happened there. People were fleeing from their villages in and around Wiriyamu, I was told. Some headed toward the mission; others, more wounded, straight to the hospital where Irmã Lúcia was the head nurse in charge. I went to the hospital. There, I met some children whose names I now cannot remember. All I can remember is the name of António Mixone. I talked to the wounded. The first people I came in contact with were the wounded from Chaworha, and this is what I was told: Portuguese helicopters had gone to that village and dropped airborne soldiers who encircled them.

"We were caught. We could not get out of the village. They ordered us to gather in one large place in the center of the village. '*Tu es Moçambicano? Tu es Moçambicano?*' they shouted again and again. They then asked us for our identification cards to see if Frelimo were among us. They did not find any."

I was then told that they were interrogated at gunpoint. Near the end they were told to clap.

"Now, you are gonna die. Say goodbye to everyone," they were told. "We clapped our hands as told. They started shooting at us, right there in the middle of the village."

They fell, some dead, some wounded, and others out of fear. The soldiers, I was told, half-covered the fallen dead with hay from thatched rooftops and set the bodies alight— perhaps because of it, some regained consciousness. Others attempted to escape. They fell, shot dead by soldiers lying in wait. Some victims succeeded in getting away. Perhaps because they were less wounded, they managed to escape. While others returned to salvage what they could, bicycles, sewing machines, etc., after hiding under the shade of trees, a distance away from danger. Some that escaped were children, six- or seven-year-olds. I found a girl of four badly wounded at the hospital during that first visit.

In fact, that is where António Mixone, one of the survivors and the grandson of the chief of Chaworha, told me what had happened to him. I asked him to repeat his story to me to make sure he was not exaggerating. When the soldiers saw him run, they shot him but missed. He ducked and dodged the bullets and ran as fast as he could, disappearing into the nearby bush. The soldiers radioed for help. The helicopters arrived and searched the area for escapees. António hid under the shadows of the big boulders near the dry creek, west of the villages of Wiriyamu and Juawu. He stood still, frozen and stiff. The helicopters hovered. They finally gave up and left. He then walked to the hospital. You must remember he was only a small boy. To this day he still carries burns and scars from the bullets. On the whole, some half a dozen had managed to escape from that inferno at Chaworha. I was shocked. I could not bear to see what had happened to them.

"Something has to be done about this to let the world know what is happening here," I said to myself. "This massacre is a new twist in the liberation war. Nothing like this has happened before. Yes, we had the massacre at Mueda, but that was nothing compared to this," I mumbled to myself, shaking my head side to side.

That very same afternoon, I decided to write down what had happened—yes, on that same day. Now that I recall, yes, I started putting pen to paper that same day. I began to interview the wounded who were in the hospital because the other wounded, predominantly from Wiriyamu, went to the base. Others had not suffered directly. Just they got out of their villages, taking a few things, leaving all behind in the huts. It was only after that that they went back to salvage what they could, pots and pans. Some of them had returned too early; they were shot dead. The PIDE and the military were still active in the area to catch Frelimo off guard. As a result, many died in an attempt to salvage goods. It is because of this that they were forced to come here to the mission and seek shelter under that tree over there.

But did you see with your own eyes people bleeding with wounds?

No, seeing people on the street with blood and bullet wounds, no—I saw nothing of the sort. They were only people who ran away out of fear. And of the wounded, only a minor portion came to us, as I said.

In fact, I used to visit them where they had gathered beneath that tree. They had nothing, not even straws to thatch a roof over their head. They were without food! Imagine that! None had pots to cook with; some later brought pots, retrieved from their villages. They would gather tree leaves to boil, add salt, and there it was ready to eat. The rains then fell, unusually hard for that time of the year. A whole week passed. The following week not a drop fell. Another week, rain again. With the result that all the children who sought refuge under that tree died under pelting rain. One or two may have escaped this fate. The adults managed as best they could. Look, with rain above for a week, and nowhere to go, what could you do? Nothing; you had no way to survive. As I said, the majority from the Wiriyamu and the adjacent villages, however, went to Raimundo's base to be looked after. They fared much, much better there, in part because we were able to help them with medication while the base took care of food and shelter.

Lists Are Formed; Concerns Are Expressed

How did you devise the list? Can you talk a bit about that process?

I made a list of the survivors and also of the dead. I included their approximate ages. I talked to perhaps half a dozen to a dozen survivors. I did not interview children, adults only. Among them were some women; this child who survived Chaworha, António Mixone; and Domingo Kansande, a youth who worked as a teaching assistant while he studied at the school in the Missão São Pedro. He had come to the mission asking for medical help. I used him as my go-between. He only had fourth-grade education. He was neither from Wiriyamu nor from Chaworha. He lived on the road to Gama, in a village there, but in the same direction of Chaworha and Wiriyamu. He could go there and back on foot and not attract the attention of the secret police, who were already prowling the area looking for survivors, Frelimo informants, and anyone who knew what had happened in these villages.

I put him in charge of going there to find out about the dead and the wounded. It was through him that I organized the medical supplies needed for the fighters and the wounded seeking shelter. He delivered the supplies and in return got me the information I needed.

I sent him back and forth with questions. "How many wounded? How many dead and their ages?" He went to the base, got the information, and came back, and I recorded it.

"Now go again and ask this," I would say.

He would go back and bring what I needed—that is how I produced the list. I continued this way with the investigation of the dead, the dead at Chaworha, and the dead at Wiriyamu proper. What happened at Wiriyamu was terrible, and the reports I compiled told the story in facts and figures. You see, I was only interested in the names and the ages to assess at least how many we could account for as dead. I also collected the data on Wiriyamu and then set to write the second part of the report. This second part came out in January 1973. That is it—that is how I wrote what happened at Chaworha and Wiriyamu, in two parts: part one and part two.

As I was about to write the accounts of the dead, I contacted the other priests here and told them I was about to compile the data of what had happened.

"I cannot write it and publish it as well," I said to them, "otherwise the PIDE would be all over me, I will be done for!" I added.

So I wrote all that happened, and the other fathers took the responsibility of sending it outside Mozambique. The Spanish Burgos and Combonian Fathers sent this first report overseas. A contact of Padre Castro, one of the Burgos Fathers, smuggled a copy of the report overseas. He was an engineer from Zamco, the firm that was heavily involved in the construction of the Cahora Bassa Dam.

So you gave them the report, right?

Of course, I gave the report to the Burgos Fathers because they were my colleagues, and because I worked with them and trusted them. Afterward, I also sent the report to the Combonians and to Padre Luis Alfonso Costa, the slender-built, blue-eyed priest of Marara.

I never gave my report to Bishop Félix Niza Ribeiro—he never knew of it. Only Dom Augusto César did, and he came to know of it in late 1972, and only after rumors began circulating about its existence. The agents of PIDE used to go to the bishop to ask about the report, and he avoided the question.

"It can't be true. I know nothing of a report," he would say. And he was not lying. In all fairness to him, he did not know of its existence, nor that I was its main author.

Finally let me stress I did not give the bishop of Tete a copy of the report. He may have received a copy, but I was not the one to give it to him. All the Burgos and the Combonians obviously knew of my work and that I was doing this. But many times, I did things I did not want to tell them, so as not to compromise them. This thing of sending drugs and medical supplies to Frelimo—no, this I did not tell them. One person who can tell you more about this thing of medical supplies is Irmã Lúcia.

Yes sir, when I needed medical supplies, I would go there and say, "Irmã Lúcia, I want this and this." She would organize the supplies to reach the base. She too saved many lives. Many times, the wounded in the bush would be placed here to get better before the PIDE interrogated them. Sometimes, they were not fully recovered before the PIDE came to interrogate.

"We want to take him," they would say.

"No," Irmã Lúcia would say, "He is not fully recovered. He is under treatment." She knew he was mended but just wanted to buy time. Many times, when she saw the men had recovered, Irmã Lúcia would turn deliberately careless, allowing them to run away. All of this happened with my connivance, always.

Then the local health services here began to express concern over the dead. They said, "Look! What happened there poses a public health hazard. We have to go there to find out what really happened."

The health services organized an assessment party and sent Irmã Lúcia along with others from the hospital. They too could not deny what had happened—even though they failed to touch down with their helicopter. I was later told, they had hovered but had seen dead bodies and dead cattle everywhere. When they returned, they wrote their own assessment. I am told it nearly coincided with what we had written. But the government here in Tete refused to accept the medical team's findings. They prepared their own inquiry. They contacted me to ask questions.

I said, "Yes, the massacres did happen, without a doubt."

"*Sim Senhor Padre, Vamos—la ver*" (Very well, we shall see then), they said—and left.

Well, during the year in which Hastings did what he did—publish the report in *The London Times*—Frelimo sent their own team to investigate. It confirmed that the massacre had happened; at least that is what I was told by Marcelino dos Santos. I remember him confirming the events. He said that my report did more for the cause of liberation than eight years of fighting in the bush.

The Escape and the Cover-Up

In the meantime, the PIDE began looking for Domingo Kansande. An informant ratted on him. They finally caught Kansande. He was imprisoned. He received the PIDE's most prized treatment reserved for suspected *terroristas*. He was first suffocated, lost consciousness, was reanimated, and then was suffocated again, and was given electric shocks.

"Are you working with Padre Domingo and Frelimo?" they asked him again and again. The PIDE wanted evidence to arrest me. Bless his heart. He said nothing.

That boy, António, got better eventually, and I collected him and kept him at the mission. Generally, he was not hidden in a room, no. We used to let him play with the others, let him walk free—sometimes I was with him to protect him. Some of the other students and boys knew who he was, yes. They were the senior boys in the boarding school. The others, the majority—there were, after all, 1,000 day students at the mission—did not know who he was. I never called out his name in public; "António" yes, but not "António Mixone!" There were many Antónios in the mission. Also hiding him in a room would have led us to feed him and take care of him; it would have raised suspicion. Let him be among the boys, and we shall see what happens. But we also knew it was only a matter of time before he was discovered—and discover they did.

One day I saw Sabino himself in search of the kid. He was with two agents in a car with an African driver. They came here. I was in my small office. He came and parked the car outside, quite a distance from the door to my office. The others stayed behind. Sabino came in; the office was full of kids, screaming and screeching.

"Excuse me, Father," he said.

"Do come in, please," I said. He had brought with him a girl of thirteen or fourteen years old. She was one of the survivors.

"How are you, Padre Ferrão?"

"Well, do sit down, please." He sat.

"Do you know this girl, Padre?"

"No, I do not know her," I said. She was a survivor, I later found out.

"This girl here is a cousin of António Mixone."

"Ah, very well," I said. Then Sabino said to me, "António Mixone is not here among these boys."

"No, there is no one of that name here."

"Look to see if António Mixone is here," said Sabino, looking at the girl. The girl said, "This is my cousin, António Mixone," said the girl, pointing at a boy.

"This is not António Mixone," I said.

The girl said, "Yes, he is."

"No, he is not," I said, "Mr. Inspector, this girl is denouncing out of fear. It is not her who is replying to you. She has such a fear of PIDE, this girl, that she is just saying whatever. Believe me, this boy is not António Mixone. If you like, you can have a look at his identification documents. He is not António Mixone, and he does not live here."

"Ah, but this girl says so."

"This girl speaks out of fear." The girl was trembling.

After this altercation he let the boy go. Sabino then left. This boy, whose parents were dead, was then sent off to Angónia, where he trained as a teacher and returned to work. In fact, I saw him last month. After this incident, we used to call him António Mixone. Everyone did. The real António Mixone was already gone. [*Laughter in the background.*] That is why I am telling you the story.

A few days before Sabino's visit, we grew concerned for António's life. I and the other priests planned his escape, and it had to be done with caution. We first met to discuss among ourselves. We decided we had to risk everything to save the boy. We did not want him caught and killed, but we also knew that there was great risk that, if left in Tete, he would be caught one day. This fate he could not escape. We risked the very integrity of the Church.

We knew the PIDE were constantly keeping an eye on the mission. At nights they would send someone to spy on us. During the day they would not. They would leave us alone. They did not think it necessary because they saw that there were many people at the mission, and it was dangerous for them as they would be easily discovered. Besides, we suspected, they were too busy torturing people. That is why we chose a daytime escape. We asked Padre Sangalo to do it. I could not participate in this directly. Sangalo was above suspicion—he was not stationed at the mission, and his visit to the mission was perfectly natural because that is where his fellow priests worked—a social visit was in order. He was to come from his Matundo Mission on his Suzuki motorbike, get the kid, and take him to Marara. That was that!

Sangalo arrived on his bike, took the boy from where he was living, and left.

But wasn't that risky? Carrying someone on your motorbike so openly in full view of the PIDE?

You see, it was not unusual to see a priest riding with someone behind. When I visited somewhere, I carried someone on the back seat. This was not unusual—no one would suspect this as unusual.

At Marara he was handed over to Fernando Napulula Tocote, the famous guerrilla commander of First Battalion of Frelimo's 4th Motorized Infantry Brigade, which was fighting on this side of Mucumbura. Fernando took António Mixone to Tanzania.

Once published, my report attracted journalists to Tete. Before they swarmed the place, Jorge Jardim paid me a visit. He owned cement factories all over Mozambique. Incidentally, after the massacre he came to see me regularly. It was he that escorted the first corps of international news media. They discovered nothing.

"You see," he said, "nothing happened here."

At first, he would seek to strike a friendship with me.

"We acknowledge our flaws, you know," he said, "We Portuguese have committed many errors, but our aim after the discovery has always been equality of men—there are no blacks, no whites; we are all equal. But things degenerated, and we fell in this pit of colonialism. This was a grave error. I do not want this kind of thinking. You know, you and I are friends," he then said. "Look! There is a corps of international news media in town. It is better that you say nothing about the massacre. Because they want to know if there was massacre. It is better not to say anything."

He then went to get the corps. He came back and greeted me as if he had not seen me. "Eh! Good morning, Padre Ferrão. How are you? Look, I brought this corps of international new media etc. . . ." as if he had never seen me in his life.

Well, I could hardly say, "There was a massacre here." I would look foolish. I said instead, "Look! You investigate. I know nothing. I won't tell you what is and what is not. Go and find out for yourselves."

He always did this. Every time there was a press corps in town, they would come with him first. He would come to me. In the end I felt inhibited to talk. I could do nothing. Do you see? Even though Jardim tried to cover up, he could not. Some years later, I got confirmation that they had massacred people.

One of the commandos who was there told me. I did not recognize him at first, though then I did. It was he who told me how they went there again. "We went there, but everything was rotting and smelled terrible. They gave us handkerchiefs to work with and asked us to collect the corpses and place them in a hole"—but you know some corpses were left out. The animals too had their share. There was enough to spare. It was these remnants that they collected and placed in a common grave.

António Mixone went to Tanzania and returned. He appears here every week. He lives in Chaworha, just before Wiriyamu on the left at a fork on the dirt road, where he is a chief of the village, a Frelimo chief, that is. And he tends to his flock, keeps the faith, and keeps the flames alive about what happened to his grandfather's village.

Interviewee:
Irmã Lúcia Saez de Ugarte
Date (yyyy mm dd):
1995 05 19
Duration (hh mm ss):
0h 47m 45s
Place:
Tete
Language:
Portuguese/Spanish Mix
Interpreter:
None
Redactions:
None

Checking Bodies from the Air

I am Irmã Lúcia. My full name is Irmã Lúcia Saez de Ugarte. One Sunday in the afternoon this boy called António Mixone came to us in the hospital.

He was running and babbling, "Irmã Lúcia, Irmã Lúcia! Many dead. Many dead, wounded. Irmã Lúcia, many people, many dead, many dead, many . . . attack, attack, attack . . ."

He was so catatonic that I thought, "This child must be going clinically mad or near it." I then realized the poor boy was in shock. I tried to calm him down.

I said to him, "Oh! António, tell us where have you come from?"

"From Gandar," he said.

They called Chaworha Gandar because Gandar was the *régulo* (chief) for the Chaworha region.

"But look, you are bloody! What happened to you? Come here, come here." I nodded my head to him to come near me.

He did, and I saw that he had a bullet wound here in his shoulder. I had never seen the boy before and did not know anything about him.

So I asked him again, this time calmly, "But what happened to you?"

"Boom, boom, soldiers, soldiers. Dead, dead, dead, dead, many dead. Shots, shots, more shots, they got me, they shot me," the boy went on and on like this.

"Oh! My God, who did this?" I muttered under my breath. I asked him how he managed to survive and get here.

He said, "Sister, I was with everybody there between two trees. There was this big tree like this, and one big tree like this. I hid and then ran, ran, ran, ran until I got to Tete."

That is all the boy could say to me.

This is how I was introduced to the massacre. I did not come to know of the magnitude of the massacre until much later when I discovered that there were many other victims that I knew nothing about. This is not to say that others knew less than I did. Padre Ferrão for instance maintained closer contacts with Frelimo than I did, and he may well have known more about the situation. As you know Padre Ferrão was very important here in Tete and played a crucial role in the local church and for Frelimo. He sent many of his boys to join Frelimo, as did Padre Vicente. Padre Vicente Berenguer was a true Frelimista. I then tried to reach Dr. Paz, the director of the hospital, but he himself was not feeling well.

I eventually got him at the hospital and told him "Something is the matter with this boy here. Have a look." I showed him the bullet wound. "If there are more wounded like him, we need to fetch them to treat them here," I said to the director. And from the looks of it, the boy had already had the wound for a day or so.

Surveying the Dead

Dr. Paz called the governor. It was not until days later that Dr. Paz was lent the trucks to fetch the survivors and wounded.

Were they military trucks?

I do not know if the cars were military or civilian. All I know is that these were sent by the administrator. By late that afternoon people started trickling in. It was the wounded that came first. Most of them were women, and nearly all had bullet wounds—from machine guns, in my opinion.

How many wounded?

I cannot tell you now how many of them came to the hospital. We did have records, but they no longer exist today. They were ripped and torn as a colonial legacy and ultimately destroyed once the colonial war ended.

But thereafter came refugees and survivors. The wounded stayed in the hospital. The survivors were taken to M'Phadwe *aldeamento*. They were given clothes and food. We gave them money to buy maize, to buy basic necessities. Everybody was deeply affected by the sight of the wounded and the refugees, and what had happened, and did what they could. Even the bishop contributed. In fact, our Bishop Félix Niza Ribeiro wanted to know exactly what and how the massacre had happened, what was happening to the survivors, and what needed to be done. He pressured Dr. Paz to fly over the zone to assess the situation. The bishop was acting clearly out of a sense of duty and conscience as a Catholic prelate, and Dr. Paz consented out of public health concerns. It was a difficult moment for all of us, even the Portuguese. They could not help but see that this way would not bring them any nearer to an end of the conflict.

After ten days or so we flew to Wiriyamu to see the dead. We were given a helicopter from the Portuguese Air Force from the Matundo base.

Was the bishop with you?

The bishop did not come, no. Dr. Paz, did not either. Dr. Paz was still unwell.

Really?

That is why he sent me. I went after consulting my bishop and therefore on his orders. There was no one else with me but one orderly called Vasco. They sent the two of us to the air force base that was here at the airport where the air force barracks were. When we saw the helicopter with a mounted cannon, Vasco panicked.

"Look, sister, I am frightened. I do not want to go."

I realized he was going to be a problem. I said, "You are right! If you are frightened it is better that you stay behind. But stay here until I return," I added.

He was relieved.

"Oh! Thank you, thank you, thank you very much, sister," he said with great relief.

Well, then I boarded the helicopter and went off. This is how I became the first to survey the wreckage after the massacre—and without the boy, the orderly who had elected to stay behind at the air force base waiting for me to return.

The helicopter got out in the morning before lunch. We entered from the back end of the village not directly into Wiriyamu. I could see on this side of the village big trees. They looked like tamarind trees to me, and on the other side mounds and rocky outcrops. We did not descend on Wiriyamu. We just flew over it. The area had only the dead and the unburied. I cannot recall flying specifically over or near the boulders at the mouth of the Wiriyamu village. I do recall we covered three villages. Anyway, as we flew over the area, the pilot was kind enough to lower the helicopter for a good view. I could see the dirt tracks crisscrossing the villages. On one side of the tracks, there were burned huts. One could see human remains strewn inside smoldering huts amidst roaming chickens, pigs, cows, and goats.

"If only the animals could speak," I said to myself.

At this point I said to the pilot, "is it possible to land there to get a closer look from the ground." He said,

Sister, our strategy is like that of Frelimo. When we carry out military operations, we place mines under the dead in case the enemy lifts these. Then, Boom! We get them alive this way, you see. I am afraid we cannot land. We will have to fly over the area. We can do nothing else. That is why we have this cannon: in case we are attacked.

He was, however, kind enough to go as low as he could get to let me have a closer look. I can't tell you at what altitude, but I could see clearly the place and both big and small objects. And that is how I did my survey.

I saw many dead. Some of the dead were less eaten than others. None were buried. There were quite a few left on the dirt roads. And the animals were alive, going from place to place. I spied two vultures [deep amidst flesh] in a hut. I found it ironic to see that the animals were more numerous, mobile, and well fed in this Wiriyamu of the dead than in other live villages we had flown over on our way to this place.

I do not know what else to convey about my impressions of what I saw on that day, except to say that I was truly sad to note the devastation. I said nothing to the pilot.

I could not. You see, I was neither Mozambican nor Portuguese. Do you see my point? I kept myself to myself. Silence was the best course of action here. I must say he, the pilot, was pleasant to me. Once we had flown over the area, he did ask me at that point if I wanted him to fly over the villages once more for one last look.

I said, "Yes, but this time please fly over that area and that area for a better view."

Later after I landed I said to myself, "But why did they do this?" But then the colonial war did not make any sense to me from where I stood. In the end it was a war of waste with hate. At the hospital we received the wounded from both sides, with one side not knowing who was who on the other side. They would share the same room, and as they convalesced, they passed the time playing cards with each other. Did that make sense? One would say, "This is my country, and I won't leave." The other would claim the same. I would be in the middle, laughing at the absurdity of it all. Anyway, when I got back, I wrote a report.

Do you remember how many pages you wrote?

I now can't remember how many pages I wrote. All I did was simply say that I had flown there over Wiriyamu as requested and had found the villages destroyed, with many dead from bullet wounds, and that I could not count the dead as there were many if not hundreds. I then gave it to Dr. Paz. Dr. Paz then gave the report to the bishop. I do not know if Dr. Paz gave a copy of the report to Tete's governor. Neither Dr. Paz nor my bishop made me change the content of the report. Neither said anything negative to me about the report. I know that the bishop was deeply affected and saddened by the events and told me that he had sent a copy of the report to Rome. As to the others in the military, I cannot tell you their reaction. I have the impression that those in the lower ranks were sad. As to the bigwigs that had ordered the military operation that led to this massacre, I do not know. It is difficult to say. There the matter was to rest for the moment.

Interrogation and the Mobbing Journalists

Six months later we then heard of the publication of the Wiriyamu massacre in London by Father Hastings. That was really sad and unnecessary in my view. Hastings should not have done what he did. After all, there had been enough of suffering already. The dead were long gone; the wounded had recovered. I think Hastings was politically motivated. People of the cloth should stick to religious matters and not get involved in matters political. Hastings' report was revealed to coincide with Caetano's visit [to the UK] and proved a major cause of embarrassment for the Portuguese government. Caetano had a rough ride in London, you know. Our interest as priests and nuns was to help these people and not to ensure poor Caetano's political fall. But that was the political reality of Mozambique at the time. In the context of its politics, I think the Portuguese could not behave otherwise. They did help, though, with the evacuation of the wounded. The governor himself came and gave money. We then surveyed the *aldeamento* at M'Phadwe and placed the survivors and the refugees there.

Anyway, when the story was published, I was to be found, as was my habit, in the hospital.

The hospital surgeon said to me, "Did you hear what happened?"

"No," I said.

"Yes! Caetano went to London, and they revealed everything about Wiriyamu. I do not know what will happen to us here."

I said something like, "Nothing will happen to us."

"I don't know, but I think they already took Dr. Paz to Nampula for questioning."

"Dr. Paz?" I asked.

I was puzzled and could not understand why. I shrugged my shoulders and thought nothing of it, and I got on with my work. On that day we had many wounded to operate on.

Then on Friday of that week, one official from Tete, a tall man whose name I cannot recall, came to the hospital to look for me.

I met him and he said, "Sister Lúcia, get ready because a car has arrived to take you to Nampula."

"Right now? To Nampula?"

"Yes." he said.

"How come?"

"I have my orders. Go home; prepare to be taken to the airport."

I got going and was a bit nervous. I went home to change since I was dressed in hospital whites. I was taken to the airport and given a boarding pass. I got into the plane and off to Nampula I went.

Waiting for me at Nampula airport was Dr. Paz and two big commanders. As you know Paz had taken an earlier flight to Nampula.

I said, "Hello, Dr. Paz, how are you?" "I am fine."

He was sad. He remained motionless. He was really sad, I felt.

Then one of the big commanders spoke. "Sister, since it is Saturday tomorrow, you can rest to recover from the heavy work load in the hospital. On Sunday, you may do what you want, see Nampula or visit whoever you want. On Monday we shall begin work."

The commanders then left me—except for one. I saw and noted that Paz remained quiet and sad.

Well, the officer who had accompanied Dr. Paz to meet me at the airport then took me to my hotel, but I felt numb with so much war going on.

The truth is, one young boy at the hotel asked me, "Sister, do you want to eat or drink something?"

"No, I am off to bed."

But I could not sleep. The whole night I kept wondering in my head, "Why am I in Nampula? Shall I ring my sisters in Tete? No, you had better not in case they are listening. What shall I do?" I kept fishing like this the whole night.

The next morning, Sunday, I asked the bellboy, "What time is Sunday mass said in the local church?"

He said at such-and-such time. Well, I went to mass. After mass, I sought out my fellow sisters. As you know, we are very few here in Mozambique.

"Ah! Ah! We have someone new here, someone new here," they said excitedly.

"Yes, I came from Tete."

"Ah! From Tete?"

"Yes."

"Very well," they said.

We began to get acquainted. It was time to go.

Just then the fathers said, "Sister, wait a minute. What is your name?"

"Sister Lúcia."

"Wait a minute, and we will take you home."

"Very well."

We got into the car. The fathers sat in front, and I [sat] behind.

"Where to?" they said.

I said to hotel such-and-such.

They said, "At Hotel Morgado?"

"Yes," I said.

"But you are lodged there. That hotel is where the military stay."

"Yes, I know."

I would rather they thought I was with the military than reveal why I was really here. I did not want to speak about the matter to anyone.

"But are you in the military?" they asked.

"No, I am not."

"This is strange," they thought out loud.

Well, mercifully they dropped the subject, and I was left at the hotel.

I then decided to pay a visit to the bishop of Nampula, Monseigneur Vieira Pinto. In fact, I had already decided on that, that morning. "After the Sunday mass I am going to speak with the bishop of Nampula," I had said to myself as I left for the church. Why not? They had given me a chauffeur-driven car, you know, imagine! And in my whole life I had done nothing but serve people and do so without wheels! Also, no one in Tete knew where I was. I wanted the bishop of Nampula to tell my bishop in Tete that I was here in Nampula and to let the hospital staff in Tete know that for all purposes I was visiting my sisters here in Nampula, and not to mention Wiriyamu as the real cause of my journey here. I got out, and the chauffeur appeared.

"Sister, would you like to go for a drive in Nampula?"

I shook my head no. I said, "Where is the bishop's residence? Take me there. I want to pay my respects."

He took me there.

I got to see the bishop and said to him, "I am from Tete, and my bishop in Tete does not know that I am here. I myself don't really know why and how. I suspect it is because I flew over Wiriyamu. I found Dr. Paz here also. He looks very sad."

"But why have they got you here now, six months after your trip?" he said.

"I don't know."

"Very well," he said. "Could it be," he said, thinking aloud, "because of this story that came out in the newspapers in England? You must be somehow linked to this story. You had better be careful with the journalists. What do you think?" he said sympathetically.

"I want to have nothing to do with journalists. They won't find me."

"I think you had better not speak to any journalists as the other Spanish priests have done," he added.

Well, we then spoke of other matters.

He then asked, "Where are you staying?"

I said, "Hotel Morgado."

"Near Hotel Morgado you mean? Ah, that is not very far. It is near here."

"No Senhor Bispo, IN Hotel Morgado."

"In Hotel Morgado? What a strange world we live in," he said.

"Yes, and without a watch or a book, it is very difficult to pass the time," I said.

Anyway the bishop was really nice to me.

On Monday, we went to look for Dr. Paz to begin work. When we arrived by car, I saw him coming out accompanied by the new commander-in-chief of the Armed Forces in Mozambique, General Machado, to receive me.

"How are you, Dr. Paz?"

"So-so," said Paz.

Just as he said that, an army officer came out of the nearby barracks together with a military or security policeman or something like that and said to the general beside Paz, "Sir! You have an urgent phone call."

The general dismissed the men and went in to take the call. Paz and I were now alone, together.

"Dr. Paz, what happened?" I said.

"I am in very bad shape, Irmã Lúcia, because I was responsible for the flight over Wiriyamu. I should have gone there personally. Instead I sent you," he said.

I understood what he meant by that.

I therefore asked him point blank. "Is it because I am not Portuguese but a foreigner?"

"Yes," he said with great relief, "and that is why I really do not know what will happen to me. And I do not know if you are thinking of talking to journalists about Wiriyamu. They are going to ask you that question."

"I want nothing to do with journalists. All the journalists want is to get to the story. And that is it. Dr. Paz, rest assured that I will not talk to journalists."

"Thank God," said Dr. Paz, "you are going to save my life."

Dr. Paz's reply and his emotional state gave me an added incentive to keep silent about the whole affair.

Upon the return of the military officer, we got to work. An important-looking officer interrogated me about my helicopter trip and asked me what I intended to do about what I knew concerning Wiriyamu.

I said, "Nothing. I intend to do nothing about it."

All I did, I said, was to obey orders: fly over the site, return, and report what I saw.

"I am a nurse and of a religious order. I am not political. I went there because Dr. Paz was ill and could not go himself and because I was asked to go there to make an assessment as a professional."

"Very well. I am pleased to hear you say that," he said.

I later came to know he was the new commander, General Tomás Basto Machado.

The interrogation lasted for eight days. During this period the military comported themselves with the utmost respect for me, I must say. They looked after me well. They took me to sightsee the Island of Mozambique and treated me to dinners of seafoods and things I had never tasted in my poverty-stricken existence as a nun. Also, remember that the Tete hospital was a fully equipped, 100 percent hospital. Therefore, all the wounded would come here directly first, and if we had no beds to spare, which was more often than not because this was a highly militarized province, the wounded would be evacuated elsewhere. So when they took me to Nampula's military hospital for a visit, several nurses and staff recognized me.

"Hey, Sister Lúcia, what are you doing here?"

"I have come to visit you."

"Ah, well, how are things with you in Tete?" they asked.

"Things are going well with me in Tete," I said.

I thought what a peculiar question. How did they come to know why I am here?

On the eighth day I was dismissed. The military commander from the Tete region had been dismissed following pressure from the authorities in Tete. Also, I was later told that the bishop of Tete was very unhappy about the way the military was conducting the inquiry with me.

The military officer who had come to the airport with Dr. Paz to receive me then came to me and said, "Irmã Lúcia, you are lucky! You must have a powerful saint on your side. You can return to Tete tomorrow."

"Many thanks, Sir."

I got into the plane and came back to Tete. Dr. Paz never returned to Tete thereafter. He stayed in Nampula or went to Maputo or somewhere, I don't know where. Our hospital never recovered. We went through many, many directors thereafter, including military directors.

Then the journalists came to Tete. They spoke in English. I could only hear and understand my name. "Irmã Lúcia, Irmã Lúcia." I managed to avoid them. Then the Spanish priests wanted me to tell them what I had seen. I said no. I said I had recorded all my impressions on the report and had given the report to Dr. Paz. I was not going to speak to them, either. I had to go to Maputo and all that. I just wanted to get back to work, to my hovel. In fact, I was deeply affected by what happened to Dr. Paz. You know after that trip that caused me so much trouble, I never returned to Wiriyamu. I never found out if they buried the dead. I never saw António, the wounded boy. Eventually, he was taken to Frelimo by one of the fathers, and I never heard of him since. Now it appears he is here. He is in Wiriyamu, is that right? Anyway, for myself, I maintained absolute silence—until today.

Not Wiriyamu Again!

So when I heard that someone wanted to speak to me about Wiriyamu again after all these years I said, "Oh dear, oh dear, oh dear me! Not Wiriyamu again. Who wants to talk to me about Wiriyamu? After all these years! May God rest my soul and theirs. It was so long ago. Poor me and poor Wiriyamu."

And so here we are, back with the dead and that poor, helpless, wounded boy!

4
THE FIRST PUBLIC OUTING OF THE WIRIYAMU NARRATIVE

This fourth group of interviews is by two priests, Miguel Buendia and Padre Alberto Fonte Castellã. Buendia's is a clear-cut text, Cartesian in texture though heavily interpolated, that begins as virtually all these interviews do, with personal details. He is very clear about where he stood on issues of social justice and the role he played in smuggling parts of the massacre report when ordered to leave the colony. Significantly this same sense of clarity affects his reasons to leave the Church and the role he played in the Wiriyamu revelations once he reached Madrid.

Padre Alberto Fonte Castellã, now in his eighties, is still active as a missionary priest in Changara, where he was interviewed for this book. Once the conflict around the mission intensified, he was ordered to move out and eventually expelled from the colony. His interview ends with his account of smuggling the Wiriyamu report in his undergarment as he successfully boarded the plane for Madrid via Lisbon. Padre Castellã's account ends with his departure to head the church mission in Mutarara, before he is expelled from the colony. Upon his return he is seconded to head the mission in Changara, then headed by Padre Sangalo.

Photo 10 Miguel Buendia, Maputo. Photo by Mustafah Dhada, © 1995.

Interviewee:
Miguel Buendia
Date (yyyy mm dd):
1995 03 14 and 21; 1995 04 04 and 14
Duration (hh mm ss):
4h 30m 29s
Place:
Maputo
Language:
Portuguese
Interpreter:
None
Redactions:
Heavy

How I Smuggled the Report

I am Miguel Buendia. We became, I became a Burgos Father because they were secular
priests attached to a Spanish diocese with missions abroad. Of course, things changed
a bit later—but that is another story. In my case, I met them through a member of my

family, a nice man very interested in missionary work, who later left the priesthood. I cannot tell you exactly why. I first entered the seminary in Murcia in my diocese, after trying to join the Jesuit order, and stayed there until I got to go to do missionary work abroad.

Today, the road to becoming a Burgos Father is less complicated. In my time, we were connected to our diocesan bishop but not connected to each other, in a way, isolated. So Padre Vicente, for example, who remains a Burgos Father to this day, depended on his bishop in Valencia, who was financially responsible for him. So we were linked only via our diocese but not [where we did our missionary work]. This was a struggle for us, which was resolved [a bit later on] so that bishops and [Burgos] fathers from different dioceses could [fraternize with] each other [on social visits].

Thereafter things changed. Fathers doing missionary work would meet their brothers from the missions in Moatize and the Burgos Fathers from neighboring Zimbabwe. A new solidarity developed, with the national seminary in Spain holding us together as a congregation, sending missionaries to Latin America and Africa and other places. Mind you, we always remained faithful to our mission. We were a congregation of secular clergy. That is it!

To understand us better, let me tell you this: As Burgos Fathers, we were unique. We worked in Burgos with the disadvantaged: the rural poor and the urban working class. I used to work with young people. It gave me a start, [an appreciation for a simple life], reflective of my surrounding, which eventually [brought me to question] our theology, [particularly to entertain] the possibility of connecting Christianity with Marxism. All these theories [preoccupied me the more I got involved with] the young and the working class. Others, like Padre Vicente, worked in hospices for abandoned children. [As Burgos, we felt deeply connected to people in the social context of their poverty and deprivation.]

We were committed to [improve the lives of the poor, to a life of] simplicity, and to work with the downtrodden. In the Burgos city, our instructor priests would go biking throughout the neighborhood, connecting with people as part of their social ministry. This was understood to be [our cardinal mission], and [we all Burgos] lived that lifestyle. Another common theme among us who served in Latin America in the 1960s was the war. We were already socially conscious [of violence and deprivation] during our formative training, when some of us fought clandestinely as priests against Francoism. I didn't directly work in this [anti-Francist] group, but I did work with individuals linked with the communist party, the only party in Spain at the time involved with clandestine work.

All our contacts with the workers [and union workers and leaders] was undercover. Numerous Catholic movements helped us [to pursue our cause] for social justice. Many of these social justice activists later came to form the last batch [of priests] to enter the Burgos [priesthood]. I also think that the civil war between the Basques and the Catalonians made us even more [self-conscious to help] heal the wounds of division. We lived together with them, together with Andalusians, which helped us and them think and heal as one. In my case, my family, my father especially, suffered a lot because of General Francisco Franco. He was jailed for being a communist. I came to develop a different vision of Spain. What happened to people, young and old, during the civil war was terrible for Spain.

How old were you when your father was arrested?

I can't tell you. I remember him well. He was tied up in a tree, beaten and tortured. He never [talked about this] afterward, [nor revealed to us who tortured him; some of my family members though thought they knew his identity]. He was never bitter or vengeful; on the contrary, he forgave [his oppressors]. He was educated and taught us to forgive people. That impressed me most about him.

[These experiences affected my] vision for Spain, not as a militant against Franco; no, but as a socially conscious person. This feeling became stronger when I [became a Burgos priest]. I began to distrust this idea of winners and losers with winners taking all. My home education, my schooling, and what I saw later in Burgos, a conservative city, told me there was a better world view. Let me give you an example. I remember a well-respected Catalonian priest at the seminary—he was a professor of philosophy, with strong opinions—opposed to Franco. As a Catalonian he was openly republican. But he took trouble to study and treat us, his students, as individuals, and that impressed me. In the end his position and the socially focused ministry of the Burgos clashed with the conservative politics of Burgos city—and we, as an order, had to leave that place and move to Madrid. That was in 1973 or 1974. That did not mean we were trouble-free. We faced other challenges, but that is another story!

The Bulge

In the last interview, we talked about Padre Ferrão, the person who put the report together first. He is a Mozambican priest from Tete, who heard the witnesses speak and took their names to make a list.

Do you know where is the original list?

I do not know where the original list is. A lot of the documents we had with us were left in Madrid at the Burgos house. I have no idea what my other colleagues did with what they had. The Burgos headquarters where they housed the press and public relations department was in Garcia Morato Street. It was later moved. I believe all the archives were left behind, including our dossier. We even did a special dossier of massacres worldwide. We spent a lot of our own money, collecting newspaper articles and collating information on this subject. These materials should be there. I hope they are not destroyed.

Of course the Wiriyamu dossier had numerous original documents. Copies of some of these we gave to Father Hastings. He used these for his book on Wiriyamu. As I said before, I saw the report first, when it was brought to me by another Burgos, Padre Jesus Camba Gomes, on February 13th or 19th of 1973. The exact date must be recorded somewhere.

Why did he bring this report to you? Can you tell me the story?

This is how it happened.

I returned from my visit to Lourenço Marques to support the Macúti Fathers on the 26th of January; a week later a friend informed me that, according to information received from the bishop, they wouldn't renew my immigration visa. I was then put under surveillance. I guessed I probably had fifteen days to get out of the country. But the orders came sooner than expected. A day before I was expelled, I had gone to Lundo for church business, but I had left my [identification] papers in Muraça. That was when it happened. They told me to leave [Mozambique]. On the train from Muraça to Manga in Beira, the PIDE [Polícia Internacional e de Defesa do Estado] agents accompanied me. I talked to them. It appears they were afraid that we would incite public protests. They had to do their job and apologized to me.

"Father, I know this is a horrible way to live our life; we don't agree with many things."

I told them I was walking tall, head up, and not embarrassed by what I did as a priest with a social conscience. "I would do it all over again. I am leaving this place with a peace of mind, knowing that I had never stolen, exploited, or hurt anyone. I am convinced that someday I will be back."

Manga was close to the airport mission.

Finally the day arrived. Júlio Moure and I were told to leave.

Do you know where I can find him?

Júlio Moure is now in Mexico, married as well, to a Mexican citizen. We lost contact with each other. Perhaps Padre Vicente Berenguer might have his contact for you to interview him. Unfortunately, I never got to see him again or got contacted—except once when he wrote to Padre Vicente.

We were at the Burgos Fathers' house in the airport parish. The house is still there.

Can you describe the house?

No, I don't remember the number of rooms it had, and in which room we were, but if I remember well, we were standing in the front room with our luggage, ready to load the car. Perhaps at lunchtime, thirty minutes before we left, Jesus Camba Gomes arrived in his jeep. Officially he was there to say goodbye.

Did he come from Chimoio?

No, I do not remember if he came from Chimoio or not; he sometimes was there and at other times travelled visiting missions. He said it had taken him two hours to get to the house. So he must have come from Chimoio, 200 kilometers away. He came and left the same day.

What time?

I can't tell you that. I don't remember if we had already had lunch that day, or if he just came a few minutes before our lunch. I know you like to know details, but I cannot be sure now. It has been a long time, you know.

What did he look like then?

He was skinny, had dark hair, and was beardless. He is no longer a father; at that time, he was responsible for the Burgos Fathers in Mozambique. As Burgos, we generally dressed casually. All this happened very quickly.

He gave me a packet, a folded document.

"Miguel, take this to Spain. It is about Wiriyamu. Don't lose it. Keep it in a very safe place."

Had you read the document?

No, I had not read the document, but I know Jesus Camba had commented on what had happened at Wiriyamu. We then left for the airport. I was shell-shocked, defeated, and so sad to leave Mozambique. You see, we were expelled after the Macúti Fathers' trial, which I talked about earlier. You remember [that trial], right?

Yes, I do.

Then you also know that [the Portuguese had jailed] two Burgos Fathers, Padre Martins and Padre Valverde. They were freed a bit later, at the end of 1973, before the April Revolution.

I put the report in my pocket. It was much safer than putting it in the luggage, which they could search without permission. When we got to the airport, the PIDE agents were shooing people who had come to say goodbye away from us, as if we were prisoners. Of course I wasn't. I protested, forcefully. The PIDE agents must have contacted their superiors. They said they were awaiting new instructions from Lourenço Marques to let us talk to our friends waiting to say goodbye. Finally they let us talk, and [we said] our goodbyes. Just then one of the defense attorneys for the Macúti Fathers [who were Portuguese and had been jailed, accused of sedition] approached us and said the PIDE were going to search us before we embarked.

They put us in a room and opened our luggage for inspection. I had taken only a few clothes that fit me and left the rest behind. At that time I weighed fifty-eight kilos. I had lost twelve kilos since my arrival. I didn't want to take too many clothes that no longer fit me. [I didn't want] my mom to notice how skinny I had become. I had very few belongings, in fact. I carried two books on liberation theology. They flipped through the pages. After they were done with the luggage inspection, one of them looked me in the eye and asked:

"Do you have anything on you to declare?"

"No," I said. At the time priests were still respected as men of the church. After our departure, all the fathers expelled from Mozambique were strip-searched. We were the lucky ones.

The defense attorney for the Macúti Fathers had warned us that they were after currency [smugglers], since the Mozambique escudo at the time could still be negotiated for Portuguese money at the Portuguese National Bank. There were people lining up to fly beside us who were not subjected to a similar search. I think we were put through this ordeal to denigrate us as people and as priests. That is what I think. All this took us an hour. We got to Lourenço Marques, and at five in the afternoon we boarded the next plane for Europe. It was a 10½-to 11-hour flight. By the time we left, it was dark. During the entire flight, I was curious to open the packet and read it. I didn't, not until I got to Madrid. I was afraid. PIDE agents could be on board. You see, it was a TAP [Transportes Aéreos Portugueses] flight, jumbo. On the way to Madrid, we stopped in Lisbon. In Lisbon, nothing happened. There was nobody to meet us, not even the immigration. I think from there we got a different plane, maybe Iberia, but I don't remember. It was just a connecting flight. We left at 9 a.m. the next day.

In Madrid, our colleagues were waiting to greet us. I don't remember if Enrique Ferrando was there to greet us. [He had already left Mozambique, if I am not mistaken.] I believe he was there at the airport, but I can't remember anyone else waiting to greet us. Again, we were so tired that I cannot recall [now clearly all these details]. The first thing Júlio and I did was to read the document. It later became clear it was incomplete. It had several pages missing. The situation was resolved a bit later when a colleague, I can't remember if it was Padre Vicente or not, smuggled the remaining pages out of Mozambique to Spain.[1] How he evaded the PIDE's strip-search, I do not know. When we arrived, we went to the Burgos house in Madrid and delivered the document. We then [rested to recover from our ordeal] in a guesthouse downtown. We were very tired and slept for a long time, up until our hostess called us to come and eat.

I then went to see my family and travel a bit. I stayed with them for about a month.

What did they say when they saw you?

Oh, I did not have to explain much. I told them, with clarity and without shame, we had been expelled and told them why. They understood. They knew this was not because of politics, because they were worried this to be the case. My father had been tortured, remember? So, we were, how do you say it . . .

Sensitized?

Yes, sensitized. They did not want to suffer another stigma. They did not ask many questions, except my mother was very concerned I had lost so much weight.

She had good reasons to worry about me. After the Macúti trial and before our departure I had fallen ill and did not take care of myself, like taking medication and resting. In fact, I nearly didn't make it to Lisbon because I had been in the middle of an epidemic zone [surrounding] my mission . . . and the Spanish doctors did not want to give me any medication in case I was carrying an epidemic virus. I was put to bed rest during my stay with my family.

The Revelations

After my rest, Padre Júlio Moure, Padre Ferrando, and I met at the [Burgos] house in Madrid to plan what to do next. We wanted to help free our colleagues in prison in Lourenço Marques and publicize the massacres in Mucumbura, Wiriyamu, and other places. We met with a high-ranking minister in the Spanish government.

When?

Oh, this must have been between February and June, well before Father Hastings contacted us. We told him what we were planning to do. We were worried that our plans to publish the stories in the Spanish press would harm [the cause] of our [incarcerated] brothers in Lourenço Marques.

---

[1] In all probability it was Padre Castellā.

The minister and his staff were [sympathetic] and advised us not to worry about a backlash. The story was unlikely to cause waves or be widely published, they thought. Often, he said, there was an agreement . . . an understanding between Spain and Portugal. The Spanish government did not intervene in Portuguese colonial politics. In return, the Portuguese respected Spanish sovereignty. The main newspapers toed the line accordingly, he added. We also suspected that the PIDE was active in Madrid, and they [advised] to be careful getting in and out of the metro. I also remember this minister wrote a letter to the foreign ministry in Lisbon demanding Portugal release the two Spanish priests languishing in prison for the last two years. The letter was very strongly worded. He didn't ask for freedom. He demanded it. They showed us the letter.

Do you have a copy of the letter?

No, I don't have the letter. I must have lost it during one of my many moves.

We then went back to the Burgos house in Madrid. We organized all the information on the massacres of Mucumbura, Wiriyamu, and other places into a dossier. We discussed our publicity plan with some people who could help us. They in turn introduced us to other people in the newspaper world. It dawned on us then that Spanish newspapers would really not touch the story, as we were told, and we did not want to use the left-wing press. It would have been seen as biased . . . and therefore not credible. So we found an Italian one.

Bruno Crimi perhaps?

I do not know if the writer Bruno Crimi was involved, but our contact came from a well-known elderly Spanish theologian and his younger colleague. Their names escape me. They were the ones who made contact with the Italian newspaper. Not all the "dossier" materials were published on the front page, just the denouncement.

Was it the IDOC dossier?

No it was not the IDOC [International Documentation on the Contemporary Church] document. Also I do not remember the exact date, but it may well have been May 1973.

Well, that strategy failed. The Italian publication of the story did not get any attention. We felt so responsible, so disheartened, and we did not know what to do next. It was hard to believe we lived these facts. Then Father Hastings contacted us. The story then developed not as we expected. Hastings had gone to Zimbabwe. I don't know if he asked or the subject came up during a conversation with our Zimbabwe colleagues, also friends of the Burgos Fathers in Bulawayo, who told him they knew people who knew more about the subject and could provide useful information, and that some of us had already been expelled and gone to Spain. Hastings came to visit us in Madrid. He talked clearly about his opportunity and the role he could play in getting the story out. He said he was invited as part of a group to a parliamentary conference that was celebrating 500 years of Anglo-Portuguese Imperial Alliance. And Marcelo Caetano was going to be in London for the occasion. He wanted to know from us if the documents and accusations we had were true because he wanted to expose these in Caetano's presence. What an opportunity!

Hastings' intervention, however, was later cancelled because perhaps the British discovered what he was about to say. His conference in the [House of Commons] didn't happen, but he convinced *The London Times* deputy editor to [publish it]. This was for us probably the best thing that could ever have happened because this newspaper had some prestige and was not associated with the left. It was like a bomb. To us this was what we had dreamed: This story was on the way to the United Nations. We didn't want just newspaper news, but a worldwide movement. We also wanted to solve the problem of freeing colleagues who were in prison with no trial in sight for them. Suddenly, no sooner than the story broke in *The London Times*, the Portuguese freed them [our colleagues], without trial, after two years of prison, imagine! Therefore, our strategy had succeeded.

From the moment the story broke in the month of July 1973, journalists from all over the world came to interview us. There were so many that most of my day, from 9 a.m. to 9 p.m., was [spent] being interviewed. There were different types of interviews. Some were looking for contradictions in the story we told in order to defend Portugal. I remember telling an old German correspondent that if he wanted information of this type he should talk to the Portuguese embassy.

"What you are really asking us is to write their version and defend them in what they were doing in the colonies."

There were others, perhaps more subtle. They tried to associate us with Frelimo and therefore imply we were their spokesmen. Essentially, they were misrepresenting our testimony, to make it more questionable. I used to say Frelimo was there, among the people; there was no way to know who they were.

I had to learn very quickly to navigate these tricky waters. It taught me to be aware not only of the power of journalism, but also of the organizations and individuals supporting points of view in reporting. Once a journalist asked me if there was really a massacre, and I replied to him:

"Look! Do you think the Portuguese are being truthful here? Every colonial war was like that; Algeria and Vietnam were like that. There is no colonial war without a massacre. Therefore, what else do you want? This war has to be denounced so it can end."

Of course the Portuguese denied all this, until Peter Pringle confirmed the story with his visit to Mozambique. He had been invited by the Portuguese government to go to Mozambique. However, when others went to Mozambique, the guides that they were provided with wouldn't take them to the exact place. They took them to an area they claimed was Wiriyamu. Of course it wasn't [Wiriyamu]. We knew the PIDE and their tactics. Therefore, through Hastings, Peter got in contact with us in Madrid before going to Mozambique. We told him:

"When you arrive in Beira, Mozambique, get in touch with Jesus Camba Gomes. He will send you to the right place."

Jesus Camba then took him to Tete, where he made some contact with survivors.

PIDE agents tailed him, arrested him, and confiscated all his material. Luckily, he got to save the pictures when the PIDE were too busy looking through his things. That roll of pictures was the only evidence he brought back to England, and it was enough to be published as evidence of a massacre. Peter had taken with him a photograph of António

Mixone, who was a survivor and witness of the massacre, and who had seen his parents die during the massacre. It was on that visit that he also saw Padre Sangalo.

Sangalo was in Moatize then. After Peter left, Sangalo heard the BBC of London talking about the Wiriyamu massacre and one of the survivors, the boy António Mixone. Sangalo went to where Mixone was with his relatives and took him away, to a place safe from the PIDE. Sangalo was lucky in finding Mixone before PIDE did. When the PIDE arrived there, the villagers told the agents Mixone was gone. A white man had taken him. When asked to identify him, they described Sangalo's face, body, and what he was wearing. The PIDE agents dashed to the San Pedro Mission in Tete, and together with one relative of Mixone, to look for Sangalo among the other fathers. They didn't find him. The PIDE then went after Sangalo, threatening to kill him to reveal Mixone's whereabouts. That did not work. So they begged Sangalo to reveal what he knew, or else he would have to bear the consequences.

Sangalo was tortured and suffered terribly [but he did not disclose what he knew]. Even Jorge Jardim, who was in Tete, joined the PIDE, threatening his life unless [he revealed Mixone's whereabouts]. Finally they had had enough. One day they came to his house, arrested him, and deported him to Spain, without even a passport. He landed in Madrid, without a passport or any of his belongings. He was scared because they were capable of killing him on the flight to Madrid. The PIDE, through TAP, took him to Lisbon and then, through another TAP, took him to Madrid. All this happened because of one survivor, Mixone. Clearly, with Mixone dead, the story would have weakened the truth. With him alive, the Portuguese had to work harder [to deny the massacre.]

I believe Wiriyamu had major repercussions [for Portugal and internationally], and even Frelimo recognized it. Júlio Moure and Vicente Berenguer, in one of these meetings during the revelations, had told me that [Frelimo leaders recognized that] we did in a few days what Frelimo had failed to do in twenty years. The Wiriyamu denunciations were a push to decolonize Portugal's Africa. And that is how this part of history was made. And we contributed to it. For something like this to happen, a lot of people and facts were involved, and great care was taken to navigate the story, and a deep pressure from history was felt among those involved.

Photo 11 Alberto Fonte Castellã, Changara. Photo by Mustafah Dhada, © 1995.

Interviewee:
Alberto Fonte Castellã
Date (yyyy mm dd):
1995 05 17
Duration (hh mm ss):
1h 21m 11s
Place:
Changara
Language:
Portuguese
Interpreter:
None
Redactions:
Heavy

The Wiriyamu Narrative Escapes Undetected!

Hello, I am Alberto Fonte Castellã. I was born near Barcelona in Girona on December 19, 1931. I graduated from the lyceum of my village in philosophy and theology. We are six, five brothers and a sister, and I am the eldest. My father was a peasant farmer. God knows why I chose the priesthood. I had already finished with my lyceum studies and was deep in philosophy and articles on overseas Catholic missions. I discovered there were many countries mentioned in these articles that were not Christian. Perhaps that was where I was meant to go. I then went to the Burgos. For four years I studied theology.

That was also where the Burgos Fathers had their world headquarters at the time, in Burgos. Now it is in Madrid, you know.

When in Burgos I was chosen to go to Mozambique. My parents were not happy. They felt I no longer loved them. "To be a priest, yes, but to go on overseas missions, no!" They did not want me to go. Even now, when I go for holidays, I still hear protest from them, particularly my mother.

"Son, leave missionary work for your colleagues now. Come back home. You have spent too many years away from us."

You see, my colleagues who stayed behind were in various parishes, but in Spain.

She said, "It is your time now to stay put and let your colleagues exchange places with you."

As a secular priest, I was attached to my diocese of Girona, whose bishop at the time was José Cardenal I. I was also linked to the Burgos as a missionary. So I reported to both of them and also of course to my bishop here in Tete. When my work finishes here, I shall go home. I intend to die there in my country, Spain. But for now we are here in Changara, from where Padre Vicente Berenguer was once expelled. That was perhaps in 1971 or 1972; I don't know exactly. The Portuguese had constructed this house we are in, because he lived down there in the bush near where Frelimo was and where they could help him. Frelimo had great faith in him and would visit him at night. He too knew that famous commander Raimundo Dalepa. I don't know where he is now. Some say he died, that he committed suicide. What a shame! I came to know him there up in the north, near Unkanha.

Expulsions

I then left Mucumbura for holidays in April or May of 1971. I therefore cannot tell you much about the Mucumbura massacre, which happened in that year, because I was not there. Padre Valverde did a report on it. He is in Madrid now; you know that, don't you? He talked and wrote a lot about it. All I can say about Mucumbura is that I heard that Raimundo fell in love with a woman from Mucumbura and got married to her eventually. I never returned to Mucumbura again. When I got back in November 1971 from my sabbatical, I was sent to Mutarara in Inhangoma.

When I got to Mutarara in late 1971, I had to change the method of my work. Unlike Unkanha, Mutarara is very rich in cotton. The Portuguese exploited African forced labor for this purpose. I mean, really exploited them. The good, most fertile land was given to the people of Azores and Madeira. The Africans were given poor soil and small parcels for cultivation, three acres, two for cotton and one for maize. It is here that my eyes were really opened.

"Yes, sir, there is reason for revolt," I said to myself. "One day they will be free."

What really filled me with horror was what one person confided with me one day. He said that cotton produced by whites was worth seven escudos a kilo, but Africans only got three escudos for their cotton. Same cotton, same land, different skin. It was shocking!

This was a stupefying discovery for me. I was changed. In my catechism lessons and in my sermons, I preached what I saw.

"Brothers! Do you not see you are being exploited? Your cotton is dirty. It is bought at three escudos. What do you think? What is wrong with this picture?"

It was then that I began to speak openly about the situation using biblical analogies and stories focussing on how God had sent Moses as a savior to set the people free.

"Friends, you too have a Moses amidst you. I know of this Moses. And it is in Frelimo that the liberation from slavery shall reside. There is no justification for the type of life that you are forced to live and lead, without clothes, with little sleep, just to enrich the Portuguese."

The African catechists liked what I said, and it helped them to hear it.

It was then that I was interrogated by the secret police. Earlier, a group of young men sent by our brothers, the Burgos Fathers, at the mission in Beira and Muraça had come to my mission on their way to join the liberation struggle. They came for a bit of rest and food and then left. This was normal to see young men at the mission on their way up north. Many were from the Burgos missions. But this time the group was caught at the border. The secret police interrogated the members of the group. They were asked where they were coming from, and they told the agents they had been to Inhagoma last, where they had spent the night before heading for Malawi. The result was predictable. I was now under suspicion for aiding and abetting terrorists.

Soon thereafter, five secret agents, two from Beira and two from Mutarara, came to see me. I cannot remember details of the fifth agent. They interrogated me for five hours. Three months later I was expelled. In the meantime, they began harassing me with frequent calls, ordering me not to speak of political issues in my sermons and to stick to godly subjects.

"Look, we are white. We need goods and have children in schools in Portugal. 'Os indígenas,' the local Africans, need nothing. They can survive on maize flour, and they are happy. We need more."

I said, "Forgive me, but this is claptrap. They have the same rights as the whites have. This issue is not negotiable whether you have a car or a refrigerator or not. They labor and sweat to produce maize and produce cotton, and they have the right to be paid the same as the whites for the cotton you buy."

"Ah, Padre! You can't talk like this."

"Look, if you don't like what I am saying, order me to leave. I have to contend with and live according to my conscience."

I knew that my time had come to leave, though I was the last one from the group of Burgos Fathers to leave. The first Burgos Father to be expelled, as you know, was Miguel Buendia, who is now a university professor. He is no longer a priest and lives in Maputo, I am told. In my case, the bishop from Tete, who was a Portuguese, had so far successfully intervened on my behalf and managed a stay of execution. Finally, the bishop could do no more. On the 10th or 11th of May I received the orders. I went to Beira to be deported.

In Beira I elected to stay at Sister Elvira's place. I had chosen to stay with her because she was very active in recruiting young African girls and because she was intelligent and a Mozambican, and I generally preferred to stay with Mozambicans than with whites. It was then that she told me of the Wiriyamu report. We were at the table sitting.

She said, "I have received a copy of the report of the Wiriyamu massacre."

I said, "Show me, show me, please." I did not bother to ask where she got it from.

She said, "I am sorry, but I can't let you see it."

She finally relented. I saw it and did not know that there was a copy of it in Spain.

"I need to take this to Spain."

She said, "Please, no."

"Rest assured, no one will know it came from you."

It was then that I decided to smuggle the copy of the four- or five-page report on Wiriyamu folded tightly in my underwear.

I was taken then to the airport in Beira for a flight to Lisbon via Lourenço Marques. Many of my colleagues and priests had gathered there to say goodbye. They even had a minute of silence in protest over my expulsion. I was then taken to a room by the secret police. I was terrified of being discovered with the report in my underwear. They opened my bags to see if I had anything suspicious. I got into the plane bound for Lisbon.

I arrived in Madrid on the 14th or 15th of May, in the morning, after a short stay to change planes in Lisbon. No one knew I was coming. I took a taxi from the airport to the Burgos headquarters. When my friends saw me, they burst out,

"By the grace of God, you are here!"

I said, "Yes. Like you all, I too was expelled!"

We started talking and talking. Sangalo was there, as were Miguel Buendia, Vicente Berenguer, and others. I told them what I had brought with me.

"Ah, you brought another copy."

It was then that I found out there was a copy of the report. I showed them mine. I handed over the report because Buendia and another Burgos priest were working on publishing it. It was during this time that Hastings came to Madrid. I can't tell you how he got to us, but he did.

I got back to Tete in the beginning of 1974, and it was there that the bishop decided to relocate Padre Vicente Berenguer from the Changara mission to the São Pedro Mission in Tete city, where Padre Ferrão was, and he asked me to go to Changara to replace Padre Vicente. I did not know Changara, where I was going to be for the rest of my life. I had spent my life in the north of Tete in a matriarchal society, but not around Tete city, which was predominantly a patriarchal society. So when I arrived this second time around, I braced myself for the worst. It hasn't turned out badly.

"Isn't this glass of iced water deliciously cold, Dhada!" said Alberto Fonte Castellã, as he ended the interview.

5

THE FINAL REVELATION

The fifth group has three testimonies, all by members of the Catholic Institute of International Relations (CIIR), which hosted the venue to discuss the Portuguese imperial alliance with Britain, during which the Wiriyamu massacre was discussed at length. The authors of the first two texts, Mildred Neville and Hugh O'Shaughnessy, give us the broader context of the CIIR driving Father Hastings' Wiriyamu narrative. Neville's text focuses on the CIIR's formative period and its goals to push a progressive agenda of the Catholic Church as a global human-development agency. With this brief context out of the way, her testimony reflects on Father Hastings' revelations from the CIIR platform, which she views as unprecedented in the CIIR's history of social activism. Her meditations end on the impact of Adrian Hastings' revelations on the institute and its future, which in her view was indelibly altered by the Wiriyamu story.

Hugh O'Shaughnessy attests to the veracity of Mildred Neville's narrative, in that the CIIR played a central role in the Wiriyamu affair, hosting leading figures of the Portuguese opposition. Two additional themes the text discusses are the handling of the story with The London Times' *deputy editor, Louis Heren, and the historical background behind the formation of the CIIR's Education Committee, to which Father Hastings was appointed, and which enabled him to launch the Wiriyamu revelations.*

The highlight of this group is the last text, by Father Adrian Hastings, recorded from his home in Leeds. It is a lengthy text, studded with facts, dramatic in places, and it clearly lays out several broadly defined topics for discussion: his formative years and the Vatican II's influence on his thinking on missionary work in Africa; his perspectives on Portugal's Caetano regime and colonial rule in Africa; the prism through which he viewed the Wiriyamu massacre; the intricate negotiations he undertook to have the story published in the pages of The London Times; *and the subsequent revolution that toppled Caetano's regime and Wiriyamu's place in it. Hastings' story is a page-turner and uplifting in demonstrating the success of a moral right in the face of mass violence.*

Interviewee:
Mildred Neville
Date (yyyy mm dd):
1996 03 nd
Duration (hh mm ss):
1h 7m 59s
Place:
London
Language:
English
Interpreter:
None
Redactions:
Light

Development Issues, Father Adrian Hastings, and the Opposition

My name is Mildred Neville, and I work for the CIIR. The CIIR was originally founded by Cardinal Hinsley in 1940 as the Sword of the Spirit and led by a group of lay Catholics committed to unite us in support of future peace. In 1965 it changed its name to CIIR and thereafter transitioned to relate much more to development issues. Now in 1958, my predecessor had convened a conference on the Church in Africa, which was in direct response to the postcolonial situation or pre-end to the colonial situation. The Papal Palace asked the Churches in Europe and North America to transform a clergy and to provide the resources available for Churches in the newly developing countries and the postcolonial countries of Southern Africa. So my predecessor, whose name was Margaret Feeny, convened this conference. Then she set up a thing called the Africa Centre in Covent Garden, London, which still exists and has now become a cultural center. In those days it was very much a center that looked at the whole future of Africa from the point of view of economy, politics, culture, religion, and so on. In those days it was sort of an educational center.

She had very much moved the organization in two ways: one, [moving] away from the persecution of Catholics in Eastern Europe and behind the Iron Curtain, which is what it was concentrated on; two, being outward-looking and at the service of the world much more. When the freedom-from-hunger campaign came in 1962, this very much firmed up the work of the organization. It became clear that if we were ever going to be of use at any real significance, we had to specialize. We couldn't simply be a general organization in international affairs. In a sense, we had to take sides. We took sides in favor of the newly developing countries, and we worked a lot on development issues.

In 1965, two years before I took over the CIIR, we set up our own overseas program for sending qualified people to work as volunteer professionals and technicians in some developing countries, and one of the areas to which we sent people was Central America. This was just at the end of the Second Vatican Council and around the first famous episcopal conference for all the bishops in Latin America, which was held in Medellín, Colombia. At Medellín, the Church took the preferential option for the poor. Although they didn't use this terminology, in effect they recognized for the first time, as a continental church, the situation of poverty, illiteracy, and illness in which the mass of population lived. For the first time they took some sort of responsibility, because previously the Church as a whole had been a church for the better-off and the well-to-do. The mass of the population in countries like Brazil were completely lacking in resources from the Church. So this was a huge regeneration of Church commitment to the poor.

This influenced the thinking of all the people that we at CIIR were working with in Central America, so much [so] that they came back to us very strongly about what did we think our role was, and how could we be part of an oppressive and dominative colonial economic power, while at the same time send people to try and help people in Central America pull themselves up by their boot straps. They felt in fact that we were a lot of the source of the trouble. This was one of the factors that began to readily change CIIR in this country. We began to see our role in completely different light. We began to realize that what we had called development was actually modernization, economic modernization. I was in my forties at this stage, and we were dealing with people of the younger generation in the 1960s when everything was possible. So there were a lot of different things going on as well. I think a very key understanding was that development, so called, of the kind that we had wanted to promote, very often wasn't development at all. It was national modernization, and the new terminology was coming out of Latin America's liberation and liberation theology.

At the same time, we had begun to work in Southern Africa. Just about the time of Wiriyamu—well the year before, for instance, the Heath government had been elected. One of the first things it talked of doing was selling arms to South Africa. The papers were full of the possibility that the British would start the sale of arms to South Africa. That galvanized a section of the CIIR. We wrote a publication about that and sent it to the people who had been working in Africa. They came back to us and said, "Our lives have become extremely uncomfortable when this announcement was made. Thank God the organization we're working for in London recognized and took a stand about how this is perceived." So we began to understand that what we did and said here was just as important as what the people working in the field were doing. The organization became greatly politicized as a result. We had an important committee for this type of work. The members of this committee, called the Education Committee of the CIIR, were myself, Hugh O'Shaughnessy, Hugo Young, Adrian Hastings, Eileen Sudworth, Father David Konstant (who is now the Catholic Bishop of Leeds), and Tim Sheehy, who was on the committee and also an important staff member. He was the person who handled the South African work. He was a very young man and went on to do all sorts of other things in Southern Africa. I can't remember offhand who else was on the committee. But Hugh O'Shaughnessy was certainly very important.

Adrian and the Detractors

Adrian went to see Louis Heren on a Sunday afternoon, I think. I picked him up from the station or from his sister and drove him to *The London Times*, where he discussed the whole matter with Louis Heren. I think, in Adrian's mind, the report would be published the next day. I think the decision must have been taken very quickly because I'm sure Louis Heren said to him, "Well, if it's not published tomorrow, it will never be published at all."

And I think it wouldn't have been. I can't remember how many days [articles about Wiriyamu in] *The London Times* did come out that week, and I can't remember at which point *The London Times* stopped publishing [them] at all. I don't remember meeting Louis Heren before. We knew him because he was the foreign editor, and he was a Catholic, but I don't think that his Catholicism had anything to do with it. Since then I have only met Heren casually once or twice.

Adrian said that when he told me that he got this documentation about the massacre that I said people don't like to talk about massacres; don't talk about that. And I'm sure that was true. We were concerned with Portugal, and we didn't see the significance of it. Wiriyamu, the whole of this event at Chatham House, and the press conference that followed were way out of our league at CIIR. My concern was more with the CIIR than it was with Wiriyamu, and whether or not we could handle it, whether the organization would be skewed. So I think that my concern was much more at the level of the survival and management of the organization in terms of, Could we do the work with the press that was required? We never had any money, and the practicalities of survival and what to do with that. Seeing where this fitted into our long-term road and long-term program, I think I was more concerned with that. We were a very small, very under-resourced organization with a handful of people. You know, in a small organization, it isn't always possible to drop everything and just concentrate on one thing. We had never held a press conference in our lives, and suddenly we had television from Sweden, the United States, Columbia Broadcasting System, CBS, and everyone else you could think of.

In the end, from the point of view of an organization coming up, CIIR handled it well, I thought. We found the staff was solidly based, knew their stuff, were not playing games, were very committed, were clear, could handle a much higher political profile, and could handle working with the media and the press. Wiriyamu ratcheted up our self-awareness and CIIR's self-confidence as an organization, which was actually very important because subsequently from 1975 on to 1980 we worked at a very high-profile level, particularly on Zimbabwe. We were constantly being accused of being communists and berated in the House of Commons as "that Marxist organization, the Catholic Institute of International Relations." So this, in a sense, was one of the turning points for the CIIR.

Wiriyamu did sort of hijack the event and the press conference, which was for Mário Soares and for Adrian Hastings. They hardly addressed one single question to Soares. I chaired the press conference, and I was very conscious of this because Soares was supposed to be the star, and he wasn't. They were much more interested in what Adrian had to say. And I'm sure I, artificially, as the chair of the press conference, brought in Soares once or twice to make sure he was able to say something. He didn't speak any

English at all, so everything he said had to be translated, which slowed things down a bit. Certainly, Hastings' revelations totally hijacked the event, and that was perfectly fine. We were not rooting for Soares or anything. He didn't need us as time went on. The next time he came back, the Labour Party officially invited him. We went to see him. After that we didn't really need his contacts. I think that Soares needed this information on Wiriyamu. It was mutually beneficial in the sense that, from Soares' point of view, to be identified with a meeting where this revelation was given credence, was something he couldn't have done for himself. Maybe he had been publishing documentation in the courts, but he certainly had never had that kind of opportunity, a bandwagon to get on.

John Biggs-Davison came to the meeting as well, I believe. Biggs-Davison and Patrick Wall started a little organization of right-wing Catholics, the name of which I can't remember,[1] and they wrote to the Catholic papers and tried to get people not to support the National Catholic Fund. It was a collection that the bishops held in every parish once a year to make contributions toward the work of Catholic organizations, and one of the organizations to which money was given was the CIIR. Pat Wall, Biggs-Davison, and a group of people said the CIIR wasn't really a Catholic organization because it supported Marxist groups, and therefore people shouldn't support the National Catholic Fund, even though the bishops set that up. Biggs-Davison was an extremely nice man, but he was very closed-minded and old-fashioned. He was a convert to Catholicism. He and Pat Wall used to be supporters, but that was before my day. They were early supporters of the Sword of the Spirit, but they didn't favor the transition to its becoming a partisan organization.

We also had a brush with the Roman Catholic bishops with the question of our posture on Portuguese Africa. We had published a comment on Mozambique before this event, and this had been very much criticized by the Portuguese ambassador in London. He had complained to Cardinal John Heenan, who was the archbishop of Westminster, about a Catholic organization publishing what he said were untrue statements about Portugal. I had gotten a letter from the archbishop listing these points and saying that we had to answer them, which we did. One of the points that we made was that we were not an official Roman Catholic organization; we were a Catholic organization, but we had an independent line.

The Cardinal accepted this position, which was quite surprising. He came to our annual general meeting several months later, and he talked about this, and he said it was a very good thing to have Catholic independent organizations that could develop their own policy and public response. This was actually a bit of a breakthrough. I have to say, we were very excited about what we were doing. We succeeded in getting an extraordinary amount of people to this meeting, and we were able to pull it off. It made a mark, and it certainly had an impact on the visit of Caetano. I'm sure it had a huge impact in England in preparation for the new Portuguese regime. What influence it had in Portugal precisely, I couldn't tell you as I do not know.

---

[1] The Monday Club.

Interviewee:
Hugh O'Shaughnessy
Date (yyyy mm dd):
1996 03 26
Duration (hh mm ss):
0h 53m 55s
Place:
London
Language:
English
Interpreter:
None
Redactions:
Light

Wiriyamu and the People of London

I am Hugh O'Shaughnessy. The CIIR became the CIIR from the Sword of the Spirit. There was a fundamental change of gear, so to speak, from the Sword of the Spirit to CIIR. From what I can gather, it reflected not only the context of the secular time but also the ecclesiastical reorientation of the Vatican. Mildred Neville would be most helpful here on details. I'm sure that whatever Mildred tells is right. She was the principal factor in the CIIR's reorientation. She was charming, dynamic, modest, talented, and intellectual.

I also knew a little bit about Portugal. I first went to Portugal in the early 1950s as an adjunct to my studies of Spanish. When I was still in school, I got a scholarship to study in Salamanca, where I did a course in Spanish. I took the train for the first time down to Rossio, Lisbon, and became very interested, charmed, and fascinated by the Portuguese culture. I hardly did any formal studies thereafter in Portuguese. I did take some lectures at Oxford, but not a lot, since I read French between 1956 and 1959 with Spanish as my area of interest. I've always been a bit bashful about my spoken Portuguese, and I speak Brazilian much better than I speak Portuguese. When I joined the CIIR, I was the only one who spoke Portuguese. It was good enough to do television for the BBC on Rede Globo in Brazil, which was a couple of years ago, where I interviewed Brazil's head of state.

I started my writing career in 1960 and was a journalist for *The London Financial Times*. From the late 1960s on, I was writing for both *The Financial Times* and *The Observer*. So my working life was devoted very much to Latin America. In 1966 and 1967, I took my wife and our three children to Chile. I was gathering interest and expertise about Latin America, but always in the background was an interest in Portugal. I was at that time not terribly politically conscious, but one of the turning points of my life was in 1961, when I was reading the very powerful piece written by Peter Benenson in *The Observer*, which was basically the foundation of Amnesty; later, it became Amnesty International. I was thrilled and electrified by what Peter wrote as a young journalist at the age of 26. I wrote to Peter and asked if I could help. To make a long story short, I was a member of the first committee of Amnesty International and was there, as many of us were, I believe Eric Baker and a number of others, planning the first steps of Amnesty.

I was a young journalist then and made editor, and I proved to be a very competent editor, of the first publication of Amnesty. That was very thrilling for me as it was the first bit of activism that I had gotten into. I kept in contact with Amnesty for a number of years and was, in the very first days of Amnesty, sent on missions, one to Tehran and the other to Lisbon, to find out what I could about political business and the political repression in that time. However, I wasn't given the official status that Amnesty delegations and missions have at the moment because Amnesty was of very small size compared to what it is now. So it was very much more informal, and I had a list of contacts to go to and, a list of prisoners to ask for, and I did make informal inquiries and produced a report, which I'm sure is still in the Amnesty archives. We'd be ashamed of the archives today because it wouldn't be of the sort of fairness on which Amnesty currently carries out its duties, but it was something at that time. For the first time, my linguistic and cultural interest in Portugal were linked into a political interest. So that was the background over above and beyond my interest in Latin America.

It was common knowledge, in London at least, that I am a Catholic. At any rate, around 1970, Tim Sheehy, who was then one of the people most closely involved on the staff of CIIR, which he was running under Mildred Neville, called me up. We had a pint of beer near *The Financial Times* office.

He said, "You've got to join the education committee of the CIIR."

I said I had made a rule to not be a professional Catholic. Tim was very persuasive. So I said I would give it a go. I therefore joined the Education Committee, which was at that time a very lively, influential, and interesting body to join under the inspired leadership of Mildred Neville as general secretary of CIIR. I did several terms on that committee. My activism in Amnesty and my interest in Portugal already established made it easy to make the jump in CIIR.

I don't know whether Hugo Young was a chairman of the Education Committee at the time I joined, but he certainly was for some time. I remember him well. He was tall and thin and wore spectacles. He was on the staff of *The Guardian* newspaper. He was also the chairman of the Scott Trust, which controls *The Guardian* media group. At the time of the Education Committee, he was still on the staff of *The London Sunday Times*, whose shift rightward was one of the reasons why he left it. He joined *The Guardian* as a columnist and then became chairman of the Scott Trust and overall one of the senior men in control of the whole *Guardian* empire. Other people on the Education Committee and the Executive Committee were people like Adrian Hastings and Pat Davis.[2] The whole lot was made [up] of very interesting, politically aware, and committed people in whose company I was very happy to be.

[2]Patrick William Hardy Davies. www.indcatholicnews.com/news/15673.

However, Tim Sheehy and Julian Filochowski were two people who played key roles in CIIR, I must say. They were key lieutenants of Mildred Neville. Tim left the CIIR later on to be a representative of the European Commission based in Amman, where he was the person who distributed European Union aid to the Palestinians. Before that, he was the European Commission Representative in Pretoria, South Africa, during the apartheid time. He moved into European Commission circles directly from CIIR. Julian became head of the Catholic Agency for Overseas Development (CAFOD), based in Britain, and had a very considerable position in Catholic life in Britain.

He and Tim were commissioned with the doings of the Education Committee, which at that time was the heart and motor of the CIIR. There was an Executive Committee, which at that time was more of a rubber stamp than a real executive decision-making organization, which it later became. Things were going on in two places in the CIIR: one, in the brain of Mildred Neville, and two, in the form of the Education Committee.

After the Story Came Out

In 1973, Hugo Young suggested that the Caetano regime was going to come to celebrate the 600 years of the Anglo-Portuguese Imperial Alliance. In that meeting, I remember suggesting that we should take advantage of that visit to bring the question of Portuguese colonialism more clearly onto the British scene. I said we should make some counter-establishment gesture, seizing his planned arrival, but not in a rabble-rousing or street way, but a dignified protest at the way in which the British government still cozied up to the regime in Portugal, despite the fact that it was clearly undemocratic and a member of North Atlantic Treaty Organization (NATO), an alliance with supposed democratic values. NATO in itself was hardly better; it was bad, but not quite as bad as the Franco regime, though Franco wasn't in NATO, other than through the US alliance with Franco.

I can't remember anybody being against my recommendation of handling Caetano this way. We decided, if I'm not mistaken, to form the John of Gaunt Committee. In fact, John of Gaunt was one of the founders, if I recall, a well-known historical figure, and prominent in English politics at the time of the first consolidation of Anglo-Portuguese relationships. I thought that John of Gaunt would be the figure easily recognized in Britain and would give some sort of political historical context to the relationship, when the name Marcelo Caetano might not mean very much to the ordinary Englishmen and Englishwomen. Letters called it the John of Gaunt Committee, and we used it, but we never formalized it. During this time, I had no idea of Wiriyamu whatsoever. After that meeting, Adrian went off to Rhodesia on a lecture tour. It was there that he was told about Wiriyamu. In the process, he decided he should go to Madrid to try to find out more about this since he was going to be in Salamanca soon anyway. In Madrid, Adrian went to the Burgos Fathers who had the documents. He had them translated from Spanish, and then he came to London and was picked up by Mildred Neville and taken to Louis Heren at *The London Times*.

Mildred and Louis were two very different people. Socially, Mildred Neville was at the far end of the spectrum whose other end was occupied by Louis Heren. So the social issues whose absence perhaps cost Louis Heren the editorship of *The London Times* militated in favor of Mildred Neville. Mildred Neville was upper-class, and Louis Heren was not. All this is only auxiliary, and I wouldn't want to be quoted or be understood by anybody as saying: "CIIR depended on Mildred Neville's social class." CIIR and its very considerable works depended in the first instance on Mildred Neville's very, very great human qualities, just as the founding of Amnesty, later Amnesty International, depended on the very great human qualities of Peter Benenson.

Eight years after he led the Wiriyamu story, Louis Heren left *The London Times* where he had been foreign editor. He was then a columnist for *The Tablet* until he died in 1995. I'm a regular contributor to *The Tablet* as well, but Louis and I have never had any intimacy; our paths have not crossed. Louis Heren was a very truthful guy. Evidently, he really wanted to become the editor of *The London Times*. I have absolutely no idea why he didn't become one. I have never written for *The London Times*, but I would say that during his life I was an acquaintance of his. I knew his name, but I didn't bother myself in finding out more. Though, do remember, Louis was Catholic. I would have thought that his lack of success in becoming the editor of *The London Times* would have been due more to his class background than to his religious background. Although I would add that until comparatively recently there were anti-Catholic clauses in the articles of association of *The Observer* newspaper. It didn't affect me because I was never aspiring to become editor of the paper, and I don't think it had any effect on their views of my writings. Certainly there was some anti-Catholic miasma, which has now subsided.

My reaction when the story broke about Wiriyamu was sorrow for the loss of life, a sense that the happenings in Mozambique fully justified, though justification was not needed, for the attitudes we had taken at the time of the Caetano visit. It fully justified the attitudes we were assuming within CIIR toward the government in Lisbon. After that conference with journalists and reporters, I can't recall precisely the date, I was at the flat of Mildred Neville for a supper party, and the guest of honor was Mário Soares, who had recently came back from São Tomé via Paris. The recollection I have is not of wines or of what we ate at the supper party, but more of the attitude and pride of Soares. He was a very considerable figure, and it was clear to everybody who came into contact with him that he knew this fact himself. He behaved as a statesman, and then as I have seen him, encountered him, and heard him, my first judgment I made of his character had been that he had been brought up by his subsequent attitudes as prime minister of the state. He possibly knew that the revelation of Wiriyamu was about to explode, but I can't recall if this dinner was before or after the revelation came out. I can't recall who else was at this dinner, but it was a jolly, frank, interesting supper.

In my personal point of view, the revelations did have an impact on Portuguese politics, and it was clear that the revelations were the first strands moving in front of an avalanche. I'd be very interested in seeing your work once it's completed, however many years it takes you.

Photo 12 Father Adrian Hastings, Leeds. Photo by Mustafah Dhada, © 1995.

Interviewee:
Father Adrian Hastings
Date (yyyy mm dd):
1996 03 nd
Duration (hh mm ss):
3h 0m 0s
Place:
Leeds
Language:
English
Interpreter:
None
Redactions:
Light

The Final Revelation and Vatican II

I am Adrian Hastings. This interview is long overdue, but I haven't been thinking about Wiriyamu much at all. There was a paper I gave about ten years ago that was more about Portugal, and it was published. It was sort of about Wiriyamu twelve years afterward, and I can give it to you. It was mostly my reflections on what I did in Portugal after Wiriyamu. It came out in a book of mine.

When I left Oxford I joined the White Fathers, and I started my training with them. After four years, I decided that I wanted to be a member of the African Church, a secular diocese priest. The White Fathers' general at the time was Bishop Louis-Marie-Joseph Durrieu, who was a really rigid person. Theo van Asten, a White Father, was aware of my uneasy relationship with the bishop. Theo van Asten and I didn't keep in touch much, and I certainly had nothing to do with their withdrawal from Mozambique, where Theo led the White Fathers. I maintained good relations with the White Fathers after I left them. In Rome, where I did a brief stint, they would sometimes invite me to the headquarters, much to the discomfort of the bishop, who clearly didn't want to have anything to do with me.

I then went to Uganda in the end of the 1950s, where we started the *African Ecclesiastical Review*, and it moved steadily into the 1960s. A Dutch missionary, Father Guedes, was the editor. This publication was meant to liberalize the Church, but in a very cautious and limited way. It was really a way for new ideas for changes under the Vatican Council to take place, which we knew were fast approaching. The African priests in my own diocese in Uganda were really conservative, understandably. They had been educated that way in the Catholic Churches of the 1920s and 1930s, and they thought that was exactly what they had to do, and they did it. They weren't in touch with anything affecting the Church because they read almost nothing. So in their eyes I was a fairly dangerous radical. They were very kind, but they were also alarmed by anything that I did. It was a strong, old, African clergy. Many were weak at reading any European language, but of course they read Latin. They didn't read any other languages, and I could only speak Latin or Luganda to my parish priest; they wouldn't speak one word of English. This was strange. It was only really in the second half of the 1960s that a program like mine, designed to be progressive, was used, but I don't think my own diocese took notice of that program very much.

By then I had moved to Tanzania. My job there after 1968 was to write commentaries on all documents of the Vatican Council, which we circulated to all the dioceses of East-Central Africa. I was doing that and going around giving seminars for two years. That was a very big exercise of reeducation of the clergy. We saw an enormous difference between groups of missionaries, bishops, and priests. A missionary here would start making all sorts of changes like establishing different relationships to Protestants; another sought big changes in attitudes toward Muslims. Others advocated a shift in politics and African culture. All of these areas were changing at the same time.

Some said, "Let's get rid of our European hymns and use African tunes and musical instruments, everything African."

The White Fathers pushed forward to Africanize the Church. They got busy translating everything into local vernaculars everywhere else and adapting to African rule.

Every side was moving. It was the sharpest contrast from the tradition-bound Church before the Vatican Council. However, each side moved differently based on the society and nationality. For example, the Dutch or the German missions were much more progressive than the Irish. There were societies like the Franciscans, who were entirely devolved and governed by national provinces. The Portuguese group of priests, however, was by and large insulated from Vatican II. Thus the Portuguese Franciscans may not have been affected by this wind of change.

The documents we dealt with in the Church, like the missionary decree of Vatican II, and missionary activity were very certainly not liberation theology in any sense. They weren't terribly radical, yet in developing things, it strongly stressed the building up of a local church that relates to the local culture. The values of Vatican II were democratic and pluralist. This meant different languages and cultures were accepted, along with the expectation you distanced yourself from the state and government. At last the Church was free to speak up.

Not so in Mozambique; the special system of a missionary agreement in place for the Portuguese colonies was utterly unacceptable and impossible for missionaries exposed to the Vatican II teachings. In a way, that is why Theo van Asten could say and do what he did, get out of Mozambique rather than continue with a tradition-bound church. We cannot function in the situation in the way the bishop of Nampula found all of them in; that was his argument. The more you focused on the Vatican II views of the Church, the more utterly impossible it was to go on with the old Portuguese missionary agreement model. With the colonial war in full swing, you had to take sides. You didn't need a complex Marxist theology or theology of liberation, especially if you read the early documents of Vatican II, to become radicalized. And the Burgos Fathers reflected this radicalization. They had previously been a conservative group. In Rhodesia, it was clear how progressive they were. In Mozambique, they were isolated and had very few African priests trained traditionally to slow down their progression to embrace the new evolving Church.

Those documents of the Vatican Council II had an enormous influence, in other words, and the change was terrific. I think the trouble with the Spanish priests was that they moved so fast from a sort of Francoist position to this sort of revolutionary fervor. It did unbalance them, and I felt that was a difficulty in a way. The Burgos Fathers were such delightful people individually, but they picked up every bit of the most extreme kind of Marxist interpretation and liberation theology of every sort. I think that for the Burgos Fathers, each being freed from prison in a different country and expelled— one from Colombia, one from Rhodesia, one from Mozambique—filled them with this enthusiasm of being revolutionaries. In a way it was very extraordinary.

A few years earlier, all of this would have been quite unthinkable, and they did come around. So in a sense I was a sort of good liberal who never altered very much to move to the progressive left. The Vatican II encouraged me, yes, but it was really the line I had always followed. The Dutch swung less violently because they were liberal before; van Asten was a liberal, so he was just being encouraged a little bit more. Even a few of the Portuguese were as well, but it wasn't all just that. Clearly the group of liberal Portuguese in Beira dioceses was following on this reverent kind of liberalism. Soares de Resende, the Bishop of Beira, was a case in point, but it was the old bishop of Porto, António Ferreira Gomes, who had the influence over Resende. It was very funny because he had been banished from Portugal by Salazar for ten years for being critical, but then he was allowed back. He had great status of being a powerful, politically acceptable bishop. In 1975, Mário Soares called this International Socialists' Conference to try to get backing for his party against the communists and the Movimento das Forças Armadas (MFA), the Armed Forces Movement. I went to attend the conference, and I was the only person from Britain who did so. The funniest thing was that they got the bishop of Porto to speak on Sunday morning. He spoke at an enormous length and in a really terrible old-fashioned way; he quoted Voltaire!

Caetano and the Wiriyamu Revelation

The fact is that when this Wiriyamu story came up in the beginning of 1973, I wasn't terribly well informed about the precise situation in Portuguese Africa. When I was in Zambia in 1969, I tried to get some information then, and the Mindolo Ecumenical Foundation where I was staying was in touch with another organization called COREMO [Comité Revolucionário de Moçambique]. Their leaders had made contact with us, and we went to one or two meetings with COREMO. COREMO was saying that Frelimo was cooperating with the Portuguese, and that COREMO was the only genuine resistance. I wasn't terribly impressed with the COREMO people. So I had that little bit of detailed information that I got in Zambia, but I wasn't greatly informed of the situation until the planning of the Caetano visit.

In 1972, I had just come back from Uganda, Tanzania, and Zambia and had become a member of the Education Committee of the CIIR, which was based in London and directed at that time by Mildred Neville. At that time, the CIIR was a small institute trying to help the Third World, in particular Africa, raise political issues, and so on. It was actually just getting more professional during this time, and it has now grown a great deal and is very influential. Wiriyamu was actually very important in the development of the CIIR after the story broke out.

In early 1973, it was announced that Marcelo Caetano, invited by the Heath government, was coming to London on an official visit to celebrate the sixth century of the Anglo-Portuguese alliance. I was already somewhat concerned with what was going on in Mozambique and Angola, although they weren't areas that I was directly familiar with, as I said. I was familiar with their neighbors, such as Malawi, to some extent. I was particularly concerned with the Portuguese territories from the point of view of Catholic Churches and their involvement in Portuguese government; and of course, I was concerned by the evidence of conflict between Catholic missionaries and the Portuguese, which manifestly showed with the withdrawal of the White Fathers from Mozambique. The final decision to withdraw had been taken by Theo van Asten, the superior general of the White Fathers, who was a close friend of mine. When I moved from Uganda to Tanzania in 1966, I went to the Kipalapala Seminary, and Theo van Asten was the director of Kipalapala. Very shortly afterward he was elected superior general of the White Fathers, but we had established a very good relationship. He was very liberal, radical in fact.

So for a lot of reasons the CIIR and I were very concerned with what was going on in Mozambique and Angola. So when the Caetano visit was announced, we felt that we must make some sort of countermove because there was obviously going to be an attempt to get British support for Portuguese policy in Africa and to convince people that the Portuguese had a very liberal, humane, and non-racial policy. So we decided to hold a meeting as close as possible to the date of the Caetano visit in London. It was going to be a public meeting. I can probably find you the exact dates when we decided these things since I have my diary from 1973 with me. We wanted to hold it in the House of Lords, but we couldn't get suitable room, so we decided to have it at the Chatham House. We booked the room at the Chatham House for July 11th, and Caetano was coming to London a couple of days later.

We decided we would invite Mário Soares to speak. We were very anxious, especially Mildred Neville, because she didn't want to give the impression that we were anti-Portuguese, but rather that we were backing the Portuguese opposition. Mário Soares was in exile in Paris at the time, so we invited him. Then we invited Lord Caradon, who had been a British ambassador to the United Nations and was now retired. Like the other members of his family, he was somewhat of a radical. We invited him to speak in terms of general politics and how Britain shouldn't be backing this kind of regime.

But neither of these people, we realized, knew much about Africa. And clearly from our point of view, we had to have someone who could actually speak on Africa. When we thought about it, we couldn't think of anyone except me. So, the Education Committee decided that I would be the third speaker. I was going to be speaking on Africa, but after we received acceptances from Lord Caradon and Mário Soares, they were clearly our top speakers. Now all that was arranged before we knew anything about Wiriyamu at all. That meeting was absolutely fixed, and it was going to have a general, well-informed critique of the Portuguese government and its African policies in particular. What we would endeavor was to get members of parliament, journalists, whoever, to come and listen to us in this highly respectable atmosphere. This left me with the need to learn more details about what was actually going on, particularly in Mozambique, where there was clearly the most trouble at that point in time.

Before the Chatham House meeting, I had to go to Rhodesia for several weeks to give lectures. I went on April 23rd, and I was there until May 13th. I was in Rhodesia giving lectures in three dioceses. The first week was in Bulawayo, and then the second week was in Wanki. I went to Wanki on April 30th, and I was in Wanki until May 6th. The Burgos Fathers ran the Wanki diocese, which was the crucial factor here. I was wanting to find out from them what I could about what was going on in Mozambique next door; and of course when I asked the Burgos Fathers, they said,

"Oh yes! We know all about that, and we have our own Burgos Fathers in Tete, and two of them are in prison in Machava for making protests about massacres in the Mucumbura area."

So at this point I felt I was onto something. However, they didn't actually have very detailed material. They could tell me that Padre Valverde was in prison, but I don't think I received very precise information about anything else. Their brothers in Spain did. I knew that after getting back to Britain, I had another engagement, which was to go to Spain about a month later to speak at a small conference in Salamanca. This engagement too was already arranged.

This conference was a Catholic-Anglican affair to be held in Salamanca from June 19th to June 22nd. So the trip to Rhodesia, the conference in Salamanca, and the meeting at Chatham House were completely unrelated and all arranged without prior knowledge of Wiriyamu. They had no relation at all, but they actually fitted amazingly together. When the Burgos Fathers in Wanki told me about their problems with their colleagues, they told me that there was documentation, but I had to get it from the Generalite, or the missionary headquarters, in Madrid.

I said, "Well, I am going to Salamanca in June, so I will stop in Madrid and visit them."

The Salamanca meeting was small, about a dozen people, Anglicans and Roman Catholics who met once a year, and Anglicans who were based in Europe on the continent. They had invited me to give a talk. So, on June 18th, I reached London, and then my sister, Susan, drove me to the airport for Spain after breakfast. I got to Madrid at about one in the afternoon. I found my way to the house of the Burgos Fathers. They welcomed me, and I had a second lunch with them. They spoke of their fathers in Mozambique, particularly those now in prison. I then went to the station, getting there around four-fifteen in the afternoon to head to Salamanca.

I arranged to call again on my way back from Salamanca. So four days later, I met them again, and we went to lunch and were joined by two other young priests with firsthand experience of Mozambique, one of whom was Padre Júlio Moure.[3] I learned a great deal on Mozambique from these two. They had very clear answers to my questions. On June 22nd, they said,

"Yes, we've got a lot of documentation, and we'll send it to you. We can't just hand it over. We will put together a large parcel and send it to you."

So by the 22nd, I still hadn't received the documentation as promised.

It was now getting pretty close to the July 11th meeting. Then, sometime around the end of June, I received a huge parcel from Madrid. The documents were all in Spanish, and I didn't really read Spanish, but I could more or less see what was going on. When I looked at them, some were fairly general accounts of the deteriorating situation or the problems of the Church. Then there was full documentation of Mucumbura, which was good but to some extent had been published already. Then there was the Wiriyamu document. This document did not include the Chaworha report. When I looked at all these papers, I realized that this Wiriyamu document was very precise, and that it happened about six months prior and hadn't been published yet, as far as I knew.

I was quite horrified by these accounts. Around July 4th I began preparing a draft summary of my speech and decided to refer to them.

"We must publicize them as well as we possibly can," I said to myself.

I was still pretty vague at that point how I would do this. What I did was I gave that document to a friend at Selly Oak College [Birmingham] to translate in full into English for me. By the time I got it back, it was July 6th. So that was a crucial day as far as I'm concerned. Two or three days had passed since I had given the paper to translate. I had

---

[3] The other priest was Miguel Buendia.

then realized that I did not have the rights to publish it should I want to. I sent a telegram to Madrid asking for full publication rights.

After I got the authorization to publish, I phoned Tim Sheehy at the CIIR to tell him what I was going to do. He advised me to get on to Louis Heren, who was the deputy editor at *The London Times*. I think we decided that it was better to give it to *The London Times* and not to *The Guardian*, because *The Guardian* was pretty anti-Portuguese, so we knew they would take it, and it would be just the typical *Guardian* story. If *The London Times* took it, it was going to have more authority. I think we were lucky that Rees-Mogg was away at the time and Louis Heren was acting editor. It was up to Heren to decide whether to publish or not.

By then, I had already decided to focus my speech on Wiriyamu, no matter what happened to it with *The London Times*. I sent the summary to the CIIR. The CIIR didn't like it a bit. On July 7th I had a long telephone call with Mildred in the morning. They felt I must try to avoid such words as oppression, fascist, etc.

"We are to have a very distinguished gathering," she said.

Two days later, I received a telephone call from Louis Heren to say that *The London Times* wanted to print my article on the Wiriyamu massacre. I wanted them to wait until Thursday. Heren said he would call back—and he did.

"Can we publish it tomorrow [July 10th], as a printing strike could start any time now?" "It would be on the center page and must prove a great bombshell."

So, really, this was not planned! I had only sent the article on the evening of July 7th, and on the morning of July 9th, Heren accepted it, and they published it on the 10th.

Political Neutrality and the Press

The London Times is usually reluctant to come out and be very challenging. Obviously they came under great attack after the Wiriyamu article was published. It may be that Rees-Mogg would have been more prudent, but maybe not. Maybe he would have seen that it was worth doing. Rees-Mogg and Louis Heren were actually both Catholics. Louis Heren was a very different kind of person. I liked him very much; he [has] passed away now. He died a year or two ago. He was a very working-class, London background, but a very tough journalist. He was a very nice, good man. It was funny afterward that the Portuguese government attacked *The London Times* and said it was all a liberal "Oxford plot" because Rees-Mogg and I had been together at Oxford. That's true. We had been together at Oxford. We were both studying history at the same time, but we never met until long after Wiriyamu. They sort of linked these facts up to suggest collusion!

Anyway, *The London Times*' front-page story with an editorial appeared on July the 10th. Caetano was coming two or three days later. They published the whole document in full, so really there was no article of mine. It was simply the full text of the document with my name on it. This caused an absolute storm. I knew it would cause something, but I didn't realize that the media, TV, and all other newspapers were going to focus on this. In fact, on that very Tuesday morning, the phone rang. It was the BBC wanting me for an interview for the *News At One* program. This meant that the meeting at Chatham House on Wednesday the 11th was transformed. It became the Wiriyamu meeting. Everybody came, not because it was a nice, general discussion, but because I was going to defend my accusations against the Portuguese at a grueling press conference [at] three in the afternoon, almost wholly directed at me. Lord Caradon sat on one side of Mildred and me on the other. Some people, particularly a BBC man and a *Daily Telegraph* man, were very hostile and persistent. Although I was being scrutinized, I did not budge one inch. Lord Caradon said a few nice words at the end, followed by a brief German television interview, followed by another conference.

The CIIR people were alarmed at first that it was not what they truly wanted. It was all too violent, but once they saw the immense impact that it had, they were happy. In fact, the Burgos Fathers too were unhappy. They had wanted to publish it and nothing more, and I found out later that the story was published two months earlier in a missionary or church magazine, and nobody ever noticed it. The whole story just totally changed the Caetano visit, who was coming two days later, and because the full document appeared in *The London Times*, people just jumped on it, despite the lack of human planning and organization involved. If it were planned, it would have all been different. I wouldn't have been able to do it if the CIIR had not put me in charge of the African perspective, if I hadn't been to Rhodesia, and if I hadn't been to Salamanca. These were quite different things, but they just led on perfectly.

It became absolutely world-shattering news! Harold demanded a special debate in the House of Commons, and I had to go to the UN within ten days to speak there. *The Daily Mail*, *The Daily Telegraph*, and *The Express* were all very bitterly opposed. My problem was that I couldn't actually tell them where the village was, and the Portuguese denied it existed. And that fact that I could not prove it troubled two journalists associated with the CIIR: Hugo Young, who was a leading journalist and now a *Guardian* columnist, a deputy editor of *The London Sunday Times*, and also a member of the Education Committee of the CIIR; and Hugh O'Shaughnessy, who was an avid journalist for *The Financial Times* and also on the CIIR Education Committee. Also there was a great debate at *The London Sunday Times* on which side they were going to come out on, but Hugo managed to swing the discussion to back me. What was crucial was that I could not answer some of their questions.

The London Sunday Times paid for me to go to Madrid to get more information from the Burgos Fathers. The result was that the very next day, the 12th, I flew to Madrid, and I stayed a night there. In Madrid, the superior general of the Burgos Fathers, Padre Artazcoz, and a Burgos Father, Padre Miguel Antoni, who had just gotten back from Rhodesia and Mozambique four months ago and knew Wiriyamu personally, met me. So Padre Antoni was crucial. However, he hadn't been expelled, so we had to be careful how we used him. In that evening, I believed I had gotten all I needed. Padre Anoveros, a senior Burgos priest and editor of their missionary newsletters, came in during the afternoon, and I had supper with him alone when the rest had gone.

Some irritating business transpired, adding to the problems we had. When I was in Madrid on that Thursday, I went to see the Burgos Fathers and encountered some

BBC people there. Everyone in attendance was in enormous excitement because of the happenings in London, and most had arrived the day before I got there. The members of the BBC and other journalists had been trying to get information out of anybody there. Unfortunately, some of the young fathers there said they had a film about Mozambique, which others said was about massacres or whatever. Anyway, when I got there, we actually removed the BBC people from the house and said they could come back later. We did this because when they learned of this film, they wanted to take it away. I said to the superior general, "We must see what is actually on this film, first of all," before any decision could be made.

When we looked at it, we saw that there was really nothing to it. We saw some burning villages, but none of the Burgos Fathers claimed it was Wiriyamu. It was just some villages being burned by the Portuguese army authorities. But there was no massacre on it at all. It was good as background, but it wasn't anything more than that. Despite this, a BBC member wanted to take the film away, but I advised the superior general not to let him do it. Then I said that I would take it to England, and I would explain that no one suggested it was evidence of the massacre, but that it could be used as background. The BBC man was very annoyed about this.

I flew back on Friday morning into Heathrow, and my flight was delayed due to rain and a thunderstorm around Madrid airport. I arrived in London at about one in the afternoon and was met by various photographers and journalists. So when I arrived back in London, I was met by, among others, another BBC man who wanted to get hold of this film. I was expecting a car to be sent from *The London Sunday Times* to pick me up, but apparently it wasn't there. So the BBC man offered to take me back into London, and I went with him. I allowed the BBC man to take the film and look at it without permission to use it. I carefully explained to him that the film was made in August of 1969, and therefore contained nothing whatsoever about Wiriyamu.

But other journalists had also been at Heathrow when I got off the plane, and they all heard already that I was bringing a film back, which gave evidence of the massacre. So then the BBC stated that they had rejected the film because it didn't show anything to do with the massacre. And *The Daily Telegraph* published something to this effect: "Hastings' film is rejected because it doesn't prove anything of massacre." So of course, I had to write a letter to *The London Times* demanding that the BBC should state that I had never told them that it contained anything to do with the massacre, but on the contrary, I had turned it over to them, and that they didn't have permission to publish.

The BBC did do so, but of course it took days. By the time they published their correction, one of the things going around was that my film had been disproved. I believe it was in due course that we got the film back. In fact, I remember later that the Dutch television asked if they could show it. They said they knew it wasn't anything to do with the massacre but wanted to show something on background. I don't know what they did with the film after. I suppose it went back to the Burgos Fathers. It wasn't a very good film; it was just on some small camera that some Burgos Father had filmed.

The London Times called me about one or two in the morning because they had just seen the earlier editions of *The Daily Telegraph* that had just come out.

They told me: "For goodness sake, tell us quickly, so that we can get into our edition and reply."

For about two weeks *The London Times* took a really partisan take on it, which was unusual for *The London Times*, and then they pulled back and refused to take any more comments. They said they didn't want to take up sides. They didn't like it at all that some conservative MPs or others had raised concerns at the press council that their journalism had been irresponsible in regard to this.

I spent many hours the same day I flew into London, on Friday, at *The London Sunday Times* with their Insight Team giving them all the information I had received. Days later, the *Daily Express* attempted to trick me by telling me that they would be willing to pay for me to go to Mozambique with a journalist to identify the village. I thought to myself, Was I prepared to go or not? Of course if I said no they would have published something like this:

"Father Hastings is unable, is not willing to identify the village."

But of course if I had just said, "Yes, I can go," I would have gone and been completely lost. So instead I told them I would go if Padre Antoni accompanied me and the Portuguese officials guaranteed us safe passage. The *Daily Express* just never rang for me again. Of course, the *Daily Express* knew the Portuguese were in Wiriyamu! What they were attempting to do was to discredit my document. They hoped that I would appear a fool for not being able to find the location of the massacre. It was also very valuable and important that Antoni was able to say: "I know the village. I know where it is."

Saturday then rolled around, and this was when the bulk of the interviews took place, and I saw no end in sight. I interviewed first with the Italian *Famiglia Cristiana*, and then I had an interview with the Independent Television Service (ITV). I then headed back to *The London Sunday Times* and worked at correcting and advising the Insight Team for an article all that afternoon. Of course, Peter Pringle was on the Insight Team, and he was the first person to see António. They finished the article two hours late. On Sunday, I read the papers, particularly *The Sunday Telegraph*'s massive attempt to exploit the whole thing. Then I got down to *The London Times* to reply to the critics. I met Louis Heren the first time that day and had a chat with him.

To the UN and Back

The next morning, Monday the 16th, Ivan Smith, the director of the UN office in Britain, contacted me and asked if I would go to New York later that week to testify before the Committee of Twenty-Four. I said yes. A week then passed by, during which I continued to receive hostile calls. One man from the *Daily Express* insisted quite savagely that I go to Mozambique on a *Daily Express* expedition. They had been very hostile, yet I agreed to go under three conditions: One of the Spanish Fathers was to go with me, more specifically Padre Antoni; we were to be sponsored by some other papers as well; and we would have certain guarantees about our work there. He promised to phone back, but I had my doubts from the beginning, and even if he had phoned back, I ignored it because I figured there was absolutely no way that the Portuguese would let me into Mozambique.

In the meantime, I began preparing for my trip to the United Nations. I returned to London on the 18th, and at Euston I met Ivan Smith, who took my passport to obtain a US visa and gave me various instructions. He was the head of the UN office in London. After that was done, I had a long interview with a French television reporter. I knew that there was still so many letters from *The London Times* that needed to be addressed. Then I had yet another interview, this time with an American TV reporter. After that, I went to the House of Commons and spoke to the liberals there before returning back to my hotel.

On the 19th I left for America. Everything was behind schedule by two and a half hours, but I made it to the John F. Kennedy Airport, where I met a young French man who led me to supper at a Japanese restaurant on 49th Street. On the 20th, I was preparing to speak with the Committee of Twenty-Four. While I was wrapping up my preparations and finishing my breakfast at nine, I was interviewed again. Peter Daly came in, along with a photographer for the *National Catholic Reporter*. Daly and I walked into the UN building together up to Akihiko Tanaka's office. I decided during the night that I should not share a platform during the press conference with Frelimo's Marcelino dos Santos. It would give new ammunition to *The Daily Telegraph*. I realized if I had dos Santos beside me and we were photographed, then they would say that we were afraid of going after them. So I always had to maintain my complete independence.

At ten-thirty in the morning we headed down the hall to the Committee of Twenty-Four. We began around eleven and ended at two-fifteen in the afternoon. I spoke for about forty minutes, and my speech was very well received. The people at the UN told me afterward that they were very surprised that *The London Times* had made such a strong statement by accepting the story. I was followed by dos Santos, who also spoke at some length and gave an extremely warm thanks to me. He then came around to embrace me, and there was some clapping. Following, we had statements from the ambassadors of Sweden, Australia, Tanzania, Yugoslavia, Iraq, the USSR, India, China, Chile, Indonesia, and the Congo. They all had nice things to say about me, except China. The statements became rather tedious after a while. Lunch was at two-thirty. At three-thirty there was a press conference that was followed by a TV interview by an educational network. I left for London the next day on July 21st. Eight days later, Peter Pringle was expelled from Tete after three days of being there. They had confiscated his papers and tapes, and they were frightened that the material he had would compromise all sorts of people.

He published his piece nevertheless. His article appeared late in the evening while the editors of British papers debated the merit of the case. The principal players were the *Daily Mail* and *The Daily Telegraph* against the *Daily Express*. On our side were *The London Times*, *The Observer*, *The London Sunday Times*, and *The Guardian*. But *The Guardian* was always general on us. That's how they always were. *The Daily Telegraph* declared the Burgos Fathers to be, in fact, a highly tainted source, and denied any massacre existed. On July 31st, I wrote a long article responding to the denials by *The Daily Telegraph*, citing the evidence I had for Wiriyamu, and sent it to *The London Times*.

A few days later on August 2nd, the article containing all the evidence was published. A few weeks had passed, and other things continued to occur.

One was the Portuguese defense, which was weakened by contradictions, I thought. They were obviously very worked up. The people in Lisbon later told me that they felt this was the point in which everything started to unravel; they felt that the world had been convinced that our story was true. Their Armed Forces Movement had received and used the material about Wiriyamu, which added to the conflict with the Church. Eventually, Bishop Vieira, the bishop of Nampula, was expelled, which was undermining in every way that the regime was in popular demand.

The other was the poor boy, António, who we hoped had not already been tortured or killed in the prisons of the secret police. We knew that we must do everything that we could. Peter Pringle wrote to Bernardus Johannes Alfrink, the cardinal of Holland, and the letter made a big appeal. Peter also went to the UN; they were all trying. Padre Mateus Carbonell was in England at that time, and on August 9th, I knew that I should go and see him and get his evidence. I had paid too little attention to his evidence when we previously met, having had too many other things on my mind. So I drove down to Chilworth near Guildford, to the address I had of where Padre Carbonell was located. We spoke at great length about the case and António, and we had supper together.

The next day, August 10th, Carbonell held discussions with Eva Blumenau, Sean MacBride, and Martin Ennals, all at Amnesty International, regarding António Mixone and what could be done for witnesses like him. Mrs. Blumenau devised a plan to get António Mixone into Zambia, where she had a home for him. *The London Times* offered to pay, and McBride went to see the Pope the following week.

The next day, I put together the text of what I hoped would be my last article on Mozambique, a more general discussion of the issues, which included some very good material from Padre Carbonell. I began typing that evening, and on August 12th, I finished and began revising the article in order to encompass a wider context in the significance of Wiriyamu. The revised article was sent out to Louis Heren that afternoon.

On the 14th, Heren said over the phone that *The London Times* no longer wanted the article and that someone was threatening to take them to a press council for publishing the original report; why they allowed themselves to be somehow intimidated by that, I can't imagine. He sent it across to *The Observer*, and they considered it. The editor's secretary said he was going to get a second opinion on it. Then, August 16th, I was in Cambridge. *The Observer* rang up in the morning to say they would take my article, but that they couldn't find room for it in that Sunday's edition due to a very long report on torture in Greece, but they published it on Sunday the 26th. It may have, in fact, worked out for the better because it was nearly the end of the holidays. There was no particular hurry; on the contrary, it was more valuable to keep interest [in the story] going, especially if the trial of Valverde and Hernandez took place as scheduled. After that I took a holiday in Bellagio, Italy. On the way back from Bellagio, I went to Dortmund, Germany, and we had demonstrations and a peace march. I was in Dortmund for several days. The peace march occurred on September 15th, and I spoke on Sunday 16th.

A bit later I was putting the book together on Wiriyamu, and I had to do it very quickly. It took a total of about two weeks for the book to come together, which contained mostly documents. The first publisher who looked at the book turned it down. I got to thinking about why it was turned down, and I came up with the idea that the Anglican publisher had gotten cold feet about the work. Almost immediately after it was turned down, a different publisher accepted the work but stated that it had to be finished within two weeks. So I worked hard, very effectively, and completed the book on the 25th of October and turned it in. It was to be published within two months by the Society for Promoting Christian Knowledge (SPCK). To my amazement, SPCK turned down the book five days later. Their reason for denying the book was because they did not think they could sell it. I called another, smaller publisher who had already told me they wanted it, but they gave me a deadline by Thursday so they could have the book out by the following week. The day following the rejection from SPCK, October 31st, I returned to London to do the final revising. The first book was published in November, and eight or nine editions followed. There were many versions of the book, including English, Dutch, Swedish, German, and Polish, and a Portuguese version emerged later. I attended the launching of the German book, which occurred during the springtime in Germany. The French edition was cancelled because the French did not see a point in publishing the book. After that, Search Press took over and published it. It didn't entirely bring activism. I went back to Germany for its launch, and it coincided with the Portuguese coup of April 1974.

In the meantime, the Wiriyamu story continued, and the pace of events accelerated. Fourteen days before the coup, I drove over to Totteridge to see Padre Sangalo, who had arrived in London to give evidence to *The London Times*. I talked to Sangalo and also to Miguel Buendia. I met with Valverde in London also, the following week. They gave me some useful documents, especially the statement of February 12th signed by the bishop of Nampula and numerous priests and sisters. They also gave me a copy of the important statement sent to the Pope by the bishop of Nampula that past August. Before I could do anything with this, *The Observer* printed news of the expulsion of seven Verona Fathers. It was Easter Sunday. I decided that we had to publish more information about this. There were a lot of phone calls to make. I took a document to Louis Heren, and on April 14th, he passed a copy across to the *Catholic Herald*.

Back in Mozambique, the bishop of Nampula himself had been expelled from Mozambique. That was on April 16th. On April 17th, Collin Legum of *The Observer* called me that afternoon, wanting me to do an article for them that Sunday on the ecclesiastical background on Bishop Vieira of Nampula's expulsion. It was due Friday morning, so it was going to be a busy two days. The next day, April 18th, I left for Padre Alfonso Valverde's press conference at two-thirty, held at Amnesty International, London. He had just been released from prison and expelled. He was excellent, impressive, and very sweet when we met. He was extremely precise in his account of Machava prison and his experiences there. I realized that he actually shared a prison cell for a time with Padres Sampaio and Mendes, the two Portuguese priests from Macúti, Beira. Afterward,

I met Polly Gaster and also Janet Mondlane for the first time.[4] Buendia and company were planning a meeting of Mozambique's missionary exiles in Holland for the following week to put pressure on the Vatican. They wanted me to go to the meeting, but I decided that I should not appear to influence them but instead retain my own independence of action.

On Friday 19th, Colin Legum came in around nine-fifteen in the morning to pick up the article, and he drove me on his way into town. They seemed very pleased with the article and only wanted a few small changes. That was a big, important article for *The Observer* on Sunday the 21st. It was about the expulsion of the bishop of Nampula and the conflict with the Church. It was on the whole ecclesiastical, but it was in fact amazing that we got the article done in two days. So that was the 21st of April; then I was working on something else in Mozambique on the 22nd.

Immediately before the coup, on April 23rd, 1974, the morning's *Guardian* was full of Mozambique information, the full text of an officer's report from Lisbon, the precise confirmation of Wiriyamu, and much more. On April 25th, my department head came to my office at mid-morning to tell me there was a revolution in Portugal going on and Mildred wanted to speak to me about it. That of course was called Portugal's Revolution of Carnations!

Wiriyamu and the Portuguese Revolution

I then paid two visits to Lisbon, and I think on the first visit that I went out to see what was going on in the confusion. I wanted to see someone from the military, but I received no response from them. Then, a journalist from one of the papers came to see me and said they wanted me to give a full account because there had never been a full account of Wiriyamu in the Portuguese press. And we did; they gave full two pages, and I still have a copy of it. Immediately after my meeting with the journalist, I got a message from the Committee of the Armed Forces Movement, the MFA, saying that it was arranged for me to see someone or other that day at the barracks. So I went, and there were two members of the Armed Forces Committee, and they were extremely upset about the publication of the article on Wiriyamu.

They said the Armed Forces did not want to hear any more about Wiriyamu "as we are in a revolution. We are very grateful to you, of course, for all that you did. You helped bring about the revolution, but far too many soldiers were involved in these things."

They had put pressure on the UN and Frelimo to stop the inquisitions about the massacres.

---

[4]Polly Gaster was then working at the Mozambique, Angola, Guinea-Bissau Information Center in London, and the American-born Janet Mondlane was heading the Mozambique Institute in Tanzania. Janet was Dr. Eduardo Mondlane's widow.

"We don't want anything of the kind now, and we have no intention of setting up a military dictatorship."

So they didn't want to talk to me about anything else; they just wanted me to say that I would shut up. And this was very revealing.

Then they instructed a young officer to drive me back to my hotel. This young officer proved to have a different viewpoint, and he asked if he could take me to dinner at some restaurant. As the young officer drank more and more, he then told me that his commanders had told him not to say anything to me at all. Also in the restaurant with us was the wife of General Kaúlza de Arriaga, who had been in prison since September of 1973. The young lieutenant went over to speak with her, but he took care to not reveal who I was. From the conversation, it became apparent that some people, including the general's wife, were upset that General Arriaga and other men like him were imprisoned without due process. I put some of what the young officer said in the new published paper. It was written nearly ten years ago, but it just failed to get published. So, when I published a collection of papers last year, I put this one in. This was just at the point at which Mário Soares got elected.

I had not imagined that everyone in Portugal was aware of my name, or that I had become something of a folk hero. Person after person came up to me and said how much I contributed to the fall of Caetano, among other things. I think those at the Commission of Coordination were rather frightened at my presence there. After the restaurant I arrived home at midnight and went to bed at two in the morning.

It was clear to me that the people in the army had been involved in many massacres of one sort or another, whether small or great, and that many people were implicated in such a manner that they couldn't take any unnecessary risks. Although they had initially put a lot of the PIDE [Polícia Internacional e de Defesa do Estado] people in prison, they couldn't even bring them to trial because the PIDE would have claimed that they did one thing, while the army did another. They couldn't make a separation, so no one was ever tried for anything.

And that is how Wiriyamu was revealed, and the stories behind it!

6

THE BRITISH FACT-CHECKERS

The sixth group in this volume showcases the work of journalists who fact-checked the story to fight Portuguese allegations, of whom two failed and one, Peter Pringle, succeeded. Here then are their stories. Knipe's text begins with his near "illegal entry" into Tete. He is expelled once the colonial secret police discover he is getting too close to the truth.

Christopher Wain, made famous for saving the life of a girl fleeing a napalm bomb with her back on fire during the Vietnam War, too, fails to fact-check the revealed narrative. His text testifies to Knipe's failure in ferreting out the facts behind the story before recounting his visit to Williamo, an abandoned village, which the Portuguese staged to waylay journalists on a trail for hard-core evidence.

Peter Pringle comes last in this group of evidence-seeking journalists. Pringle's erudite text covers six aspects of his journey to Tete and back. After a brief introduction on the formative period of his life, his narrative unveils the kind of in-depth journalism he did as part of an investigative team at The London Sunday Times, *which brought him to Tete, after taking precautions to evade the colonial secret police to get to the story. The second half of his record tackles measures he took to get the story out, the attempted blackmail instigated by South African secret police operatives in the colonial capital, and the impact that Wiriyamu had on his professional life in London and later in New York.*

Photo 13 Michael Knipe, London. Photo by Mustafah Dhada, © 1995.

Interviewee:
Michael Knipe
Date (yyyy mm dd):
1996 03 nd
Duration (hh mm ss):
1h 30m 59s
Place:
London
Language:
English
Interpreter:
None
Redactions:
None

Knipe Combats Fake News

My name is Michael Knipe. I come from Portsmouth, Hampshire, southwest of England. My father was a builder and decorator. I went to grammar school. I left school at the age of 16. After wanting to be a pilot or a priest, the usual, I wanted to be a newspaper reporter from the age of 11. I joined my local newspaper, *The Portsmouth Evening News.* I then did three years of my probation period there as a cover reporter. Then I had a year working for Southern Television on the sports program. But my ultimate goal was to get to Fleet Street. So I left Southern Television after a year and started freelancing in London, working for various newspapers. I eventually got myself a job at a paper called *The People*, which was a campaigning newspaper, popular at the time. It had an audience of about four to five million people, so it was very successful. I spent five or six years doing that, which was very enjoyable.

I was now 27, and I realized that this wasn't the sort of journalism that I really set out to do. I always wanted to be a foreign correspondent, and the area that interested me the most was Africa. The reason Africa interested me, I think, was because I'm a jazz enthusiast. I play the drums in traditional jazz bands, and for a long time there was the question, "Do I become a drummer in a jazz band or a journalist?" I found that the average drummer doesn't make much money, so I chose journalism as a career, and I played in jazz bands on the side. With my interest in music, black music, it led me to do this sort of terrific thing. I wanted to know where it came from, who were the people, and that led me [to] Africa. I wanted to know how to become an African correspondent. After five years on *The People* and realizing this was a dead end and wasn't where I wanted to go, I wrote to the foreign editors at *The London Times* and *The Daily Telegraph* and said,

"I want to be an African correspondent; how do I go about it?"

To my great delight, *The London Times* was courteous enough to invite me for interviews, and then they said, "You can either join the home side staff, and if you are very lucky get an opportunity to go abroad, or you can go and freelance in this country, and you may eventually get a job; either way they are both long shots."

I decided to take the first option and joined *The London Times*. They were in fact looking for an investigative journalist, which was the sort of thing that I had been doing on *The People*, exposing crime and corruption and vice rings, etc. I applied for that job based on my private agenda to get to Africa, and I joined a team of reporters called the news team. Teddy Hodgkin, the foreign editor at the time, interviewed me, and I was hired at the beginning of the year in 1967. *The London Times* had just been taken over by Lord Thomson. Rees-Mogg had just been appointed editor, and he wanted *The London Times* to have a team of reporters like the Insight Team on *The London Sunday Times*; that is where Peter Pringle was.

We had just had the Aberfan disaster, the coal miners' disaster in the Merthyr Tydfil village in Wales that had killed 28 adults and 116 children. The *Daily Express* had sent twenty reporters, and everyone else had sent a lot of reporters. *The London Times*, true to tradition, had sent one man to cover it. Rees-Mogg said, "This isn't the way you cover this sort of dramatic story; we need a team of reporters who would work as a cohesive whole and work together."

So he set out to create this team, and he wanted an investigative reporter because they wanted a team that would do day-to-day disasters, such as mad cow's disease or airplane crashes or whatever, and also, when it was quiet, to do investigative matters. So that was my value to this team, and I joined on that basis.

Experiencing Africa

At first, we were doing the big crashes and the big stories of this nature. Then one day Rees-Mogg asked, "What ideas have you got?"

And I said we should look at the liberation wars going on in Africa, which were virtually unreported in British press at this time. He said that this was an interesting subject, but how could we broaden it, how could we fit it into our other priorities? There was also a lot of concern at this time about "Black Power" and a lot of talk of revolution in Britain. This was 1967, so coming up on the student protests, etc. So together with my colleagues on the news team, we decided to look at the black man in search of power and look at Black Power in its manifestations in Britain, America, and Africa. So one of my colleagues went to America; two or three of them concentrated on the rebellious element in Britain, and I was the colleague who went to Africa.

Bill Norris was not on the news team then, but he was *The London Times* Africa correspondent. We decided we needed to look at both sides of the situation. There was very little coverage of the liberation wars. So per my suggestion, we decided I would first go to Addis Ababa and talk to the United Nations' people there. Then I would go to Tanzania, Zambia, and the Congo. This was indeed what I did. While I did this, Bill Norris went to white Africa: Mozambique, Angola, and South Africa, looking at their perceptions of what was going on. We were hoping to find out and report what was going on the ground because it wasn't getting attention. I had an interview with the chairman of the liberation committee of the Organization of African Unity (OAU), in Addis. I then went on to Dar es Salaam, Tanzania, which was my next stop, where I had three goals: One was to interview Frelimo; another was to look at what support there was [at the grassroot level]; and then to look at where the [external] support was coming from, whether it was Chinese support or Russian support.

This was my first time in Africa—my great goal for all these years. The first day, I went to the Frelimo headquarters; I had a very useful talk with Jorge Rebelo, their press secretary at the time, who filled me in. He gave me a lot of details. Later, he set me up with an interview with Eduardo Mondlane. I was interested in the Chinese activity there, so I got a cab and went out to the Chinese textile mill. I took pictures of the building and that sort of thing. Then I went back into town and had more interviews. A few hours later, a police car came up alongside me and picked me up, and I was arrested. I was taken down to the police station where a huge black police officer said to me, "You've been behaving kind of funny, jumping around taking pictures."

I said that I was just taking pictures. I also had previously put in an application for an interview with President Nyerere, and that had been agreed, and I already had the date set for it.

Well, the police took a statement from me and demanded to see my passport. So they took me back to my hotel, collected my passport, and went back to the police station. Then they said to take off my socks, shoes, tie, and belt, and then they threw me into the prison cell there. This was very nerve wracking as this was my very first time in Africa.

Anyway, after a couple of days, I got more and more desperate. They finally let me out. Once I was out, I carried on and had my interview with Nyerere a week or so later. Then I interviewed Mondlane. My meeting with Eduardo was at his home and was very casual. There was virtually no security. His children were playing there. He was charming, relaxed, and a big, good-looking man. In fact, I tape-recorded this interview, and I'll try to find it. I also met a Scandinavian journalist who I think was Swedish. He was doing much the same as I was, and he travelled into the bush and wrote a series of articles about being with Frelimo in the bush. I'll try to remember or find his name.

I went back to South Africa a week or so before the 5th of May, and a week or two after I got there, I went to Malawi. I can't really recall, but I spent time first in Zambia, then in Malawi. While I was in Malawi, this was the period when Caetano, the Portuguese president, was going to Britain on a state visit. It being a state visit, it had that much more resonance to it. Father Adrian Hastings approached *The London Times* with an account of a massacre in Wiriyamu. *The London Times'* foreign editor, Louis Heren, took one look at this and thought this was one hell of a story. Without much more regard than that, he published it. I think he published it literally on the eve of the state visit without any reference to me. I mean, I had been in Mozambique, and I didn't know anything about this. It was suddenly in the paper; the first I heard of this was on BBC *World News* that *The London Times* has reported a massacre. I was either in Malawi or on my way there. I thought it was a tremendous story and wondered why I didn't know about it when I was in Mozambique; I wondered why they didn't send me to Mozambique to find out about this story, and who Adrian Hastings was, and [what was] the strength of this story.

Anyway, I had been in Malawi for a day I think, and I got a message from *The London Times*: "Go as fast as you can to Mozambique."

I was just thinking, "Bloody idiots, what were they doing?"

I mean, I work there, and if they had sent me in before they published, I could have gotten in; to think that I'm going to get into Mozambique now when this is up in the air. I mean, because it was a huge story. There were questions asked by the UN; Caetano was on the verge of cancelling his state visit to London. It caused huge waves diplomatically.

In the midst of this, *The London Times* was telling me to go to Mozambique and find out more about this massacre. I went to the Portuguese consulate in Malawi, Blantyre, and asked if I could have a visa to go to Mozambique. I couldn't get it the first day, so I went back the next day, and it was like this for a few times. I thought to myself I wasn't going to get anywhere like this. So, I looked again at that visa entry for Mozambique that I had gotten before going to Malawi, and it had expired on the 5th of May 1973. And I thought, that five could very easily become an eight; so, I changed five into an eight. I didn't bother going back to the embassy after that. I just bought myself a ticket to go to Lourenço Marques, Mozambique.

I departed the next morning at about lunchtime. I was very anxious and nervous, as I had already been to jail in Africa once before and didn't want to go again. When I got on that plane, I thought I should take some precautions. So, I found another Englishman and got talking to him. He happened to be a doctor, an anesthetist. He was going to see his brother who was in South Africa. I was feeling confident about him after talking for a while, and I told him that it was possible that I wouldn't pass through immigration. I then told him to please explain to *The London Times* about this incident if anything happened to me.

Into the Bush and Back

Thankfully, with this visa I passed straight through immigration without any problem, and we went to a hotel. My desire was to get to Beira and of course to Wiriyamu. By the time I got to Beira, the newspapers were full of stories that said: "The *Times*' man arrives in Mozambique."

I was a celebrity. Somehow, they got to know this story, so there I was seen in the local paper, a picture of me; it was in Portuguese, and I can't read Portuguese, but someone gave me the gist of it. We headed for Tete. On the plane we were talking about Wiriyamu. He was fascinated about this story. He asked me if he could tag along. By the way, his name is Jonathan Ward, and we became very good friends. He is still alive and living up in Newcastle, and in fact we exchanged Christmas cards recently. I was able to see him about two or three years ago. He will fill in a few details because for him it was even more dramatic than for me.

When we got to Tete we booked into the hotel. Things then got interesting. The hotel staff informed me that they were told that my visa application, which I had put in when in Malawi, had been sent to Lisbon, which had looked into it and had turned it down. Lisbon then issued a statement to *The London Times* basically saying *The London Times* correspondent wasn't allowed to enter Mozambique. So *The London Times* took the story and put in the paper: "*Times* man barred from Mozambique." So it appeared I was on my way into Mozambique but not in Mozambique.

The first thing the hotel did was to take our passports, normal procedure. The next morning I went down and asked for mine, and they said there was a small administrative matter, and it would be there later that day. I thought to myself, Someone is looking into that passport. I better work fast on my Wiriyamu story. All I knew was that *The London Times* had published a story about a massacre. I had to try to find out whatever I could about it. I discovered that before I could get anything done, I had to see Colonel Videira, the military governor. In that same evening, I got in a car and went to see Colonel Videira at his house. I said:

"I'm from *The London Times*, and as you I'm sure appreciate, we have published a story saying that there has been this massacre. And you are busy saying there hasn't been a massacre. I'm here to find out the truth. I would very much like any assistance you can give me."

I suspect I had a translator, or he probably spoke enough English; either way it was dusk.

Colonel Videira said, "There's been no massacre; I can assure you that."

I said, "Well you'd appreciate that I need to see; I need to find out."

He said, If you want you can go see for yourself. He said he'd provide me with a soldier, and they'd take me there. So I said fine. He said to be ready the next morning for a long walk, and that it's very dangerous because of the mines. Jonathan Ward was at the hotel at this stage. There was another correspondent there. I think it was an Independent Television Network (ITN) correspondent, Chris Wain. Wain realized I was there for this story. [He said he] wanted to come along. So at about five in the morning, Wain and myself were met by the military. A young white soldier at the wheel of a lorry took us to where they said was close to Wiriyamu.[1] We then had a ten-mile walk with a platoon of thirty-eight soldiers with mine detectors. They were all young soldiers as it was a military operation. We then stopped. When we got out, we walked to the right of the jeep and passed through a dry creek. I don't recall any plateau or field, but I want to say I did see a baobab tree. Chris Wain filmed all of this.

We marched through the bushes. We passed through certain villages. Each time we came to a village, we hunted very desperately for any sign of a massacre. What we found was that it was clear that these villages had been abandoned rapidly. There were pots, pans, little bicycles, and many personal things that indicated that they had been cleared out. The Portuguese admitted that they were doing this, but they said it had been done in a humane fashion. We were looking for any evidence of bullet holes. At one village, the village that they said would have been Wiriyamu, we found a pot with what looked like a bullet hole in it.

And the platoon commander said, "That's not a bullet hole; if you want to see a bullet hole here's one." He then fired at a pot and said, "Now, that is a bullet hole. The other hole is just a hole."

That was it. I didn't find any actual evidence of a massacre.

This put me in an awkward position because *The London Times* wanted to have some information since they sent me there. To be clear, when I went to the village, the soldiers pinpointed it and told me I was in the village of Wiriyamu. We then turned around and marched back. We got back to the hotel, and that night, Jonathan and I went to some nightclub. I remember being fascinated because I saw a huge crowd of young soldiers clamoring at the doors to be let in. I thought it was some sort of stripper show or something like this. They were actually Portuguese soldiers. We then went to another club where, in

---

[1]The site in question was prepared to waylay journalists, and the Portuguese named it Williamo.

fact, they had some sort of floor show on. A bit later some sort of fight broke out, but I forget what it was about. Anyway, we had to get out of there. We went back to the hotel.

Expulsion and Returns

The following morning, I asked if I could get my passport back because by that time I wanted to go to a hospital or to see anybody that was around aid workers. They said my passport was still in the immigration office, at the DGS [Direção-Geral de Segurança]. They advised me to go to the DGS office. It was nothing, they said, nothing that I needed to worry about. I was nervous, but it didn't stop me from going to the DGS.

I don't really remember where the office was exactly located. I went in, and there was a man holding my passport and also holding a paper, saying,

"What the hell is that man doing [here] when he hasn't got a visa."

"But I have got a visa," I said.

He then asked me what I was doing in Mozambique. I said I was in Mozambique because *The London Times* had reported on this massacre, and I was anxious to find out the truth. He said I shouldn't be there because I'd been banned.

I said, "Well, I'm here; am I being arrested?"

He said, "No, no, no. We are just concerned for your safety. *The London Times* is very unpopular in Mozambique. It nearly caused the cancellation of our President's visit to London, and your life is in danger."

I said, "I have found everybody I have spoken to remarkably friendly."

I didn't tell him about the fight the night before. Nevertheless, I said I felt reasonably safe here, and I wanted to go and talk to people to find out more. He kept on telling me to leave. I wasn't being deported, but he was saying I wasn't safe there. He refused to let me do my research and escorted me back to the hotel to get my bags. Chris Wain was there and filming me being ejected, so that was the news item that night: "*Times'* man expelled from the Tete province."

The DGS man took me to the hotel. There I got my belongings, and I even had a drum, which I had gotten in the village in [so-called] Wiriyamu; it was one of the things left behind, and it was a sign that this village had been left, and it was a real drum, not something from a tourist shop. I was then taken to the airport to go to Lourenço Marques. It was against my will because I wanted to go through Beira. We had no tickets, so I basically told them they were stuck with me, and they couldn't get me out of there.

I was not lying, mind you. I had been having a problem with my international credit card, which I bought my tickets with, but I didn't have a travel credit card. I had bought myself a one-way ticket into Beira because I didn't know which way I would be leaving. This ticket had become used and worn by this time. It got more and more scruffy, and my signature wasn't clear on the back. One of my colleagues had said to me at some point: "Well, wash it." In that evening, while I was in the shower, I washed it. The minute it was wet, I could see a sign made up with little words that said "invalid." It looked like I had been trying to wash off the signature, but I hadn't. This worried me because it didn't look like it was going to get me a ticket; I left it in my wallet anyway.

The DGS took me to their office, where I was kept further. They chartered a small plane to come and collect me. I flew with a guard to Lourenço Marques. When I got to Lourenço Marques, they said I was free to go to my hotel and took me to it. I was left there. I immediately wrote and sent a story to London saying I had been expelled from Tete. After finishing the story, I went downstairs, got a taxi, and went to a restaurant to get a meal.

When I was halfway through my meal, the server came to me and said: "Mr. Knipe?" I replied: "Yes."

"From *The London Times*?" he asked.

I said, "Yes."

He just asked that, and that's it. On my way out of the restaurant, there was another taxi waiting on me. I certainly knew I was being tailed. They were making certain of what I was doing.

The next day I applied for an interview with the governor general, Kaúlza de Arriaga, as I continued to still ask what was going on. Funnily, they granted the interview. I got into this interview, and he gave me the Portuguese version saying that it wasn't a massacre, but it was a humane movement that moved people into less dangerous areas. Peter Pringle was in Lourenço Marques at that time, and that's where we met up. He was interested in my story. That was more or less the end of my experience, except for one thing.

About six months later or so, there was that coup. I was in South Africa for the election. It was in fact the night of the election that the coup took place. I took a plane and flew to Lourenço Marques, as it still was, to explore and to cover the story there. The story basically was that we were waiting for Frelimo to come out of the bush. The parliament in Lourenço Marques was overthrown, and there was this big peace rally. The liberals were trying to hold a big mass meeting for hundreds of thousands of people. These were fairly nice, pleasant people who wanted some kind of middle course, and they stood up to get it. It was a multiracial solution to Mozambique's problems. But they were overwhelmed.

I was in the crowd. As I stood to see, I heard a huge crowd yelling, "Fre-li-mo, Fre-li-mo," drowning out the liberals.

Suddenly, this huge crowd took up this cry, and the liberal meeting just broke up. The new crowd had no empathy for these people wanting a liberal coalition, I suppose. So these people just left, and I then headed to Rhodesia to drive over the border to Beira. I was trying to find villages where Frelimo had begun to take over the authority. I met up with some Portuguese correspondents. They said they would charter a plane and go to one of these villages. They asked me if I wanted to go, and I said yes. On a Sunday morning, we met in the center of this little village somewhere north of Mozambique and waited for the plane to take us to the village where Frelimo had taken the reins of power.

While I was waiting, some white people came down the road. As they approached, I looked at this man, and he looked at me, and he turned very white. He was the DGS agent who had held me in his office in Tete. He knew I recognized him. He was terrified that I was going to denounce him. I didn't. He didn't do any harm to me besides kicking me out. But I was intrigued. What was he doing there? Should I talk about this or not in my dispatches to London?

Anyway, I got on the plane and went to the village. Later I discovered that he was one of several DGS officials who were put in prison attempting to cross the border into Rhodesia.

Now that I think of it, my visit to Tete shed no immediate light on the massacre allegation, but it provided everything needed for the war between the Portuguese Army and Mozambique's Frelimo to be brought into a fuller perspective as I saw it. What would be wonderful now would be to meet Father Adrian Hastings at some stage. After all, this was his story.

Interviewee:
Christopher Wain
Date (yyyy mm dd):
1996 03 25
Duration (hh mm ss):
0h 52m 32s
Place:
London
Language:
English
Interpreter:
None
Redactions:
None

How the Portuguese Foiled One Fact-Checker

In 1973 I was 33 years old, and I was married then but am divorced now. I had a two-fold job at Independent Television Network, or ITN, at that time: I was a general reporter, but I also had specialist knowledge in defense matters. I was an ex-soldier in the British Army, and when I joined ITN I had come from Southern Television, which had the south of England as an area. I noticed at Southern Television that no one was covering defense as a specialization, even though their area of coverage was surrounded by important army, navy and air force bases. Nobody was covering these as such, you see, so I made it a small specialization.

When I went to ITN in January 1971, it was with that specialization that they kept me in mind. I had covered other conflicts before. I was in Vietnam in 1972; I went to Northern Ireland as well, and other stuff. So if it was something to do with defense, and Portugal was an ally at the time, I was the logical choice. I remember when Wiriyamu broke as a story. We got visas a couple of days after. I went to Lisbon, and there was a delay either with the flight to Mozambique or with getting a visa. I do remember I was cooling my heels in Lisbon for a couple of days. When I went down there, I took a straight flight into Lourenço Marques. I met my cameraman either there or in Tete. He was a stringer for ITN.

I knew soldiers who were no good when looking at them. I could also spot some of the other characters that were around. I could spot the Rhodesian Special Forces who obviously were providing some kind of backup to Mozambique because they bordered each other. The Rhodesians were very worried about what was going on in Mozambique and Tete, and they obviously had a big presence there. I think Michael Knipe came in the same day I did. He came with this British doctor, Jonathan Ward. I think I was the only television person there as the BBC people and others had already come and gone. We were that late on the scene, and it was terribly embarrassing. By the time we got there, the story was very cold. It was a question then of persuading the locals to permit us to go off and have a look at the place they told us was Wiriyamu. Of course we had no way of telling whether or not the village we went to was it or not. It was a long hike, and I take it that it was the same place everyone else had gone to and that the village I saw was the same one that others had seen.

The Bouncer and Knipe's Return!

Before Mozambique, I had met Knipe a couple of times, but I didn't know him entirely well. I think he arrived that afternoon, and we arranged to go out that evening for a drink. We went to a nightclub with a French name, Moulin Rouge or something like that. The three of us got a table: Michael Knipe; Jonathan Ward, the doctor that accompanied him; and myself. I remember there was a worry about the steak, and Ward said to order it very well done as they had many cattle diseases you could pick up. All I remember is the food was rotten. They had a floor show going on. The clientele looked like something out of the Wild West. They were in various odd uniforms. I think some were Rhodesians who were keeping an eye on us. Then they had these strippers who came in and were going through their routine. They were going through a curtain. Knipe moved the table slightly, which flipped the curtain so you could see the girls getting in and out of their tassels.

Eventually, someone complained or something, and this big bouncer came up. He gestured to us that he wanted us to move. I mean, he picked up the table and shoved it about three feet. That sent Knipe flying out of his seat. So various people stood up, and I thought this was very bad news.

I said, "Look, sorry about my friend. All we were looking for was a nice quiet drink."

Then Knipe sort of got up, and the guy tossed him out.

So I stayed along with the doctor, and things calmed down a bit, and it was okay. Five minutes later, we had killed another beer. Suddenly, I became aware of two things. One, we were rejoined by Michael Knipe. He was sitting between us. I mean, he had been tossed out on his rear, and five minutes later he was sitting with us while this floor show was going on. The second thing I became aware of was that this bouncer was standing against the wall with his arms folded. He looked highly hostile.

So I asked Knipe, "What the hell are you doing?"

He said, "I was walking back to the hotel, and I thought, why should I allow someone I don't know to trot me out like that?"

"Well, because he's going to kill you, Knipe, if you don't!"

So this was getting a bit serious. We were getting very hostile looks toward us. The people in the bar had been drinking a lot. We weren't in a place that we really knew, and this was our first night. Some of these characters were very hard men indeed. I mean, they definitely weren't the sorts of people you'd like to borrow a cup of sugar from.

While we were there, this little guy turned up. There was music playing and this floor show going on.

This little guy said to me, because I think I was the most sober one out of all three of us, "You must get your friend out quickly, or there is going to be trouble."

I said, "Well, how do you mean?"

He said, "There are only six of us."

That was the first time I realized that we had a group of minders, DGS agents. They hadn't been prepared for this gentleman from *The London Times* to start World War III in this nightclub. He implied that they couldn't protect us in there. So when the dance was still on, we got up and started to move out. We moved fairly quickly to the door. I know there was some kind of argy-bargy going on in the background, but we got out, and we walked back to the hotel. Knipe was going on about why should we have to leave. I was just very relieved that we got out in time. I thought at the very best, we would have been arrested; and at the very worst, we would have been put in the hospital.

It was just one of those things, you know. Mercifully, nothing happened. But it stuck in my mind, the fact that this guy comes over, speaks fluent English, and tells us we have to leave because there are only six of them. I believe he meant there were only six DGS agents and that they couldn't hold this lot, so get out now, don't finish your drinks, don't hang around, and just go. I don't know who this man was. All I can remember was that he was small, thin-faced, and about forty years old. When we left it was about midnight, but we still had a couple of drinks in the hotel, even though it definitely put a damper on the evening. The only thing that I thought was it was just a stupid thing to do; you know, if you get bounced by a guy that size from a place like that, the one thing you do not do is walk back in five minutes later. It was designed to cause trouble. And I could see this turning into a headline, "ITN man arrested for brawl in nightclub." I was thinking to myself, How could I have gotten into this mess?

Williamo and Departures

It was the next day or the day after that we went on the road. There was a whole group of us who went up. We had soldiers provided to us, and we took multiple vehicles. We travelled on a tarred road, and then at some point, they dropped us off, and then we had to walk. I remember it was a hell of a distance, ten miles or so. They had soldiers providing escort, but it was fairly quiet. The soldiers who were with us were predominantly white conscripts, ill-equipped, and just not very impressive. The conducting officer spoke fluent English, but I'm not sure about the other officers. They did not strike me as particularly good soldiers. They seemed sloppy and ill-trained. The soldiers seemed a bit nervous. Anyone who's nervous with a firearm is always a danger.

I walked along the right side of the road into the bush. It wasn't very much of a road. It was very bumpy. There were bits and pieces of rock, so it was not much more than a [dirt] track. I was more concerned with making sure we were stepping on the rock rather than the dirt because you can't put a mine in a rock. I remember telling my cameraman to stick to the rocks. A mine could take your foot right off just below the knee, and I didn't fancy that at all.

I didn't speak Portuguese or the local dialect. We were absolutely in their hands. They could have taken us anywhere they liked, and we would have had no idea if we were being taken to the right place. Wiriyamu wasn't on any map, and I didn't have a decent map of the area. I didn't even have a compass with me. I had an approximate idea of the area, but I certainly didn't know if it was the place that we were supposed to be going. I assumed they were taking us out of convenience to the same place they took the BBC the week before. Whether or not it was the right place, I had no idea.

Did you see baobab trees or boulders at the site or any noteworthy features?

I don't remember any large open views at all or any baobab trees once we got there. We walked for about two hours in the sun, and then we came into a village. There were a dozen or so huts. All of the roofs were gone. We poked around. There was no blast damage that I could see. It was an empty village. It looked to me that someone had torched it. It certainly didn't look like a village that had suffered from any particular military action. I mean, no grenades, no shells, no sustained bursts of fire, or anything like that. These are the things you would expect to see even if it were several months after. This was something that was supposed to have happened five or six months before, but you would still expect to see obvious signs of military activity, and I couldn't see any.

I didn't take any photographs, as I was carrying the bag for the cameraman. The cameraman took shots, and I did a piece for the camera. I think we did a brief interview with one of the English-speaking officers, and I think I may have interviewed one of the other reporters. There was very little there. I think that was the gist of my story.

Did you meet local people there?

I don't remember meeting any sort of local people since it was a deserted village. We were there for about an hour. After about half an hour of being there, the soldiers were getting very anxious to get us back, and once I got the pictures, I was anxious to get back as well. There was no point in hanging around. We had a long walk back, and obviously I wanted to write the script and get the pictures up. Michael Knipe was with me when I returned. I started to write my story. Knipe and everyone else were filing their stories, usually by telex. I forgot how we got the story out; I think we shipped it to Rhodesia on a flight because that was the priority, to get the story out to the UK as quickly as possible.

I remember feeling a deep sense of embarrassment as I did my story, in the sense that we were very late in the game. The BBC had not only been there; they had gone and had sent out the story. It was unheard of almost, being so late on the story, so when I sent back the piece I began it with, "Today we went for one last look at Wiriyamu." In other words, just to say we were having yet another look just to tidy it up, rather than, "Guess what, folks, we've been ten days late getting here. You may remember this as an ancient history story. But we're doing it because it's the first airing of it on ITN." So I started it off like that to try and freshen up the story.

Meanwhile back at the hotel, I remember Knipe was picked up by the DGS. They had discovered he didn't have a visa. He thought they were going to make waves about it, so he was worried. We were in the hotel, and these two guys turned up to pick him up. My cameraman was there, so I told him to film it because if you do get arrested, it's quite important that people know as quickly as possible; otherwise they'll just beat you up. So we filmed it. The DGS didn't like that. We filmed them putting him in the car. Then they carted him away. I then was on the hotel telex to Ian Mills in Rhodesia who was the local stringer. I told Ian Mills what had gone on, and he opened up a separate telex to ITN in London and said, "The local secret police just carted Knipe away literally this very minute."

ITN apparently instantly got onto the Portuguese embassy in London and also called *The London Times* and said, "Your man's just been lifted."

So the phone calls by that time were sort of urgently going into the ambassador, who called Lisbon, and Lisbon opened up their DGS communication to Tete. Knipe told me that by the time he had arrived at police headquarters, all hell had broken loose. People were saying, "What have you done; where is this man?" Because they were getting very intense pressure from Lisbon to get him out and to not cause any more trouble. They said deport him and put him on a plane. It was all very interesting because I was still on the telex when this whole circus had opened up.

I stayed behind but wasn't there very long. I did one more story on the hospital before I left. They brought in an injured child with his foot blown off. We got some amazing pictures there. As it turned out someone had been mining the water wells in the villages where they knew people would be going. They were really nasty, these little tiny plastic mines with tiny bits of cloth. I had seen them in Vietnam. They were vicious things. You can't detect them since they're plastic. Just a simple thing, fling them on the ground and they get covered over. They're not designed to kill; they're just designed to take your foot off, which is a standard military tactic. If you wound somebody, you tie up at least another four people, one for each corner, and they are bad for morale as the injured person is lying there screaming his head off. They had these things around all over the place. We never knew whose mines they were: Portuguese, Frelimo, it could have been anyone.

So with that story filed, I left Tete. It was shortly after Knipe was deported. The pictures from Hotel Zambêzia and Knipe being arrested may still be around, but it has been a while since I have worked for ITN.

Photo 14 Peter Pringle, New York. Photo by Susan Meiselas, © 2011. Used with permission.

Interviewee:
Peter Pringle
Date (yyyy mm dd):
2013 03 27; 2014 04 15; and 2015 03 15
Duration (hh mm ss):
5h 30m 17s
Place:
New York City
Language:
English
Interpreter:
None
Redactions:
None

"The Story Checks Out!" Said Peter Pringle

I am Peter Pringle, but you know that. I had taken an interest in Africa when I was there as a kid. My father was a fighter pilot in the Battle of Britain; he survived, and in 1946 we went to Rhodesia. He was in charge of training the Rhodesian air force pilots. We were there in 1946 for about a year or two, and so I knew about Africa and had been there before ever working there. I read geology at Oxford, from 1959 to 1961, and after leaving Oxford, I went on an expedition to Tehran because I was interested in paleontology.

I had a lot of fun, but I knew I could never really do this for a living, and I had always really wanted to be a journalist. So I decided to stay in Tehran, and I got a job with the English-language *Kayhan International* daily newspaper as a proofreader, working from ten o'clock at night to four o'clock in the morning. A month later, I became the chief proofreader, and then I became a subeditor, and I was there when Kennedy was assassinated. At some point, some very savvy guys ran it from Dar es Salaam who did all the advertising stuff. One of them asked me if I would like to start a magazine in Beirut. I said yes and got a colleague on the paper to make a mock-up of the magazine, and I went to Beirut. I stayed a year, but we never published the magazine because the guy from Dar es Salaam's father died, and he went home.

I then got a job with an Egyptian who was taking tenders out of Arabic newspapers and translating them into English and putting out a monthly digest. Then I knew I had to get serious about life and returned to England. So I joined the Thomson training scheme for journalists and went to Cardiff for two and a half years to get my union ticket. This was around 1965. When I got there, they said they never had a journalist who had a degree in geology, and I said, "Well, this is the first time, let's go!" I eventually got to Fleet Street as a feature writer on the *Evening News* and then, in 1969, as a reporter on *The London Sunday Times*, run by Harry Evans. Within a year, I was on the Insight Team. I thought I was immortal, as one does aged 28. I looked at this picture that you sent me of António and myself. I showed it to my wife, Eleanor, and she said, "Gosh, I'm glad I didn't meet you in those days!"

How I Got the Story Out

The Insight Team was established in 1963. The person who could give you the full whack on this is John Barry, who was then the editor of Insight and was absolutely terrific; he was a wonderful editor and fantastic guy! He had a bunch of people who liked to go out and get stories and not have any contact with the head office until they got their story. So that's who we were, and that's what we did, and he was brilliant in coordinating it all. Insight was one of the first, if not the first, effort at group journalism, where you all start off at the beginning of the week with a story that nobody knows anything about, but there's something fishy about it, and by the end of the week you've solved it. You can do it very, very quickly if you have five guys on the phone with the right questions and are prepared to go to places like Mozambique and make a nuisance of yourself. You know, you could come up with something really good.

There were almost no restrictions on the Insight Team's activities, as a matter of fact; those were the glory days because this kind of stuff costs a lot of money: sending a journalist to Mozambique at the drop of a hat and telling him not to come back until he has the story and then have him come back three weeks later. Those were really good times for journalism and especially *The London Sunday Times* journalism. The best outfit to belong to in those days was the Insight Team. If there had not been an Insight Team, *The London Sunday Times* may not have taken on this story of Wiriyamu. We had a lot of people on the staff that would be regarded now as sort of lefty—not liberals, but lefties—and they had contacts with people like Polly Gaster at the Committee for Freedom in Mozambique, Angola, and Guinea (CFMAG).

At some point, I had met Polly Gaster and was put on their press list. The press releases came flying. So I knew about Angola and Mozambique, and I knew about Frelimo and the liberation movements. One other thing, for two years before the Wiriyamu story broke out, I had spent a lot of time in Northern Ireland. So when Mozambique came along, I was able to say to the Insight Team, "Well, I know something about this, and I can go and get the Frelimo side. We can get to these Burgos priests."

Our approach to the Hastings' story was, first of all, let's find out who these priests were. Once we'd done that, the next step was to go to Madrid and talk to these priests because everyone else was getting nowhere. There was a string of journalists who were trying to figure out what was going on, including Bruce Louden at *The Daily Telegraph*. We, at *The London Sunday Times*, had correspondents in Rome, Madrid, and South Africa, but it didn't amount to much, so John Barry suggested that I hop on a plane and go to Madrid.

Just before I left London for Madrid, we had a run-in with the Portuguese embassy in London because the second secretary there said that they were not issuing any more visas for journalists to go to Mozambique because it was very dangerous. He said that they could not guarantee my safety. We told him that others had been there, including Bruce Loudon of *The Daily Telegraph* and Michael Knipe of our sister paper *The London Times*. The secretary said that people don't like *The London Times* and *The London Sunday Times* in Mozambique and they don't like what's being written.

He told us that they could not guarantee our safety and said, "We're not going to say that you're going to be shot, but you might be hindered."

We said that we'd like to go anyway.

So I went, and they granted the visa, and I got in. I went to Madrid, and I saw the Burgos Fathers and explained to them what I was doing. I asked if they could make a tape recording for me. I was going to take this recording to the mission at São Pedro and that would give my credentials. I said that every other effort is failing here, and if this massacre really happened, then you'll have to tell your guys to tell me what happened. That was my pitch to them. I asked if they could write a letter that I could give to them as well. So they did, and I spent a day with them in Madrid. I can't remember where it was exactly. There were three or four of them. I believe Padre Berenguer and Padre Luís Afonso da Costa were there. Costa, or whoever was in charge, made the tape. The tape was basically saying, "This person is Peter Pringle; he's from *The London Sunday Times*, and he's asked all the right questions. And we think that at this point you should tell him the story."

I am summarizing because the DGS took my tape, so I can't say for sure what he said, but that's what I asked him to say. My Portuguese was non-existent in those days, but I'm just assuming that's what he said. And he told me, "This is the best chance we have," or something like that. So I took the tape and went to Mozambique. I went from Madrid to Lisbon, and then I went to Mozambique. I landed in Lourenço Marques and went to the British Embassy to check in, which was what you did in distant lands in those days. I told them what I was doing, and they said, "Okay, carry on. But we can't help." Then I went to the local Burgos Father's house in Beira. He was the regional head of the Burgos Fathers of the Tete province.[2] I can't recall his name now. I asked him if he would accompany me to Tete and then to the São Pedro Mission. I had the tape, but I can't remember if I told him about it. He agreed to accompany me.

We went by plane to Tete. I had asked the Portuguese authorities in either Beira or Lourenço Marques, I can't remember which, for permission to go to Wiriyamu.

They said, "No. You can't go anywhere like that."

I asked again when I got to Tete, and they said, "No. You can't do anything like that."

However, at this time this Burgos priest accompanied me. We were staying at Hotel Zambêzia. The next morning, we walked from the hotel to the São Pedro Mission, which is not very far, a couple of miles maybe, through the bush. I produced the tape and the letter. The priests went away for a little bit, then came back and said, "Okay, we'll talk."

Everything went pretty smoothly. I did this for three days running. I remember going out there a lot. I'm not sure how long the regional priest from Beira stayed, probably not much longer than to introduce me. My whole idea was that I couldn't just drop in because the other journalists had just dropped in, and that hadn't worked. I knew I had to do something different. On the third day, the priests produced António. He showed me his bullet wounds, and I knew bullet wounds from my time in Northern Ireland. I knew bullet entries and exits because we had spent a lot of time talking about entry and exit wounds after Bloody Sunday in Northern Ireland. So I was quite convinced that this was in fact a bullet wound that he was showing me. He was very convincing. I took pictures of him, and they took pictures of me with him. I think they gave me something to take back to Madrid.

António is still alive today, right?

Yes.

Hotel Zambêzia, where I was staying, was quite spooky in a way, because it was obvious that three men were following me. These white agents were obviously trailing me at that point. One day I walked over to the bishopric and asked for an interview with the bishop and was told that he was not in. Finally, I was able to schedule an interview with him at eleven o'clock that Friday. Before I met with the bishop, I went out to say goodbye to the priests and thank them. I had this bag with my notebook and my camera and rolls of film I had taken. As I left the São Pedro Mission to meet with the bishop, a white DGS agent jumped out from the bush and told me to come with him. I asked him, "Who are you?"

He refused to tell me and grabbed me by the arm and said to go with him. We went to an office in the DGS building, and at this office was the famous Sabino sitting behind his desk.

Captain Sabino was a short, menacing guy and was clearly happy to have me in custody. He told me to empty out my belongings onto the desk. I told him that we needed to make a deal first, that if he took anything he would need to write me a receipt. Of course, he said no. He started going through my notebook that had maps of the area and maps of

---

[2]Padre Mateus Carbonell.

Mozambique. The notebook also contained a note discussing how I thought the people at the embassy were useless and my feeling that they wouldn't be able to help me if I got into any sort of trouble. I also had useful international telephone numbers and such in there. Sabino was clearly very happy about all of this information. Then he told me I had to leave Tete immediately and that I would be escorted to the plane and someone would be with me on the plane to Lourenço Marques. Once there, he said my materials would be returned back to me, which never happened of course. But while he and his assistant were very interested in the telephone numbers I had in my notebook, I put my hand on the table and took one of the film cassettes and put it in my pocket. They didn't notice.

So I now had this cassette in my pocket, but I had no idea which film it was because there were several. Anyway, I got on the plane, and that was the end of my time in Tete. We arrived in Lourenço Marques, and they checked me into the famous Hotel Polana. The DGS guy who escorted me said that I couldn't leave as they were conducting an inquiry and such and such. I had to stay there in the hotel. Surprisingly, the guy in the room next to mine was Michael Knipe, the *Times* correspondent. I thought they had kicked him out, but he said they didn't, but he was leaving soon. He said that staying there at the hotel was basically like house arrest. One day, I called Knipe and asked him if he had a big box sitting on top of his wardrobe.

I told him I didn't know what was in it, and he half-jokingly replied, "I think it is a tape recorder, Peter, but I don't know."

I replied, "Oh, so what should we say to each other!?"

When Knipe was absent from his room, I often saw people going in and out of there carrying suitcases. Who knows what they were up to; I have to say that it was a lot of fun, and it certainly kept the adrenaline running. The first thing I wanted to do when I got to the hotel was to type out my story that I had been arrested and send it by telex to London. So I walked out of the hotel to the government telex office in downtown Lourenço Marques. I don't know if someone was following me or not, but they didn't stop me. I handed my story to the telex operator at the counter and asked him to send it to London. He disappeared with it for almost half an hour. He then returned and told me that he was not able to send the story that day because the weather was bad. I told him not to be ridiculous and that this had nothing to do with the weather, but he still refused.

So, I walked back to the hotel and bought a box of chocolates in the lobby. I knew that there was a telex in the hotel, for bookings and stuff, and there was a very nice woman who was the telex operator.

I gave her the chocolates and said, "These are for you. Now, can you please send this telex?"

And she said of course, and so it went to London! And that is the story that appeared on the front page of the paper even while I was still supposedly under house arrest at the Hotel Polana. So the story of my arrest was published in *The London Sunday Times*, and the official reaction in Lisbon, I soon discovered, was that I needed to be interrogated and taught a lesson because I was causing so many problems and making this stuff up. I got a call the next day in my room from a DGS agent, and he said, "You need to be out front at three o'clock, and I'm coming to pick you up."

I asked where we were going, but he wouldn't tell me. So I went, and they had a little VW to pick me up and drive through the suburbs to a safe house. The DGS captain at the safe house had a big desk where he had arranged photos of airfields and railway lines and such, and he told me that I had taken these pictures and asked me why I had taken them. I said I had never taken those pictures. They told me that they had my camera, and I told them I wanted it back, along with the pictures it had in it. They said that they knew these pictures were taken by me, and as for my telex story to London, they said that it is against Portuguese law to publish the name of any member of the secret service, the DGS. I had no idea of this law, of course. He said, Well, we have a problem.

The South African BOSS and the Attempted Blackmail

At that point the door opened, and there was this huge, enormous, South African agent from the South African Bureau for State Security (BOSS). He sat down next to me.

He turned to me and said, "Mr. Pringle, do you know that you have been associating with these priests?"

I replied "Yes, that's absolutely correct; I have."

And he said, "Well, you know these priests are liars, Mr. Pringle; they're all liars, all of them."

So I said, "Can we just agree that I have done something you do not like, and you say it is against the law, but I do not understand that it is against the law. So can I just please go home?"

At that point, the BOSS agent invited me to go have a coffee with him. In my mind, I thought that he was the last person I would want to go have a coffee with, but we had a coffee in the safe house basement. It looked like an ordinary villa, but I really cannot remember the villa in detail.

Anyway, so we had this coffee, and he told me that I was going to be deported, and that I would be on the next plane. I was still in possession of the film I took off of the DGS agent's desk, and I thought that this couldn't be good because I figured they would search me going into customs and seize it. The plane was going through Johannesburg, which was good because I could meet up with our correspondent there and give him the roll of film. So I put the roll in my wash bag, and it wasn't searched. So I got on the plane, and I still had the film.

I remember sitting on the runway thinking to myself, "Come on, come on, come on. Start the engines. Let's go."

We took off for Johannesburg. I didn't have any luggage besides my shoulder bag, so I went straight to immigration and told them that I was coming to see the correspondent for *The London Sunday Times*.

The guy looked at me and said, "I'm really sorry, Mr. Pringle, but you are not allowed into this country."

I said, "What are you talking about, 'I'm not allowed'? Nobody ever told me that."

He answered, "That's right, Mr. Pringle; you are not allowed into South Africa."

I told him that I just wanted to see our correspondent from *The London Sunday Times*, of London! He told me that he was sorry, but that I was on this blacklist. I was allowed to call our correspondent on the telephone, and he said he would come out and see me at the airport. We met at the airport, but I ended up keeping the film instead of giving it to him because I thought it would now be easier for me to take it back myself.

I flew back to Lisbon from Johannesburg, so I was still within the fascist orbit. Actually, I think that I flew back to Madrid, not Lisbon. Finally, I flew back to London with the film, which, with luck, happened to be the one with António on it. Then the story was published, but we were very worried about the picture of António because while the Portuguese didn't have a picture of António or me, they did have all of my notebooks and everything else. So now they knew everything. So we published my story and then called everyone, including the British Broadcasting Corporation, BBC, to let the world know.

Just a little anecdote: There was a wonderful lawyer on *The London Sunday Times* by the name of James Evans. He was a libel lawyer. He was so brilliant, not only did he take out the potential libels from our stories, but he changed the copy to make it more literate.

He called me up a few months later and said, "Peter, you would be really interested to know that I have had communication from someone from Johannesburg. They said that they have all your notebooks, and your films, and everything that they had taken from you in Mozambique. Now they are demanding money from *The London Sunday Times* to get it back. They said it was all incredibly embarrassing to you personally."

So I said, "Really, what should we do, James? I know I said some nasty things about the British Embassy, and I know I had stuff from Amnesty International, but it's all publicly available if you want to go find it out."

James replied, "I'll tell you what we're going to do; we are going to send a note back telling them that all those notebooks and everything in that bag are copyrighted by *The London Sunday Times*, and that if they publish one word of what was in Pringle's notebook we will sue them."

That was the end of that. I never got the notebooks back. We took the ransom claim as credible because it came from Johannesburg.

Hastings, Loudon, and Gaster

I did get to meet Father Adrian Hastings at some point. My impression of him was that he was a really good, caring priest who understood that his role in life went beyond the clergy. I read his book on Wiriyamu, which was quite a courageous thing to write. I probably met Bruce Loudon while I spent six months in Lisbon during the revolution in the spring of 1974. I must have bumped into Loudon because the place was crawling with hacks, so he was probably there. I did hear that when they sacked the DGS headquarters, his name was on the list of journalists they approved of. I would love the real history of Wiriyamu to be out there; every time I wrote the word Wiriyamu people would say, "Is there such a place? Does it exist? Pringle has it all wrong." Loudon was *The Financial*

Times correspondent based in Lisbon when this story broke out in July; he also did work for *The Daily Telegraph*. He served several masters.

Before I went to Mozambique, he wrote a couple of pieces: "No Massacre: Say Tete Tribesmen," and "Priests Do Not Know About Massacre." So you have the revelation of the massacre from the priests, and then almost immediately Loudon wrote these two pieces saying it didn't happen and there was no such place.

Did you have contacts with the military during your Tete visit?

No, I had no contact with the Portuguese military in general or the operational military at all over there in Mozambique. I asked, but nothing happened. I never saw anybody. In fact, Melo Antunes and others, as you know, we all met during the revolution in Lisbon, but that trip to Mozambique was my first.[3] I had never been there in my life, so I didn't know anyone, and they didn't want to introduce me to anyone that could help me with the investigation. So that's it.

The first time I had any realization of the impact of the massacre was when I was asked by the UN to come talk in front of the committee on decolonization. And then of course when I became the New York correspondent, which of course deals a lot with the UN, I didn't work with them though, as I mainly focused on Africa. During the time in Lisbon we were just reporting what was going. I sort of realized later the importance of the story.

Anyway, I'm very happy with all of this, and I'm very happy going back over these things because it is one of many unfinished stories of my life. So I am delighted to help in any possible way now. If at some point that means going back to Wiriyamu and finding out the real place, and if the São Pedro Mission is still there, and if the house is still there, I'd love to.

Two years after Wiriyamu, I moved to the United States, first as a correspondent for *The Sunday Times* in New York. In 1980 I went down to Washington where I had a girlfriend, Eleanor Randolph, who became my wife. In Washington I was picked up by *The Observer* and became a correspondent for them for a year. After that, I freelanced for two more years, and then *The Independent* picked me up. I was working with Alexander Chancellor, the former editor of *The Spectator*. Then Chancellor left to go back to London, and in 1990, *The Independent* sent me to Moscow. While I was in Moscow for three years, the Soviet Union ceased to exist. Then I came back to New York and have been here since.

On a scale of the worst massacres to have taken place around the world, Wiriyamu is pretty high up there. But it is not anywhere near the public eye, and it is not being investigated, and it is being very easily denied. And the pictures of burning bodies I gave you are not really traceable to a source. Nobody is talking about it, and the level of violence was astonishing. And it is still being denied. You ask, How can we collect enough evidence for people to understand what happened? You have a wonderful book;

---

[3]Lieutenant Colonel Ernesto Augusto de Melo Antunes was a Portuguese Army officer and ideological leader behind the April 25, 1974, coup that toppled the Caetano dictatorship.

you really do. I think a documentary would also be stunning. Historically, Portugal needs to accept and come to terms with the fact that the massacre happened. The Portuguese government will no doubt try to fight it.

But how can you argue with the facts, which have already been presented?

The articles and testimonies about Wiriyamu that are now public have played an important role in shaping the historical narrative of Portugal.

7

THE FINAL ACT—WITNESS PROTECTION

This seventh and last group of interviews includes one by Padre Vicente Berenguer and one by Padre José Sangalo. Berenguer's account omits extensive materials on his missionary work in Tete, leaving us with a narrative of his journey to Europe to protect the veracity of the Wiriyamu narrative, Wiriyamu as a place, and Wiriyamu as a documented event in the Portuguese colonial mass violence.

Padre Sangalo's text is perhaps the more dramatic in this duet. It begins with a brief description of his early life, his work as a priest at the Matundo Mission, and his involvement with Padre Ferrão's project in collecting data on the dead. The remainder is on protecting Mixone as a witness to the massacre. This part of the story is spellbinding, told in great detail, with grace and reflective depth. Ultimately Sangalo pays the price for his role as a witness protector—he is expelled from the colony and forced to leave behind happy memories and the place he loved most as a priest.

Photo 15 Padre Vicente Berenguer, Maputo. Photo by Mustafah Dhada, © 1995.

Interviewee:
Padre Vicente Berenguer
Date (yyyy mm dd):
1995 03 02, 06, 20, and 27; and 1995 04 03, 06, and 10
Duration (hh mm ss):
6h 4m 56s
Place:
Maputo
Language:
Portuguese
Interpreter:
None
Redactions:
Heavy

An Eyewitness Confirms the Place and the Events

My full name is Vicente Berenguer Llopis. I was born in July of 1937, in Alicante Province, Spain. I have two sisters, one older than me and one younger. I am the middle child. My parents and friends didn't believe that I wanted to go to a seminary and become a priest. I was eighteen years old and liked to have fun, they said. It was even harder for my parents—especially my father—to believe that I was going to move from Valencia to the seminary in Burgos and then go to missions to other countries. They would have preferred that I stayed in Spain. Unfortunately, they passed away when I was still studying philosophy.

My mother liked the idea of my becoming a priest in the beginning, but my relatives thought differently. I was going to be away from home for about five years, and they thought I was trying to get away from them and my parents. My mother never pressured me to stay home. She always respected my vocation. My sisters were the same; it was something normal. Of course, they wanted me to work in the diocese near them, but they didn't make a big deal of it. I would go home to visit on vacations.

I was homeschooled at the beginning and then studied for my elementary grades at the local civil institute of Alicante. One summer in June, I sat for public exams for the lyceum studies. I remember studying Latin during my homeschooling years. Of course, at that time we studied Latin, but I had trouble with Latin pronunciation since I was my own teacher. When I took my Latin exam, the supervising teacher asked me who my teacher was because I appeared to have learned to pronounce in classical Latin. She was surprised to hear that I had taught myself.

After the civil institute, I went to the seminary of Valencia because my diocese is Valencia. There I studied for two years. I took more Latin and added Greek as part of my lyceum education. I also studied philosophy. After I finished my lyceum studies, I went to the Burgos Seminary at the age of twenty-three to study for five years—four years of studying theology and one year studying spirituality.

The Burgos Seminary was unlike any other seminary in Spain. It trained priests from all over Spain, the Basque country, Castela, Catalunia, Andalusia, etc. Because of this supply of trainee priests, Spain could fill the Church's missionary needs all over the world, including places like Mozambique. Ideologically, we were the most diverse, in comparison to seminarians in Barcelona, Toledo, Valencia, Murcia, and so on. There were also cultural differences among us, and between us and the rest, the seminarians in Spain—who considered us different. We were not seen as normal trainee priests, so to speak.

Many opportunities came to us because of this diversity and training. The mental outlook at the Burgos Seminary was much more advanced than anywhere else in Spain. We were exposed to missionaries from around the world in distant places like Rhodesia, Mozambique, Zambia, Japan, and Latin America. Their work opened our eyes and our horizon. So I did not have to be a priest in Spain for the rest of my life; I could go anywhere in the world and be a priest just as well.

I landed in Moatize in September of 1967. The Moatize Mission, which was established well before I went there, was about fifteen kilometers from Tete, after the Zambezi crossing on the way to Zóbuè. I don't really remember the total population of Moatize. What I remember is that I formed part of a group of three Burgos Fathers, Miguel Antoni—not Buendia—Padre João Pascoal, and myself. Padre Antoni was overall in charge of the mission. I was in charge of education, both formal and informal. Padre Pascoal was responsible for pedagogy and liturgy, and catechists at the mission and surrounding community. I stayed there for one year before leaving for the Changara Mission, where my other colleagues were, in July of 1968.

As Burgos we were mainly in Tete—close to the borders like Unkanha, Miruru, Mucumbura, Chioco, and Changara. We dominated this part of the border. We also had the Tete parish—the cathedral of Tete—but we gave it up. The Jesuits took over the parish in 1968 or 1969—I cannot remember now. We kept a suburban mission, though, called São Pedro, which is where Padre Ferrão was. Later on we established a presence in Vila Pery, Sussundenga, and Beira. Here, we were at the Sacred Family Parish near the airport.

The Massacre

As you know, Wiriyamu was located between Changara and Tete, in the interior, and not on the main road. It is about twelve to fifteen kilometers from Tete. It's interesting to read Jorge Jardim's [*Moçambique:*] *Terra Queimada*—which gives us his version of the Wiriyamu story. I think, if I remember correctly, he provides reasons why the massacre happened. In my opinion, the conflict in the colonial army between exterminators and advocates of insurgency containment was one reason for the massacre. I have no proof of this idea; it is just a thought.

Padre Valverde was the one who collected data on the Mucumbura massacre. He was not involved in gathering information on Wiriyamu—that was Padre Ferrão and Padre Sangalo. Yes, it is true that Wiriyamu was simply one of many massacres that happened in quick succession. But unlike the massacres immediately before, Wiriyamu happened in one day and a bit. Mucumbura happened over several weeks. Ten were killed one day, ten another, five the following day, and so on. Valverde collected the information the best way he could. There were more killings that escaped Valverde and the others I am sure, but that is the record we have. Here in Wiriyamu it was another story. They used helicopter gunships, air bombardments, and coordinated commando attacks—very different, you know.

Also, I want to point out, I wasn't the one who delivered the report to Padre Hastings. Although Padre Júlio Moure and I had already denounced the massacres once we arrived in Madrid, his article had a better impact. It attracted much attention. Once everyone knew of the massacre, the Peace and Justice organization of the Catholic Church invited Padre Moure and me to visit the Netherlands, Germany, Belgium, and England, and we did that. This happened exactly at the time when Marcelo Caetano was planning to visit London to celebrate the Anglo-Portuguese Alliance. When we arrived in London, he was already there.

The Portuguese government denied Wiriyamu existed. They said we had invented the story. It was not surprising, they said. We, as Burgos padres, were communists—that is why we told these stories. We were in the Netherlands at the time, visiting the Congress of Deputies, which we then followed with a meeting of the Dutch Cardinal Bernardus Johannes Alfrink. His office sent an urgent telegram to the Vatican recommending a clear condemnation of the massacre by the Holy See.

Thank God we had proof that Wiriyamu existed, firstly because the Missão of São Pedro in Tete had a document in its possession recording the teachers it had sent to Wiriyamu. The document carried some official weight since the mission was paid by the government and had to report its activities accurately. The government paid the bishops, and the bishops paid the teachers at the mission and those sent to places like Wiriyamu.

Secondly, in Wiriyamu, there was this old, huge baobab tree with "Wiriyamu" written on it. Somebody had carved it many years ago. I say many years ago because the word was noticeable, as the tree trunk stretched as it grew. You know, baobabs grow very slowly. No, we did not photograph it, but we knew where it was. By this time, we were in Germany when we revealed these facts at the headquarters of the NDA [Nationalsozialistische Deutsche Arbeiterpartei the National Socialist German Workers' Party].

We found out that three Frelimo leaders were also visiting Germany. They did not know the full extent of the massacre. Someone proposed we meet them, which we did. I cannot tell you now who organized it, but we told them the massacre details. The Frelimo leaders were Marcelino dos Santos, Mariano Matsinhe, and Armando Panguene. They did not know because news travelled slowly from Tete to Dar es Salaam. They really thanked us for informing them of the details. We had come well prepared to give a well-informed press conference in a center near the hotel where we were staying. Several journalists tried to taint us as Frelimo spokesmen. We said we were priests. Did we know Marcelino dos Santos? When was the first time we met Mariano Matsinhe? Did we have any previous connections with Armando Panguene? We gave the same reply. We do not know these people. We are priests. We knew that we needed to maintain political neutrality and speak as a moral force, not a political force, as priests, and tell the truth independent of Frelimo politics.

When we got to England the BBC interviewed us. Journalists told Marcelo Caetano that he should let us go to Wiriyamu to prove where it is. This way the controversy would die one way or the other—and we were willing to go back to Tete accompanied by Amnesty International and the Peace and Justice organization of the Catholic Church to show the location and the documentary proof from the Tete parish church school. Marcelo then asked, "Would you let elements of the Irish Republican Army enter London? I can't let terrorists enter Mozambique."

And the subject ended there.

Photo 16 Padre José Sangalo, Madrid. Photo by Mustafah Dhada, © 1995.

Interviewee:
Padre José Sangalo
Date (yyyy mm dd):
1995 06 11–21
Duration (hh mm ss):
3h 51m 11s
Place:
Madrid
Language:
Portuguese/Spanish Mix
Interpreter:
None
Redactions:
Very light

Mixone's Rendition on a Suzuki Motorbike

I'm Padre Sangalo. I'm fifty-five years old. I was born in 1940. I started at Pamplona Seminary in 1951 and continued until 1958 when I went to Burgos Mission Seminary to finish my studies. I was ordained in 1964. Ever since the age of eight, I wanted to be a priest like my cousin. Later on, I was very inspired by reading letters written by missionaries to priests in Spain with whom I was friendly. Their work was full of purpose. There was no need for missionaries in Spain itself at the time. Spain had enough priests. I considered joining the Combonians, but I was introduced to the Society of White Fathers. Many of my colleagues had joined some society. I eventually decided to join the Burgos Society of Priests. The Burgos was more suited to my way of thinking and feeling. They were laic. The local dioceses paid them. They worked where no one wanted to go. They were practical and down to earth. After I joined the Burgos, I was asked to go to Mozambique in the province of Tete—a land forgotten by God and mankind.

I had to go to Portugal for six months to study the Portuguese language before I went to Mozambique. When I arrived in Mozambique in 1967, I was asked to go to Mucumbura—which, as you may very well know, was developed and headed by well-known Burgos Fathers, Padre Ferrando and Padre Valverde. My destiny was not in Mucumbura. After six months at that mission, I was sent to serve at the Burgos mission in Unkanha in the northwestern-most portion of Tete near Zambia. I enjoyed my two-year stay there. I participated in the people's religious life—felt their joy, happiness, and pain. After two years I was sent, in June or July 1969, to serve the Burgos mission house in Tete city itself, near Missão São Pedro. The Burgos house had two very dynamic and very committed Spanish priests, Padre Castro and Padre Jovete. I stayed with them until late 1971 or very early 1972. I was then promoted to be the father superior of the Matundo Mission. I was very happy to head my own mission in Matundo.

The Matundo Mission was small. It was on the other side of Tete as you crossed the bridge over the Zambezi River on the left-hand side after those giant boulders. The mission itself was a rented house that belonged to a Mozambican. It had no telephones, an outhouse and a very small kitchen, and no electricity. There was a way to rig up electricity into the house from the outside electrical pole—but I chose not to. That is how the locals did it—and the landlord even suggested I do it. I did not want to appear as a padre to engage in something so unethical.

I had a paraffin lamp instead, with a gauze hat that glowed and gave light. So anyone outside could spy on me easily. When the house was unlit, they would know I was out or fast asleep. When someone wanted to see me during daytime they would just appear and hope they would find me home or send someone with a message or leave me a message to wait for them. I cooked for myself—other missions had cooks, generators for electricity, and running water. Here, the others and I did all our house chores; anyone staying with me and I kept the place clean.

The mission had a school nearby. It was a Portuguese school—we had no control over it, nor did we have close enough contact with the students to bring them into the fold. Despite all this, I was happy there. My life was very basic, and I liked it that way.

You see, I am the son of a *matador* (bullfighter), and I knew how to take life's hardships like a fighter. It did not bother me that I was there and not at Missão São Pedro or some other more prestigious mission with other fellow padres. I wasn't bothered, no! In any case, I was often out visiting my parishioners, covering a vast area. I did, though, have contact with Missão São Pedro and was close to Padre Domingo Ferrão. He was not a Burgos Father but liked to work with us. It was mutual, as I liked working with him. Most nights I would keep up with the news on my battery-powered radio; that is how I remained connected with the world outside my mission.

Contacts with Frelimo—and My Nemeses

Inside Tete I never had direct connection with Frelimo until after the war. I did have contact with them indirectly through my students. The first indirect contact with Frelimo in São Pedro was with the famous Raimundo Dalepa. He arrived at the mission one night and sent my former student whom I had taught at the Unkanha Mission to see me. Soon after graduating from our mission school, this student had joined Frelimo, along with two others from Missão São Pedro. I kept in contact with them but did not discuss politics, nor did I encourage them to reveal to me what they were up to. As far as I was concerned, they were my students and parishioners; believers in human dignity and self-determination, in liberty and human rights; and deep believers in the Christian faith. I kept these contacts alive in Missão São Pedro but never in Matundo.

This student asked for help from me. He told me that Raimundo Dalepa was getting married and needed clothes to wear at his wedding. I saw this as a Christian duty to help, and perhaps an opportunity to secure the place of the Church not only in Tete but also possibly in a Mozambique in a future without Portugal. My job, he said, was to bring the clothing, and this student would deliver it to Dalepa. So I did [just that]. I took pants, shirts, beautiful skirts, shoes, etc. This student, who I believe is still alive, but whose name I truly don't recall, delivered the clothes. I was never invited to the wedding, nor did I see the face of the person whom I had helped.

Raimundo didn't come to Missão São Pedro or visit its chapel until after the war. The first time I saw Dalepa was when he entered Tete along with his guerrillas from the Tete region. Then Dalepa went to Missão São Pedro, asked for me, and said, "I want to talk to that Senhor Padre and thank him for the wedding clothes he provided me."

We met. We had lunch together at his house with his wife [present]. She was from Mucumbura. I don't know who did his wedding ceremony, but I am sure he was a padre—perhaps [a padre] in Frelimo itself, who knows. If not, then it must have been one of the big chiefs in the Frelimo hierarchy.

I maintained good relations on the other side as well—and where this was not possible, I always kept myself well informed of what was going on in local politics to protect my church and my parishioners. That was my priority. I made sure I was seen as a non-partisan padre. That is why I cultivated the chief of the secret police, Senhor Inspector Sabino.

Two characters that I did not like very much and who made my skin crawl and made the life of my parishioners miserable were Senhor Sabino's agents, Chico Kachavi and [assistant] Johnny Kongorhogondo.

I had contact with both of these PIDE [Polícia Internacional e de Defesa do Estado] agents. They were both invaluable to Inspector Sabino. They provided him with information, and because of this Sabino paid little attention to complaints about them and the way they treated the population, many of whom were my parishioners. Chico in particular was an odious nightmare and brutal. People feared him and would do anything to avoid him. Chico was addicted to women. He had to have them, as many as he could. He had no respect for anyone's wife, daughter, or mother.

But of course, Frelimo got to know what Chico did to the population, as did Raimundo. So Frelimo soldiers said, "No! It is necessary to kill this man."

So they did; two soldiers *may* have done it. One was the student who had brought the wedding clothes from me to Raimundo. The other was also a former student from Marara and was chief of the Frelimo cell for Tete city. I know they killed him because the same very night of his death they came to visit my mission. They did not see me directly. They did not want me compromised. They told a catechist of my mission who happened to be outside the house, "Tell Padre Sangalo that Chico Kachavi doesn't exist anymore."

He died when he was in the shower—in fact, they put a grenade in his bathing hut. It was a near-instantaneous death.

Although Chico was a very cruel PIDE agent, he also had deep friendships with his colleagues, especially Johnny Kongorhogondo. This relationship, however, was because they were PIDE agents. Moreover, they lived close to each other, and one would often see the other. They were also close in other ways. They shared a love for torture and inflicting suffering on their suspects and victims in prison. Chico's specialty was spying on the people in the city. Johnny was more in the villages surrounding Tete. As far as I know, Chico had little if any contact with the villages of Wiriyamu and Chaworha. Johnny, on the other hand, had connections with these villages.

Johnny Kongorhogondo's father was the local sorcerer and chief of his village. He was very protective of his practices and the old ways of doing things. He was a traditionalist. He used threats and intimidation to keep things as they were. He believed in the old ways of holding power and distributing it to people who served the chieftaincy well. He did not get along with chiefs around him, particularly the chiefs of Chaworha and Wiriyamu. They were becoming "modernists" and shedding old ways [and adopting new ways of doing things]. I think he was also against us padres. We believed in educating people and enabling them to be self-empowered. That is what Christ would have wanted. And that is why I visited Wiriyamu several times to see if we could establish a school for the kids of that village and villages around it, including Chaworha.

I once told him that his way of doing things was dangerous.

"Be aware because we know that even sorcerers must be careful in using their powers. Don't think you are immortal because the bigger and mightier you are the steeper your fall will be: Even stones obey this law," I said to him. "So be careful what you do; one day, you too could fall."

He of course ignored me, and I liked him even less. He would not change, and he would continue to practice his magic and his power of chieftaincy to win control of the region.

His son was like his father, a dark, dark, dark soul. A cloud encircled him always. He said little. He lived with his father sometimes and sometimes on his own—he may well have shared his father's philosophy of life and practices of power and rulership, but I do not know. I do know he was an evil twin to Chico. They both were a pair of unspeakable afflictions on my parishioners. Johnny procured women for Chico, and unlike Chico, Johnny was an authentic cold-blooded killer.

Did you know his brother?

No, I did not know his brother Thai. I know his brother had joined the Portuguese army and had some connection with the chief of Wiriyamu. I have no details other than that.

The Visitor from London and Hiding Mixone

Were you involved in the report?

Yes, I did get involved in helping Padre Ferrão write the report and helped him publicize the atrocities overseas. I had to. With killers like Chico and Johnny, and the way my parishioners were suffering and had no voice to speak, I had to. All I did was to lend my tongue and my Suzuki, the spirit of my father as a bullfighter, and my cloth as a priest. These were the things and the only things I had to make my work meaningful in the service of God. I know Christ would have done the same. I did my way, the only way I could.

When the report was published in England, the Portuguese denied it of course. *The London Times* sent reporters to Mozambique to get eyewitness proof that the massacre had happened. Several reporters tried to get this information. The one that nearly succeeded was Peter Pringle. When Peter Pringle arrived in Tete, the PIDE was very alert and ready to catch anyone who got near the truth. Peter came to Missão São Pedro because that is where the father superior of the mission resided. Peter said that he simply wanted to contact survivors and hear their stories. I was put in charge of getting him the information. Padre Castro fetched António and brought him to Missão São Pedro in his Land Rover. Mr. Pringle interviewed him, recorded it, and took a picture with him. Pringle also took a picture with Podista and her son, who were also survivors— I appeared in the picture as well.

With this information in his hand, Peter Pringle was ready to fly back to England. Before he could step out of the hotel, the PIDE agents [grabbed and took] him to the secret police headquarters. He went there, and he found Inspector Sabino. They ordered him to take off all he was carrying along with him, and it was all confiscated. The PIDE were really happy to have caught him in the nick of time. In this excitement they forgot to confiscate his photographs with António Mixone.

Peter left on his flight to London, and the first thing he did was to publish the picture of António Mixone, a survivor from Wiriyamu. When this happened, *The London Times* newspaper confirmed the information was true; there were survivors from the massacre. The proof was the picture. Peter said he had recorded the interview for more specific information, but the PIDE had confiscated it when he was leaving the place. He couldn't show this to *The [London] Times*. On that same night, this information was broadcast on the radio, and I happened to hear it.

The night in question was in the month of July 1973, and I was in my mission in Matundo.

I was tuned to the news on the BBC and heard the announcer mention Chaworha. When he said Chaworha my ears pricked up, and I got closer to the radio not to miss a thing. Just as I did that, he mentioned António Mixone.

I said, "Oh, my God in Heaven, blessed be his sanctified name. If they find him, they will kill him. The PIDE will be on to him. I must do something right away."

I and the other padres secretly met at the Burgos mission house—we had to avoid detection from the secret police when in Tete. We were in a race against time. I do not remember who was at the meeting. We discussed what to do. We decided to send him into hiding. But where? Anywhere in Tete, he would be discovered and in the end killed. The best thing was to hand him over to Frelimo. He would be safest with them, since they were experienced in protecting themselves and others of value to them from the Portuguese authorities. But who would take him to them? And how would we engineer this?

Padre Ferrão could not get involved. He was black. He had already been in prison for his political views; and in any case the PIDE were watching him and the mission very closely. The only person who could do it and would not raise suspicion was me. I was in Matundo and far away from Tete city and Missão São Pedro. Also, I was in good standing still with Inspector Sabino, the chief of the secret police. He believed in me—at least that is what I thought. It is true I had indirect contacts with Frelimo, but they were near Missão São Pedro and not in Matundo. No one associated with Frelimo came to visit me there. Matundo was surrounded by whites, and it was risky to be seen fraternizing with suspected *turras* [terrorists]. This was very funny and a bit ironic really because Frelimo transported their guns, small arms, and other supplies, and God knows what else, behind the mission near the bridge where the Zambezi waters narrow. Eventually, that is where Frelimo launched their assaults on Vila Pery, south of the Tete province.

We also knew we could not get Missão São Pedro involved in any way. So my Tete contacts and those of Padre Ferrão were useless. We needed a place outside Tete and someone with Frelimo contacts there to help us safely hand him over. After much discussion and thought, we found the ideal place—the Combonian mission near Changara, fifty to sixty kilometers from Tete.

The next day I woke up at five in the morning, took a shower, and got ready. At five-thirty, I left for M'Phadwe on my Suzuki motorbike—I would have left a bit later if I still had my other motor-ped, my 250 cc Honda, which could reach the speed of sixty kilometers per hour. But I sold it to someone in the Portuguese Air Force who unfortunately never paid me. What can you do, when someone says he now does not have the money and he and his family are broke because of some tragedy? I let it go.

Anyway, I arrived in M'Phadwe an hour later at around six-thirty. To get to M'Phadwe, I had to go across the bridge and go through Tete and hope to not be stopped by police or tailed by the secret service. That is why it took me an hour to get there. I looked for António and found him at the foot of the baobab tree. He was up and nearly ready. He knew I was coming because I had sent a message that I was coming to visit him that morning. I had not seen him since December 1972, during his stay in Tete hospital. He had grown and really looked to me more like a man than a small boy. I liked that he was dressed discreetly, not to attract attention.

I spoke to his people, near and dear to him, his family, and explained why he was being taken. I couldn't just take him away without telling them why. After all he still had family members around him that had survived the Chaworha massacre. So, I spoke to them about the danger António was in and that the PIDE were looking to kill him. I felt it necessary to say that because that was the truth and his family needed to know the real truth, the real story. Otherwise it would have been a long morning with discussions and more discussions, and more opinions, and more "Let us not do anything hasty. Leave him with us," kind of thinking. He would have been surely dead within days if not hours. In less than one hour they could be there. Of course, his relatives didn't want the boy to die after having survived the massacre, so they hurriedly organized his small bundle of clothes, and we left at seven-thirty—and just in time.

Soon after our departure, and I cannot tell you exactly how soon, the PIDE came to the baobab tree in search of him. I did not think it right to ask his family not to reveal what happened to him, who took him, and where and why. Of course, I did not tell them where I was taking him. To tell his family members to keep my visit secret would have led the PIDE to interrogate and torture them. I left them free to say what they knew, what they saw, and who came to get him. This way they were spared pain and possible death.

To get to Changara I had to go back to Tete, cross it, and then take the road to Marara via Boroma. Yes of course, I prayed, not very hard I must admit, not to be stopped by the police. It was not unusual to see padres on motor-peds, carrying a backseat rider even *um Moçambicano Negro* [a native Mozambican].

He rode on the back holding both his bag of clothes and my waist. We left there about seven-thirty. We rested for a short bit at the Boroma Mission. It wasn't easy to ride on a motor bike for long without a break. I was saddle-sore, and I needed to rest to prepare myself mentally for the next leg of the ride. The road from Boroma to Marara and then Changara was full of potholes.

Combonians ran the Boroma Mission. You could trust them. They did not have to be patriotic like priests who were paid by the Portuguese government. We were paid poorly but by our diocese in Spain, and we did not have to be Portuguese or defend what they did to the people in our parishes. Combonians, like the White Fathers and us, were devoted to their mission and did God's work with passion and commitment to truth. They defended the truth and were not afraid to face it like a good *matador* in front of an angry bull. They believed in human values and decency.

I told them where I was going, who my cargo was, and what my mission was. With the break over, we got on the bike to go to the Changara Mission, which was also run by Combonians. By the time we got to Changara from Tete we had been on the road for a bit longer than an hour and a half.

I cannot remember the names of the Combonians in the Changara Mission or the name of the *padre superior* [father superior]. The fathers took a picture of us, Mixone and me, and then we all had lunch in the company of students at the mission's boarding school. I do not recall what was for lunch that day. All I remember was that it was nice to be in the cool shade—and among fraternal brothers. The most fortunate thing is that Mixone was among his peers, and no one asked questions. Thank God, the PIDE were nowhere to be seen. They could easily have sent someone since the Combonian Fathers had contact with Frelimo, and that was how he was going to be handed over.

I left António in the safety of the Combonian Fathers, who promised me they would look after him. They were to let him rest for a night at their boys' boarding school and then arrange a handover the following night or thereafter.

The Pendulum Swings

I hurried back to Matundo. The sun was bright and roasting me like a pig over coals from Moatize. When I got to Boroma, I rested for a bit. The ride was as I expected—awful. I missed my other bike, the Honda. The ride would have been a bit softer on my backside. Anyway, at Boroma I had a light meal with the fathers and then hurried back to Tete. Once on the road, I zoned out. The hum of the Suzuki engine was Zen to me until I got near Tete. The sun was setting—like the light on La Ribera hills of Pamplona, golden. Once in Tete I went straight to Missão São Pedro to see Padre Ferrão and tell him all was well—and the parcel was safely delivered. He was very happy that the mission was accomplished. Now that you ask, I do not remember if he told me that the PIDE had been at the mission looking for António. He might have.

When I left Missão São Pedro I was tired, too tired to go home. I went to the movies instead. The movie theater, Santiago de Tete, was located across from the house where Padres Castro and Jovete lived, a little further down the street from the Tete dioceses and parish.

Was it close to the ZOT?

No, the movie theater wasn't close to ZOT [Zona Operacional de Tete]—in fact, it wasn't in the same neighborhood. I went to the center many times. It was located on the other side of Tete.

Do you remember the movie?

I can't remember the movie, either, if it was about war, action, or a mystery. I was just there to unwind. After the movie, I paid a visit to Padre Castro and the others at the mission house. We talked and socialized a bit. I needed the comfort of my friends, and I was tired—I didn't really want to get on the bike and head to the bridge right away. In the end, though, I thought it better and went home. I had work to do the next day.

When I reached Matundo, I was still wound up from the day's events—the success of having out-foxed the police from nabbing António. Though a bit hungry, I didn't feel like eating. I didn't even turn on the paraffin light—just went straight to bed.

Much, much later I discovered that Inspector Sabino and his secret agents went to Missão São Pedro in search of António Mixone that day and, upon not finding him there, suspected my involvement in his disappearance.

Sabino said to his agents, "No way can Padre Sangalo be involved in this. I know Padre Sangalo. He is a good man, a holy man. Many people confess their sins to him. He would not do such a thing. I cannot bear thinking of him this way. He is a man of God."

"Then how come he is not where he is supposed to be at his mission in Matundo? We checked. He is not there. He is nowhere to be found. I bet you it is he. He is playing both sides," his agents said to him.

Later that day, the PIDE agents discovered where Mixone lived. Someone told them to check for him in M'Phadwe; that is where most Chaworha survivors had gone to live,

"He was supposed to be there with his relatives. He lives under the large baobab tree at the mouth of the village near the road."

The agents went there, and they were told, "Padre Sangalo was here, and he took the boy, but we do not know where."

Sabino was furious, "I will kill him. Son of a bitch! Wait until I get hold of him. Send someone to fetch him here. I will not go there again to visit him."

Sabino often came to visit me at my mission house, and we were "close."

The day after my trip to Changara, someone appeared at the house at lunchtime. He knocked at the door, which I always left ajar as a sign of welcome.

"Excuse me, Padre Sangalo, are you in?" A head popped in.

It was a secret agent's face: "I am to take you to Tete, Senhor Padre."

My heart missed a beat. I had to do what I did the way I did it. Not only was António Mixone's life in danger, but the lives of others. If the PIDE got Mixone, they could get all the population, and another massacre would begin. Besides, I said to myself, "You are the son of a bullfighter. Now go and fight the bulls."

"I am ordered to present you at the secret service headquarters for interrogation, Senhor Padre," said the agent.

He appeared timid—and that helped me a bit.

I sent word to Missão São Pedro that I was being taken to the PIDE headquarters. Then I followed the agent to the secret service building. It was an ugly building. Some of the inside walls were blood-splattered. They had not bothered to clean them and used them to show what they could do to people when they were brought there. That is how my ordeal for the week started. To talk to Sabino I had to meet him in the PIDE headquarters. I entered through the main door. Two guards were posted on each side of the door. Then I turned to my immediate right. That is where Inspector Sabino's office was. I knew the place well. I had been there many times to visit him, so I went straight to him without waiting for the agent who had come to me at the house and led me here.

First, I want to tell you that it is untrue that you helped Mixone disappear. I do not believe what I hear, and I do not believe what my agents are saying to me. They tell me you have him. If that is the case, Padre Sangalo, you better have him hidden somewhere where we cannot find him. And you too better hide yourself where we cannot find you.

Before I could say anything, he continued,

Look, Padre Sangalo, I must obey orders from Lisbon. They want me to find him. I promise you, Padre Sangalo, we will do nothing to him. No harm will come to him. If he goes to Frelimo, the whole thing will blow up. It will be a giant political mess. Is that what you want? For the sake of our friendship, please, I beg you to tell us where he is and not to hand him over to Frelimo.

Once he calmed down and I sensed that he was not going to kill me, I said to him,
"Relax *Senhor Inspector Sabino*—Inspector Sabino, Sir. If I find him or know where he is, I will personally come and tell you immediately. The truth is at this moment I cannot tell you where he is exactly."

And I was not lying. Mixone by then could have been anywhere, with Frelimo or in transit somewhere else. God knows.

We went like this back and forth. He tried to persuade me to tell him where Mixone was. I said I would tell him the moment I knew where he was exactly.

Finally, he let me go, "But you have to come back tomorrow to be questioned. We will send an agent to come and get you. I will be retaining your passport."

He wanted to put pressure on me until I confessed. I left that *monstrosidade* (monstrosity)—the PIDE headquarters—and went straight to Missão São Pedro and then to the Burgos house in the city. They were waiting for me. I told them what happened. They were very concerned and prayed that I would be safe to go back there the next day. I said I would be all right. There was nothing they could do to me. They could kill me. If so, it was God's will. I was prepared to die. Why not? The bulls will win. I still will have done God's work. But they could not afford another scandal. Imagine a headline in the world press, "Burgos priest found dead." Nah! They had to keep me alive to get to Mixone. He was their ultimate prey, not me!

I left for Matundo on my Suzuki. I could see from the back mirror that I was being followed. When I got home, I was emotionally exhausted. Once the sun set, I felt like a piece of meat in an African night surrounded by hungry hyenas. I could not eat, nor could I go to sleep. When I fell asleep, it was dawn, and the sun was up, and then—tap, tap, tap. There were the knocks on the door. I felt them in my heart.

"*Vamos la ver o que se passará hoje*—Let us see what the day brings."

I got on the Suzuki, and back I went to the secret police headquarters. By this time, I thought we would be developing a routine. He would ask questions and threaten me with disappearances, deaths, and anything he could imagine. I would respond calmly and with firmness.

But then they tortured me. Chico was not present. Johnny wasn't, either. Sabino was. I responded as I always did;

"I do not know where he is, and I promise you that I will bring you the information you need the moment I get it. I promise, Inspector Sabino."

They continued to torture me—to a point and no more. He was a practicing Catholic, and I was a Catholic priest. Yes, it is true I was not Portuguese, but I was better than a laic. Without my priesthood, I would have been tortured to death—gone!

When we ended this second session, I said to him, "Inspector Sabino, there is no need to send an agent to get me to come to your office. I will come and see you on my own once I get the information you need."

He agreed. He knew I was going nowhere. He had my passport. *No outro lado*, on the other hand, I made sure I went to see him to tell him I did not have the information he needed. I had made a deal with him, and he was counting on me to get him the information. I was not going to renege on it. Before every visit, I let Missão São Pedro and the Burgos Fathers in Tete know I was going to see "Frankenstein." After every visit I would go and tell my colleagues what happened and what I had to do next. All in all, I paid four or five such voluntary visits. During my last visit I told him I had not found the exact whereabouts of Mixone. But I also told him the truth. He had already been handed over to Frelimo, and they did not tell us where Mixone was. So, I was truthful [to a point] and did not need to confess *perante os meus colegas sacerdotes*—in the presence of my priestly colleagues.

To Spain and Back

By then, Sabino sensed I had had a hand in Mixone's disappearance. People from M'Phadwe probably told him. In fact, someone told me that they told him that they had allegedly seen a white missionary taking Mixone for a motorcycle ride on the way to Changara. By then he was convinced I was guilty. He was disappointed in me. He thought I was his buddy. Instead I turned out to be a bullfighter dressed as a priest.

A week after my last visit, the PIDE expellled me. Sabino sent two white and two black agents. He said he would not come to the house. I was no longer a *persona grata*—a friend. These PIDE agents came very early in the morning, around six. They knocked on my door. They came and were warned to watch out for Frelimo nearby or in the house in case I called on them to entrap them. That is how low their opinion of me had sunk.

I opened the door, and there they were, standing. I was told I was being expelled from Mozambique, and that I was a terrorist. I was ordered to pack. I got a little suitcase and grabbed whatever I could. What could you pack when asked so suddenly? They waited for me and watched me get ready.

"Finally, you will be among the many Frelimo supporters when you get to Spain," said one agent sarcastically, looking at me pack.

I said nothing. I did not want to make matters any worse than they were.

Before getting on the plane, I was taken to see Inspector Sabino, again, to be interrogated one last time. This last time, one person from the diocese, who was Portuguese, was also present. He was there to witness the happening. Sabino explained to him the reason why I was being expelled. I was a terrorist, untrustworthy, and a threat to the security of Mozambique and the state of Portugal. I asked for my passport. Sabino said I did not need one since I would be using state-approved transportation. By then I was ready to leave and did not argue with Sabino.

I was flown to Nampula on Portuguese civil aircraft, and from there I was put on a flight to Beira, but without my luggage. My suitcase was confiscated at Tete airport, I later found out. The PIDE put me on a plane to Lisbon via Lourenço Marques. It is just as well that they did not strip-search me because I was carrying a copy of the full report of the massacres in Mozambique. I hate to think what would have happened to me had they discovered what I had hidden in my pocket.

I got to Madrid practically naked, with only the clothes on my back and no proof of who I was. At Madrid airport, I said to the immigration police,

Sir, you must know by my Spanish accent that I am Spanish, don't you? Do you recognize me at all? I'm Spanish and was expelled from Mozambique by the Portuguese government. I don't have any identification with me. They took it away. But I am that priest of the massacre story that appeared in all the newspapers. You must have read about the story, no? My father superior is here in Madrid— here, I can write his address for you. Before you send me back, please call my father superior. They will prove to you who I am and why I am here without my papers. Please, please check with them first, before you send me back.

I then gave them Padre Anaveros' number. They called him. Thank God, they called the number. Padre Anaveros came rushing to the airport.

"I am very surprised to see you. You are unexpected. They told us you jumped off the plane and were dead. The Portuguese authorities said you had committed suicide."

Padre Anaveros could not believe that it was me that he was seeing and not some sort of a ghost. I told him to take me home and that we could talk more calmly. The Spanish immigration official noticed that we knew each other. He let me go and told us there was no problem. Padre Anaveros wasn't the superior father. The superior was Padre Navarro, and he was the general superior of the Burgos Mission Seminary in Madrid, and although he was a conservative by nature, it was he that authorized the publication of the report and gave a copy to Father Hastings.

Why Inspector Sabino initiated the rumor of my alleged suicide I still do not know. Perhaps he wanted to kill the Wiriyamu story by suggesting my death, the death of the last person who knew where Mixone was. The truth is that there was a massacre, and it was proven. There were victims, and it was proven. There was a father, and he was now in Madrid. And he was the son of a bullfighter!

Months after my arrival, I wanted to return to my missionary work, but I could not. So others and I went to London to learn English and prepare to work in countries neighboring Mozambique. That is why I went to stay with the White Fathers in their house in Tottenham. My plan was to go to Lusaka, Zambia, and be near Tete on the freer side west of the province, perhaps even near Unkanha!

But then the military coup happened in Portugal in April 1974. Others with me continued studying English. I dropped everything and returned to Madrid and asked my father superior in Madrid to let me go back to Mozambique because that was where my heart was. I went back in January 1975 and worked there until 1982, when I went back to Spain, never to return.

This was my work and my journey to Mozambique and back.

CONCLUSION

This book's introduction began with a broad sketch of the Wiriyamu massacre woven with materials from twenty-nine individual respondents on Wiriyamu. Collectively, the twenty-nine respondents and their texts prove without a shadow of doubt certain inalienable truths about the place, the events, and the subsequent narrative of the massacre. Wiriyamu existed. Vasco Tenente tells us so, as do Bulachu Pensadu Zambezi, massacre survivors, and Burgos priests who worked in missions in the Tete region. The Wiriyamu massacre happened. António Mixone, Kalifornia Kaniveti, João Xavier, António Chuva Culher, Enéria Tenente, Kudangirana, Magaissa, Baera, and Djemusse survived the massacres and tell us what they went through. Antonino Melo, the commander who led the counterinsurgent operation Marosca, backs up their story, as does Irmã Lúcia Saez de Ugarte, who flew over Wiriyamu to see for herself the rotting corpses strewn all over the killing fields. Although Chico Kachavi, the secret agent who led the interrogations, died soon after the massacre, his surviving brother confirms who he was and furnishes us with a photo from his identification card to give us a visual.

General Hama Thai, Bulachu Pensadu Zambezi, and João Xavier tell us Wiriyamu was caught between two unenviable propositions, support colonialism or fight it; their circumstantially dictated decision to support, albeit through logistics and recruitment of cadres for Frelimo, sealed its fate as a living community. From a nationalist perspective, Wiriyamu was ideally located to supply arms to General Hama Thai's forces to launch a new front in the Manica-e-Sofala, then a colonial district; this offensive ultimately led to a new massacre in Inhaminga, which was documented and reported a little after the Wiriyamu revelation.[1] Bulachu Pensadu Zambezi's dramatic testimony tells us how Frelimo entered the triangle to recruit men to join Frelimo and win over the chief of Wiriyamu, to support Frelimo logistically at least. Once that was accomplished, Wiriyamu's fate was sealed.

Domingo Kansande and Padre Domingo Ferrão's testimonies dominate the evidence-gathering section of the book, telling us about the laborious process undertaken to collect data on the dead, which was augmented with repeated data-gathering trips among survivors clustered around the Frelimo base near the Luenha tributary. Two priests got the report out of Mozambique: Both were Burgos; both were daringly courageous; one

---

[1] *Relatório dos missionarios de Inhaminga* (Lisbon: Edição do Movimento Justiça e Paz, April, 1974), n.p. Accessed February 9, 2018, www.cd25a.uc.pt/media/pdf/Biblioteca%20digital/NReg%205312_Relatorio%2 0dosMissionariosde%20InhamingaOCR.pdf.

smuggled it in his pocket in broad daylight right under the nose of the secret police, and the other stuffed it in his underwear as he boarded a plane to Madrid via Lisbon.

Thereafter, three testimonial narratives by Mildred Neville, Hugh O'Shaughnessy, and Father Adrian Hastings tell us that, after much internal debate, a powerful clutch of British Catholics backed the story in *The London Times*. Key factors aligned themselves to catapult Wiriyamu into the pages of *The London Times*, among them the CIIR's support of the story; the timing of the story, which coincided with Caetano's visit; and *The London Times*' own internal turmoil. Portugal and its hired hands attacked the story and the key facts, underpinning it as fake news. According to the evidence that Knipe and Wain provide in the book, the Portuguese would nearly have won the fight to discredit the story had it not been for Peter Pringle and Padre Vicente Berenguer. Their testimonies cemented the veracity of the London revelations, leaving an eyewitness Pringle interviewed unprotected from the colonial police in Tete. Padre Sangalo, who whisked the eyewitness, Mixone, to safety, immediately addressed that weakness. Sangalo's testimony is every bit as dramatic as it is central to Wiriyamu as a revealed truth. His rescue left a sole survivor safely protected beyond the clutches of the Portuguese empire.

These then are the inalienable truths about the massacre. Needless to say, gaps in the narrative will remain unfilled, but the integrity of the narrative is impregnably solid. No amount of spuriously argued narratives[2] for invalidation can shake its veracity, now backed by primary source evidence—and the matter should rest here, with Wiriyamu the event and Wiriyamu the revealed narrative as incontestably true.

---

[2] Anonymous, *"Wiriyamu" or a Mare's Nest* (Lisbon: Ministry of Foreign Affairs, 1973); "Lisbon Inquiry Rejects Massacre Story," *The Times*, August 20, 1973, 1; Bruno C. Reis and Pedro A. Oliveira, "Cutting Heads or Winning Hearts: Late Colonial Portuguese Counterinsurgency and the Wiriyamu Massacre of 1972," *Civil Wars* 14, 1 (2012): 80–103.

WORKS CITED

The following bibliography confines to works cited and omits interviews included in the book. These are listed in Table 1 in the Preface. A comprehensive list of texts and archival materials used but not cited directly in the footnotes is given in Mustafah Dhada's *The Portuguese Massacre of Wiriyamu*, pages 197–229.

Archives and Unpublished Papers

ADN/GABMIN, SR. 7, 0035, 047, Ofício n. º 3394/GB, Proc. PS-10-02, de 4 de Junho de 1973.

D. Altino Ribeiro Santana, Bispo da Beira, 1973–1974, PT/AHD/MU/GM/GNP/RNP/0456/07052

Arquivo da Defesa Nacional (ADN)

Arquivo Histórico Diplomático

Arquivo Nacional da Torre do Tombo (TT)

Centro de Estudos Africanos, Universidade Eduardo Mondlane (CEA):
Pasta 967. 5 25/I

PT/TT/D-F/001/00004, December 15, 1971.

PT/TT/PIDE/D-A/1/2826-10, June 11, 1973.

PT/TT/PIDE/D-F/001/00023, August 22, 1973.

Oberlin College Archives:

"Biographical Files, 1950s–2003," and Series 4, 1952–1966. Subseries 1, "Writings by Eduardo Mondlane, 1952–68, n.d.," Box 1.

The Tablet Archives: "Mozambique in London." Accessed December 24, 2013. http: //preview.tinyurl.com/o99ctgj.

Web-Based Resources

One generally useful site to go to as a starting point for any genocide-centered research is, http://www.h-net.org/~genocide/.

For Armenian genocide archives see, www.armenocide.de which holds all German materials on the Armenian Genocide in English translation. See also University of Minnesota's online archive: http://www.chgs.umn.edu/educational/ as well as http://www.chgs.umn.edu/educational/.

For Rwanda Genocide, 1994, consult the following archival holdings: Information, Intelligence and the U.S. Response at http://www.gwu.edu/%7Ensarchiv/NSAEBB/NSAEBB117/index.html; evidence of inaction at http://www.gwu.edu/%7Ensarchiv/NSAEBB/NSAEBB53/index.html; electronic repository for Rwanda related materials at http://www.gwu.edu/%7Ensarchiv/NSAEBB/NSAEBB119/index.htm. Additional Rwanda genocide related documents consisting of 4,705 declassified documents that address the situation in Rwanda are to be found at http://www.rwandadocumentsproject.net/gsdl/cgibin/library.

On the removal of the Aborigine children from their homes to boarding schools, see Colin Tatz at http://www.kooriweb.org/gst/genocide/tatz.html.

Works Cited

Secondary Literature

Adam, Yussuf, and Dyuti, Hilário Alumasse. "Entrevista: o massacre de Mueda – falam testemunhas." *Arquivo* 14 (1993): 117–128.

Alexander, Jocelyn, McGregor, JoAnn, and Ranger, Terence. *Violence and Memory: One Hundred Years in the 'Dark Forests' of Matabeleland*. Oxford: James Currey, 2000.

Alexievich, Svetlana. *Last Witnesses: An Oral History of the Children of World War II*. New York: Random House, 2019.

Alexievich, Svetlana. *The Unwomanly Face of War: An Oral History of Women in World War II*. New York: Random House, 2017.

Alexievich, Svetlana. *Zinky Boys: Soviet Voices from the Afghanistan War*. New York: W. W. Norton, 1992.

Amnesty International. *Annual Report 1973–1974*. London: Amnesty International, 1974.

"An Oral History Bibliography: A Research Guide by the Columbia University Center for Oral History." Accessed February 10, 2019. https://library.columbia.edu/content/dam/libraryweb/locations/ohro/The%20Oral%20History%20Bibliography%20--%20A%20CCOH%20Publication.pdf.

Anderson, David. *Histories of the Hanged: The Dirty War in Kenya and the End of Empire*. New York: W. W. Norton, 2015.

Andrews, Molly, Squire, Corinne, and Tamboukou, Maria, eds. *Doing Narrative Research*, Second edition. Los Angeles, CA: Sage, 2016.

Anonymous. *'Wiriyamu' or a Mare's Nest*. Lisbon: Ministry of Foreign Affairs, 1973.

Arriaga, Kaúlza de, General. *História das Tropas Pára-quedistas Portuguesas, vol. III*, BCP 21, CTP. 1. Accessed January 1, 2010. http://preview.tinyurl.com/qzeovqb.

Azevedo, Carlos A. Moreira. "Perfil biográfico de D. Sebastião Soares de Resende." *Lusitânia Sacra* 2, no. 6 (1994): 391–415.

Bilbija, Ksenija, and Payne, Leigh A., eds. *Accounting for Violence: Marketing Memory in Latin America*. Durham: Duke University Press, 2011.

Cabrita, Felícia. "Os Mortos Não Sofrem." *Revista Expresso*, December 5, 1992.

Cabrita, Felícia. *Massacres em África*. Lisboa: A Esfera dos Livros, 2008.

Cabrita, Felícia. "Wiriyamu, Viagem ao Fundo do Terror." *Revista Expresso*, November 21, 1998.

Cahen, Michel. "The Mueda Case and Maconde Political Ethnicity." *Africana Studia (Porto)*, no. 2 (1999): 29–46.

Calvão, Guilherme Almor. De Alpoím, Comandante da Marinha reformado e ex-combatente na Guerra Colonial. "Quantos Morreram em Mueda?" *Jornal Público*, June 16, 2002.

Chabal, Patrick. *Amílcar Cabral: Revolutionary Leadership and People's War*. Cambridge: Cambridge University Press, 1983.

Chang, Iris. *The Rape of Nanking: The Forgotten Holocaust of World War II*. New York: Basic Books, 2012.

Chipande, Alberto Joaquim. "The Massacre of Mueda." *Mozambique Revolution* 43 (1970): 12–14.

Collingwood, Robin George. *The Idea of History*. Oxford: Oxford University Press, 1994.

Comaroff, Jean, and Comaroff, John L. *Theory from the South, or, How Euro-America Is Evolving Toward Africa*. Stanford: Stanford University Press, 2012.

De Fina, Anna. "Narratives in Interviews — The Case of Accounts: For an Interactional Approach to Narrative Genres." *Narrative Inquiry* 19, no. 2 (2009): 233–58.

Dhada, Mustafah. *The Portuguese Massacre of Wiriyamu in Colonial Mozambique, 1964–2013*. London: Bloomsbury Academic Press, 2017.

Dhada, Mustafah. "The Wiriyamu Massacre of 1972: Its Context, Genesis, and Revelation." *History in Africa* (June 2013): 1–31.

Dhada, Mustafah. *Warriors at Work: How Guinea Was Really Set Free*. Niwot: University Press of Colorado, 1993.

Elkins, Caroline. *Imperial Reckoning: The Untold Story of Britain's Gulag in Kenya*. New York: Holt Paperbacks, 2005.

"Esclusivo: Massacri Nel Mozambico." *Cablo Press* (June 4, 1973): 5–11.

e Silva, Teresa Cruz. "Igrejas Protestantes no Sul de Moçambique e nacionalismo: O Caso da 'Missão Suíça' (1940–1974)." *Estudos Moçambicanos*, no. 10 (1992): 19–39.

e Silva, Teresa Cruz. *Protestant Churches and the Formation of Political Consciousness in Southern Mozambique (1930–1974)*. Basel: P. Schlettwein Publishing, 2001.

e Silva, Teresa Cruz. "The Influence of the Swiss Mission on Eduardo Mondlane (1930–1961)." *Journal of Religion in Africa* 28, no. 2 (1998): 187–209.

Ferreira, Hugo Gil. *Portugal's Revolution: Ten Years On*. Cambridge: Cambridge University Press, 2011.

Fields, Rona M. *Portuguese Revolution and the Armed Focus Movement*. Santa Barbara, CA: Praeger, 1976.

"From the Editors: Genocide Tourism—Educational Value or Voyeurism?" *Journal of Genocide Research* 9, no. 4 (2007): 513–15.

Funada-Classen, Sayaka. *The Origins of War in Mozambique: A History of Unity and Division*. Cape Town: African Minds, 2013.

Gellately, Robert, and Kiernan, Ben, eds. *The Specter of Genocide: Mass Murder in Historical Perspective*. Cambridge: Cambridge University Press, 2003.

Gourevitch, Phillip. *We Wish to Inform You That Tomorrow We Will Be Killed with Our Families: Stories from Rwanda*. New York: Picador, 1999.

Hastings, Adrian. "Reflections upon the War in Mozambique." *African Affairs* 292 (1974): 263–76.

Hastings, Adrian. *Wiriyamu: My Lai in Mozambique*. London: Orbis, 1974.

Hastings, Adrian, and Lowrie, Ingrid, eds. *Christianity and the African Imagination: Essays in Honour of Adrian Hastings, Studies of Religion in Africa*. Leiden: Brill Academic Publications, 2001.

Helgesson, Alf. *Church, State and People in Mozambique: An Historical Study with Special Emphasis on Methodist Developments in the Inhambane Region*. Uppsala: Studia Missionalia Upsaliensia, 1994.

Henriksen, Thomas H. *Revolution and Counterrevolution: Mozambique's War of Independence 1964–1974*. London: Greenwood Press, 1978.

Herbert Shore Collection, Oberlin College Included: Series 1. "Biographical Files, 1950s–2003," and Series 4. 1952–1966. Subseries 1, "Writings by Eduardo Mondlane, 1952–68, n. d.," Box 1.

Hochschild, Adam. *King Leopold's Ghost: A Story of Greed, Terror, and Heroism in Colonial Africa*. New York: Mariner Books, 1999.

IDAF. *Terror in Tete: A Documentary Report of Portuguese Atrocities in Tete District, Mozambique, 1971–1972*. London: IDAF, 1973.

Introduction to Oral History. Waco, Texas: Baylor University Institute for Oral History, 2016.

Israel, Paolo I. "Mueda Massacre: The Musical Archive." *Journal of Southern African Studies* 43, no. 6: 1157–79.

Jorge, Lídia. *A Costa dos Murmúrios*. Lisboa: Publicações Dom Quixote, 2008.

Karodia, Farida. *A Shattering of Silence*. Oxford: Heinemann, 1993.

Kiernan, Ben. *Blood and Soil: A World History of Genocide and Extermination from Sparta to Darfur*. New Haven: Yale University Press, 2007.

Lackner, Helen. *Yemen in Crisis: Road to War*. London: Verso, 2019.

Works Cited

Lemarchand, René, ed. *Forgotten Genocides: Oblivion, Denial, and Memory*. Philadelphia: University of Pennsylvania Press, 2013.

Lennon, John, and Foley, Malcolm. *Dark Tourism: The Attraction of Death and Disaster*. London: Continuum, 2000.

Leydesdorff, Selma. *Surviving the Bosnia Genocide: The Women of Srebrenica Speak*. Bloomington: Indiana University Press, 2015.

Lima, A. Carlos. *Aspectos da Liberdade Religiosa. Caso do Bispo da Beira*. Lisboa/Braga: Diário do Minho, 1970.

Lima, Carlos. *Caso do Bispo da Beira, Documentos*. Porto: Civilização, 1990.

Madlingozi, Tshepo. "On Transitional Justice Entrepreneurs and the Production of Victims." *Journal of Human Rights Practice* 2, no. 2 (2010): 208–28.

Marcum, John A. *The Angolan Revolution, Vol 1: The Anatomy of An Explosion*. Cambridge: The MIT Press, 1969.

Marcum, John A. *The Angolan Revolution, Vol 2: Exile Politics and Guerilla Warfare, 1962–1976*. Cambridge: The MIT Press, 1978.

Marcum, John A. (Author), Burke III, Edmund, and Clough, Michael W., eds. *Conceiving Mozambique*. London, UK: Palgrave Macmillan, 2018.

Mazuza, Abel, and Mate, Xadreque. *Vida e Obra de Armando Tivane, 1937–1973*. Maputo: ARPAC-Instituto de Investigação Sócio-Cultural, 2013.

Minter, William. *Portuguese Africa and the West*. New York: Monthly Review Press, 1972.

Mondlane, Eduardo. *The Struggle for Mozambique*. London: Zed Press, 1983.

Morier-Genoud, Eric. "The Catholic Church, Religious Orders and the Making of Politics in Colonial Mozambique: The Case of the Diocese of Beira, 1940–1974." PhD diss., State University of New York, 2005.

"Mueda evocada em Portugal." *Notícias*, June 13, 1981.

"Mueda: memórias de um massacre." *Tempo 609* (June 13, 1982): 24.

Oliveira, Paulo. "Kaúlza de Arriaga e o 'Peso de Wiriamu.'" *Público*, February 4, 2004.

Olson, James S., and Robert, Randy. *My Lai: A Brief History With Documents*. New York: Bedford/St Martin's, 1998.

Olusoga, David, and Erichsen, Casper W. *The Kaiser's Holocaust: Germany's Forgotten Genocide and the Colonial Roots of Nazism*. London: Faber and Faber, 2011.

Operacional: Defesa, Forças Armadas de Segurança. Accessed June 13, 2012. http: //preview. tinyurl.com/l7jdxrv.

Panaf Great Lives. *Eduardo Mondlane*. London: Panaf, 1972.

Papachristophorou, Marilena. "Orality, Transcription and Construction of Data." *Indian Folklore* 4, no. 1 (2003): 13–15.

Parker, Kevin. "Wiriyamu and the War in Tete, 1971–1974." MA thesis, University of York, 1982.

Ponchaud, François. *Cambodia Year Zero*. New York: Penguin Books, 1978.

Porch, Douglas. *Portuguese Armed Forces and the Revolution*. Stanford, CA: Hoover Institution, 1977.

"Quantos Morreram En Mueda." Macua.org. Accessed December 16, 2011. http://www.Macua.Org /Quantos_Morreram_Em_Mueda.htm.

Reis, C., and Oliveira, Pedro A. "Cutting Heads or Winning Hearts: Late Colonial Portuguese Counterinsurgency and the Wiriyamu Massacre of 1972." *Civil Wars* 14, no. 1 (2012): 80–103.

Relatorio dos missionarios de inhaminga. Lisboa: Edição do Movimento Justiça e Paz, April 1974, n.p. Accessed February 9, 2018. http://www.cd25a.uc.pt/media/pdf/Biblioteca%20digi tal/NReg%205312_Relatorio%20dosMissionariosde%20InhamingaOCR.pdf.

Resende, Sebastião Soares de. *Os Grandes Relativos Humanos em Moçambique*. Porto: Livraria Nelita Editora, 1957.

Resende, Sebastião Soares de. *Problemas do Ensino Missionário*. Beira: Tip. E. A. O., 1962.

Resende, Sebastião Soares de. *Responsabilidades dos Leigos*. Porto: Oficinas Gráficas da Sociedade de Papelaria Ltd., 1957.

Resende, Sebastião Soares de. *Um Moçambique Melhor*. Lisboa: Livraria Morais Editora, 1963.

"Reunião de indígenas perturbada por agitadores estrangeiros que foram repelidos." *O Século*, June 19, 1960.

Roulston, Kathryn, deMarrais, Kathleen, and Lewis, Jamie B. "Learning to Interview in the Social Sciences." *Qualitative Inquiry* 9, no. 3 (2003): 643–68.

Saavedra, Ricardo de. *Os Dias Do Fim*. Lisboa: Editorial Notícias, 1995.

Sansone, Livio. "Eduardo Mondlane and the Social Sciences." *Vibrant—Virtual Brazilian Anthropology*, 10, no. 2 (July–December 2013): 73–111.

Santos, José Rodrigues dos. *O Anjo Branco*. Lisboa: Grávida, 2010.

Sassine, Williams. *Wiriyamu*. London: Heinemann, 1980.

Schmidt, Heike I. *Colonialism and Violence in Zimbabwe: A History of Suffering*. Oxford: James Currey, 2013.

Schuman, Donna L., Lawrence, Karen A., and Pope, Natalie. "Broadcasting War Trauma: An Exploratory Netnography of Veterans' YouTube Vlogs." *Qualitative Health Research* 29, no. 3 (2018): 357–70.

Shoeb, Marwa, Weinstein, Harvey, and Mollica, Richard. "The Harvard Trauma Questionnaire: Adapting a Cross-Cultural Instrument for Measuring Torture, Trauma and Post-traumatic Stress Disorder in Iraqi Refugees." *International Journal of Social Psychiatry* 53, no. 3 (2007): 447–63.

Shopes, Linda. *Web Guides to Doing Oral History*. Murfreesboro, TN: Oral History Association, 2012.

Sin, Chich Hoong. "Seeking Informed Consent: Reflection on Research Practice." *Sociology* 39, no. 2: 277–94.

Singh, Amrit. *Death by Drone*. New York: Open Society Foundation, 2015.

Spínola, António Sebastião Ribeiro de. *Portugal e o Futuro: Análise da Conjuntura Nacional*. Lisboa: Editora Arcádia, 1974.

Stapleton, Timothy J. *A History of Genocide in Africa*. Santa Barbara, CA: Praeger, 2017.

Strong, Liz H., Clark, Mary Marshall, and Bertin-Mahieux, Caitlin, eds. *Oral History Transcription Style Guide*. New York: Columbia University Center for Oral History Research, 2018.

Sturken, Marita. *Tourists of History, Memory, Kitsch and Consumerism from Oklahoma City to Ground Zero*. Durham: Duke University Press, 2007.

Sunday Times of London Insight. *Insight on Portugal: The Year of the Captains*. London: Andre Deutsch, 1975.

Szabla, Christopher. "Against the Memory Industry." *Maisonneuve*, January 6, 2012.

Tajú, Gulamo. "Dom Sebastião Soares de Resende, Primeiro Bispo da Beira: Notas Para Uma Cronologia." *Arquivo, Boletim do Arquivo Histórico de Moçambique* 6 (October 1989): 149–76.

Tembe, T. Joel Neves. "Uhura na Kazi: Recapturing MANU Nationalism Through the Archive." *Kronos* 39 (November 2013): 257–79.

Thomas, Martin. *Violence and Colonial Order: Police, Workers and Protest in the European Colonial Empires, 1918–1940*. Cambridge: Cambridge University Press, 2012.

Thomas, Martin, Moore, Bob, and Butler, L. J. *Crises of Empire: Decolonization and Europe's Imperial States*, Second edition. London: Bloomsbury Academic Press, 2015.

Thompson, Paul. *The Voice of the Past*. Oxford: Oxford University Press, 1988.

Totten, Samuel. *Centuries of Genocide: Essays and Eyewitness Accounts*. New York: Routledge, 2012.

Totten, Samuel, and Ubaldo, Rafiki, eds. *We Cannot Forget: Interviews with Survivors of the 1994 Genocide in Rwanda*. New Brunswick: Rutgers University Press, 2011.

Works Cited

Vansena, Jan M. *Oral Tradition as History*. Madison: The University of Wisconsin Press, 1985.

Venter, A. J. *Portugal's Guerilla Wars in Africa: Lisbon's Three Wars in Angola, Mozambique and Portuguese Guinea, 1964–74*. Southhill, UK: Helion and Company, 2013.

Wiarda, Howard J. *Corporatism and Development: The Portuguese Experience*. Boston: University of Massachusetts Press, 1977.

Periodicals

Africa Report:

2 (1966): 30.

1 (1967): 30.

The London Times:

March 16, 1973, 8a.

May 17, 1973, 18h.

May 23, 1973, 6h.

July 11, 1973, 1.

July 12, 1973, 16a.

July 16, 1973, 1.

July 21, 1973.

July 20, 1973.

July 25, 1973, 1.

August 20, 1973, 1.

April 24, 1974, 8.

May 15, 1974, 5.

December 10, 1974, 1.

The London Sunday Times:

July 15, 1973, 16 and 17.

July 29, 1973, 1.

December 9, 1973, 9.

GLOSSARY

ADN Arquivo da Defesa Nacional, National Defense Archives
AHD Arquivo Histórico Diplomático, Diplomatic History Archives
ANC African National Congress
Aphani Wense! Kill the lot!
BBC British Broadcasting Corporation
BOSS [South African] Bureau for State Security
Cachaço Spirits from white flour, tamarind, and baobab fruit
CAFOD Catholic Agency for Overseas Development
CBS Columbia Broadcasting System
CES Centro de Estudos Sociais, Social Studies Center, Coimbra University
CFMAG Committee for Freedom in Mozambique, Angola, and Guinea
CGDB Cambodian Genocide Databases
Chico Kangoma Kabodzi Chico the Drummer
Chimbawas Vestal virgins
CIIR Catholic Institute of International Relations
COREMO Comité Revolucionário de Moçambique, Revolutionary Committee of Mozambique
CSUB California State University, Bakersfield
Curendeiro Herbalist
DGS Direção-Geral de Segurança, General Directorate for Security
FCT Fundação para a Ciência e a Tecnologia, Foundation for Science and Technology
Frelimo Frente de Libertação de Moçambique, Front for the Liberation of Mozambique
GE Grupos Especiais, Special Forces
IDOC International Documentation on the Contemporary Church
ITN Independent Television Network
ITV Independent Television Service
Kabandazi The corporeal intermediary for the *mphondorho*
Kadembo The Stinker, nickname given to Raimundo Dalepa, Frelimo commander stationed near Luenha
Lenha Kindling
M'zungo White person
Machamba Horticultural plot
MANU Mozambique African National Union
Massa Cornflour porridge
MFA Movimento das Forças Armadas, Armed Forces Movement
Mfumo Chief
Mphondorho Lion spirit, inducer of rain
NATO North Atlantic Treaty Organization
Ngozi Baobab tree
OAU Organization of African Unity
OPV Organização Provincial de Voluntários, Provincial Organization of Volunteers
OPVDC Organização Provincial de Voluntários para Defesa Civil, Provincial Organization of Volunteers for Civil Defense

Glossary

PIDE Polícia Internacional e de Defesa do Estado, International Police for the Defense of the State
Poço Water well
Pombe Local brews from flour and sugar
SJ Society of Jesus, missionary order
SPCK Society for Promoting Christian Knowledge
TAP Transportes Aéreos Portugueses
Thundo Sorcerer's bag
TT Arquivo Nacional da Torre do Tombo, Portuguese National Archives at Torre do Tombo
Turras Terrorists, a term the Portuguese used for Frelimo insurgents
UDENAMO União Democrática Nacional de Moçambique, the National Democratic Union of
Mozambique
UN United Nations
UNAMI União Africana de Moçambique Independente, National African Union of
Independent Mozambique
ZANU Zimbabwe African National Union
ZAPU Zimbabwe African People's Union
ZOT Zona Operacional de Tete

INDEX

Alexievich, Svetlana   xxx
Amnesty International   13, 147, 149, 161, 162, 186, 193
archives
    ADN (O Arquivo da Defesa Nacional), National Defense Archives   18 n.65
    AHD (Arquivo Histórico Diplomático)   4 n.13
    CFMAG (Committee for Freedom in Mozambique, Angola, and Guinea)   182
    CGDB (Cambodian Genocide Databases)   xxx n.29
    IDOC (International Documentation on the Contemporary Church)   134
    TT (Arquivo Nacional da Torre do Tombo), Portuguese National Archives at Torre do Tombo   209

Baker, Eric   147
baobab   11, 37, 38, 42, 46, 53, 76, 77, 86, 95, 98, 99, 171, 178, 193, 200, 202
B Caç   55
Biggs-Davison, John   145
Blumenau, Eva   161, see also Amnesty International

Cabrita, Felícia   53, 55, 57, 62
Caetano, Marcelo1, 2, 14, 15, 16, 17, 26, 66, 121, 122, 134, 141, 145, 148, 149, 153–4, 156, 157, 164, 169, 192, 193, 208
Caradon, Lord   154, 157
Catholic bishops, archbishops and Cardinals
    Alfrink, Cardenal Bernardus Johannes   161
    César, Bishop Dom Augusto   111, 114
    Durrieu, Bishop Louis-Marie-Joseph   150
    Gomes, Bishop António Ferreira   130, 131, 135, 152
    Heenan, Cardinal John   145
    Konstant, Father David, Leeds Bishop   143
    Pinto, Bishop Dom Vieira   123
    Resende, Bishop Dom Sebastião Soares de   x, 3, 6, 28, 152
    Ribeiro, Bishop Félix Niza   1, 110, 114, 119
    Silva, Bishop Dom Augusto César Alves Ferreira da   111
Catholic missionary societies
    Burgos Fathers   4, 8, 12, 13, 14, 16, 28, 77, 78, 113, 114, 128, 129, 131, 132, 134, 138, 139

Combonians   113, 114, 195, 199, 200, 201
White Fathers   4, 13, 29, 150–1, 153, 195, 201, 206
Catholic missions and seminaries
    Boroma   26, 66, 77, 78, 200, 201
    Changara   xxi, xxii, 4, 8, 11, 12, 26, 33, 101, 103, 109, 137, 138, 140, 192, 199, 200, 201, 202, 204
    Chioco   26, 31, 33, 40, 78, 192
    Lundo   4, 131
    Marara   4, 26, 28, 78, 114, 116, 197, 200
    Matundo   4, 16, 116, 119, 195, 196, 199, 201, 202, 203
    Miruru   192
    Moatize   4, 6, 57, 66, 129, 136, 191, 201
    Mucumbura   xxiv, 4, 6, 8, 11, 12, 14, 26, 27, 28, 30, 32, 33, 41, 116
    Muraça   4, 12, 131, 139
    Mutarara   4, 21, 22, 127, 138, 139
    Parish, Sacred Family, Beira   192
    Pedro, Missão São   65, 76, 77, 103, 110, 111, 113, 195, 196, 198, 199, 201, 202, 203, 204
    Pery, Vila   192, 199
    Seminary, Kipalapala   153
    Seminary, Pamplona   195
    Sussundenga   192
    Unkanha   4, 6, 138, 192, 195, 196, 206
    Wanki   154, 155
    Zóbuè   xxiv, 4, 8, 29, 191
Catholic nuns and priests, see also Berenguer; Moure; Sangalo Ferrao; Hastings; interview list; Lucia
    Anaveros, Padre   14, 205
    Antoni, Padre Miguel   157, 159, 191
    Artazcoz, Padre   13, 14, 157
    Bosque, Padre Miguel del   77
    Carbonell, Padre Mateus   161
    Castro, Padre Luis Alfonso   114
    Claudio, Padre   xxiv
    Costa, Padre Luís Afonso da   28, 182
    Elvira, Sister   139
    Ferrando, Padre Enrique   xxiv, 6, 133, 195
    Gomes, Padre Jesus Camba   130, 131, 135
    Guedes, Father   151
    Joseph, Padre   xxiv
    Jovete, Padre   195, 201
    Martins, Padre   132

Index

Navarro, Padre   205
Palagi, Padre Giacono   xxiv
Pascoal, Padre   191
Ugarte, Irmã Lúcia Saez de   xxii, xxv, xxvi, 10,
      118, 207
Valverde, Padre Alfonso   132, 138, 154, 161,
      162, 192, 195
van Asten, Father Theo   150–1, 152, 153
Catholic societies
      Fathers, Burgos   4, 8, 12, 13, 14, 16, 28, 77, 78,
            113, 114, 128, 129, 131, 132, 134, 138, 139,
            148, 152, 154, 155, 157, 158, 160, 182, 183,
            191, 195, 196, 204
      Fathers, Comboni   28
      Fathers, The White   12–13, 29, 150–1, 153,
            201, 206
      Fathers, Verona   162
Chief Buxo   27, 28
Chief Chaworha   xxi, xxv, xxvii, xxviii, 8, 9, 10, 12,
      13, 14, 27, 37, 39, 42, 46, 71–7, 78, 79, 84,
      85, 86, 87, 90, 101, 111, 112, 113, 117, 118,
      155, 197, 199, 200, 202
Chief Djemusse   xxi, xxv, xxvii, 8, 11, 37, 39,
      40, 41, 45, 46, 70, 80, 82, 85, 87, 93, 97–8,
      100, 207
Chief Gandar   30, 84, 118
Chief Gozinho   95
Chief Kongorhogondo   41
Chief M'Chenga   40, 45, 95, 96, 102–3, 104, 105,
      106, 108, 109
Chief Matambo   10
Chief Mkumbi   75, 105
Chief Thaurhu   75
Chief Wiriyamu   37, 38, 39, 40, 41–3, 45, 46, 73,
      80, 82, 84, 85, 86, 87, 88
College, Selly Oaks   14, 155
Colonial mass violence   2, 8, 18, 189
the cover up   110–11, 115–17
Cruzamento Dezoito   48, 49, 80

Davis, Pat   147
Dr. Paz   119–20, 121–4

18th Parallel   42
Ennals, Martin   161, see also
            Amnesty International
Evans, James   186

Feeny, Margaret   142
Filochowski, Julian   148
foreign cities
      Addis Ababa   168
      Alicante   190, 191
      Barcelona   137, 191
      Bellagio   161

Blantyre   22, 169
Burgos city   129, 130
Cambridge   161
Chatham   175
Chifombo   78
Chilworth   161
Dar es Salam   2, 78, 79, 168, 193
Dortmund   161
Guildford   161
Heathrow   15, 158
Johannesburg   185, 186
Lisbon   13, 15, 16, 47, 60, 61, 132, 133,
            134, 136, 140, 146, 147, 149, 161, 163,
            170, 175, 179, 182, 184, 186, 187, 203,
            205, 208
London   xx, xxii, xxvi, 14, 15, 16, 57, 121,
            122, 142, 143, 145, 147, 148, 153, 154, 155,
            156, 158, 159, 160, 162, 167, 169, 173, 179,
            182, 184, 186, 192, 199
Lusaka   23, 78, 206
Madrid   13–14, 16, 130, 132–6, 138, 140, 148,
            155, 156, 157, 158, 182, 183, 186, 192, 205,
            206, 208
Medellín   143
Moscow   187
Newcastle   170
New York City   xxii, 15, 159, 187
Oxford   146, 150, 156, 180
Paris   149, 154, 192
Plain, Salisbury   175
Porto   3, 57, 60, 152
Portsmouth   167, 175
Pretoria   148
Rome   3, 13, 121, 151, 182
Salamanca   14, 146, 148, 154, 155, 157
Tottenham   206
Valencia   129, 191
foreign states
      Algeria   135
      Belgium   192
      Colombia   143, 152
      Germany   161, 162, 192, 193
      Greece   161
      Guinea-Bissau   1
      Japan   191
      Malawi   21–5, 79, 139, 153, 169, 170
      Mexico   131
      Netherlands   192
      Northern, Ireland   175, 182, 183
      Rhodesia   6, 14, 27, 148, 152, 154, 157, 173,
            174, 175, 176, 178, 179, 180, 191
      São Tomé   149
      South Africa   27, 37, 143, 148, 165, 168, 169,
            170, 173,182, 185
      Soviet, Union   187

Spain   14, 16, 129–30, 132, 133, 134, 136,
    138, 140, 154, 155, 190, 191, 195, 201, 204,
    205, 206
Sweden   144, 160
Tanzania   16, 22, 24, 27, 41, 78, 79, 116, 117,
    151, 153, 160, 168
Uganda   151, 153
Vietnam   135, 165, 175, 179
Zambia   6, 16, 23, 24, 25, 29, 78, 153, 161,
    168, 169, 191, 195, 206
Zimbabwe   27, 28, 34, 37, 67, 108, 129, 134, 144
Frelimo
    Frelimo Frente de Libertação de Moçambique,
        Front for the Liberation of Mozambique   3
Frelimo bases
    Chioco   26, 31, 33, 40, 78, 192
    Kadembo   41–3, 72, 88, 93
    M'Pharhamadwe   41
    Nachingwea   22, 23, 29, 30, 78
    Richard   43
Frelimo leaders
    Caetano, Mariano Pinta   26
    Caliate, Zeca   33, 40, 78
    Chissano, Joaquim   78–9
    Chissone, Carlos Nunes   26
    Dalepa, Raimundo   6, 8, 26, 30, 31, 32, 39, 40,
        41, 72, 88, 93, 108, 138, 196
    Danda, Damião de Sanchez   26
    Escabalca, Zacarias   26
    Gaster, Polly   163, 182
    Gruveta, Major General
        BonifácioMassamba   6, 22, 24
    Gwenjere, Mateus   28
    Hama Thai, General António   6
    Kadembo, Raimundo Dalepa   41, 42, 43, 72,
        88, 93
    Machel, Samora   4, 25, 26, 27, 31, 33, 78
    Magoé, Pedro   26
    Matsinhe, Mariano   193
    Matsinhe, Mariano de Araújo   6, 24
    Moiane, José   41
    Mondlane, Eduardo   3, 23, 168
    Mondlane, Janet   163
    Napalula, Commandante   26
    Nenhumfica, Raimundo Dalepa   31
    Nkume, Donai   39
    Panguene, Armando   193
    Rebelo, Jorge   168
    Salvador, Commandante   26
    Santos, Alexandre dos   106
    Santos, Marcelino dos   114, 160, 163, 193
    Tavane, Armando   40
    Tenente, Alverino   40, 41
    Thai, General Hama   xxi, xxv, 207
Frelimo military strategy   103, 106, 108

Hastings, Susan   155
Hotel Morgado   123, 124
Hotel Polana   184
Hotel Zambêzia   16, 179, 183

images   xxiv
informants
    British Catholics   208
    British journalists   17
    evidence gatherers   101, 110
    eyewitness protectors   190–2
    Frelimo commanders   19, 78
    Portuguese military commander   4
    Portuguese secret police   9, 16
    survivors   xxv, xxvi, xxix, 8, 9, 10, 11, 12, 15,
        16, 51, 70, 75, 92, 94, 105, 107, 112, 113,
        115, 119, 121, 135, 136, 198, 199, 202,
        207
international organizations
    Amnesty International   13, 147, 149, 161, 162,
        186, 193
    North Atlantic Treaty Organization
        (NATO)   148
    UN   157, 159–61, 169, 187
    United Nations Special Committee of 24 on
        Decolonization   15
interpreters and translators
    Karimu, Abidu   xxi, xxv, xxvii, xxix
    Senhor Elídio   xxi, xxvii, xxix
interviewee list
    Baera   xxv, 11, 70, 97, 98, 99, 207
    Berenguer, Padre Vicente   xxiv, 8, 11, 12, 13,
        16, 28, 77, 101, 103, 119, 131, 136, 138, 140,
        182, 189, 190, 208
    Culher, António Chuva   xxi, xxv, 69, 89, 207
    Djemusse   xxi, xxv, xxvii, 8, 11, 37, 39, 40,
        41, 45, 46, 70, 80, 82, 85, 87, 93, 97–8,
        100, 207
    Ferrão, Padre Domingo   xxi, 9, 11, 12, 16, 28,
        74, 76, 77–8, 79, 103, 105–6, 107–10, 115,
        117, 119, 130, 140, 189, 192, 196, 198, 199,
        201, 207
    Hama Thai, General   xxi, xxv, 207
    Hastings, Father Adrian   xxii, xxv, xxvi, 14–15,
        17, 121, 130, 133, 134, 141, 142, 145, 150,
        158, 159, 169, 182, 186, 208
    Kachavi, António   xxi, 65
    Kaniveti, Kalifornia   xxi, xxv, 10, 69, 80, 207
    Kansande, Domingo   xxi, 8, 9, 11, 12, 101,
        102, 113, 115, 207
    Knipe, Michael   xxi, xxiv, 15, 166, 167, 175,
        176, 178, 182, 184
    Kudangirana   xxi, xxv, 11, 70, 97, 99, 100, 207
    Magaissa   xxi, xxv, 11, 70, 97, 207
    Melo, Antonino   xxi, xxv, 8, 17, 19, 47, 207

Index

Mixone, António   xxi, xxv, 9, 10, 11, 12, 16, 69, 71, 72, 74, 77, 78, 101, 111–18, 136, 161, 199, 201, 202, 203, 204, 206, 207–8

Moure, Padre Júlio   xxv, 12, 13, 16, 28, 131, 133, 136, 155, 192

Neville, Mildred   xxii, xxv, xxvi, 14, 141, 142, 146, 147, 148, 149, 153, 154, 208

O'Shaughnessy, Hugh   xxii, xxv, 14, 141, 143, 146, 157, 208

Pringle, Peter   xxii, xxv, 15, 16, 77, 135, 159, 160, 161, 165, 167, 173, 180, 182, 185, 186, 198, 208

Sangalo, Padre José   xxii, 16, 77, 78, 116, 127, 136, 140, 162, 189, 192, 194, 195, 197, 202, 203, 208

Tenente, Enéria   xxi, xxv, xxvi, xxvii, 70, 207

Tenente, Vasco   xxi, xxv, 19, 38, 44, 91, 93, 95, 120, 207

Ugarte, Irmã Lúcia Saez de   xxii, xxv, xxvi, 10, 118, 207

Wain, Christopher   xxii, xxv, 15, 165, 171, 172, 208

Xavier, João   xxi, xxv, 69, 82, 85, 207

Zambezi, Bulachu Pensadu   xxi, 8, 19, 36, 40, 207

interview list   xxi–xxii

interview methods   xix, xx

interviews excluded   xxxii

journalists and editors, *see also* interviewee list; Knipe; Pringle; Wain

Barry, John   181, 182

Chancellor, Alexander   187

Crimi, Bruno   134

Evans, Harry   181

Heren, Louis   14, 15, 141, 144, 148–9, 156, 159, 161, 162, 169

Hodgkin, Teddy   167

Legum, Colin   162, 163

Lord Thomson   167

Loudon, Bruce   182, 186

Norris, Bill   168

Rees-Mogg, William   14, 156, 167, 168

Kachavi, Chico, Assassination   9

Luso-African liberation   xxxi

MacBride, Sean   161, *see also* Amnesty International

maps

Chieftaincies of the Wiriyamu Triangle   7, 8

Church Missions and Place Names in Tete   5

Wiriyamu Triangle   xviii, 7

Massacres, Chaworha   xxi, xxv, xxvii, xxviii, 8, 9, 10, 12, 13, 14, 27, 37, 39, 42, 46, 71–7, 78, 79, 84, 85, 86, 87, 90, 101, 111, 112, 113, 117, 118, 155, 197, 199, 200, 202

Massacres, Djemusse xxi, xxv, xxviii, 8, 11, 37, 39, 40, 41, 45, 46, 70, 80, 82, 85, 87, 93, 97–100, 207

Massacres: general

Armenia   xxix

Bosnia   xxvi, xxx

Cambodia   xxx

Congo, free state   xxx

Herero-Nama   xxix

Mau Mau   xxx

My Lai   xxix, 15

Nanking   xxix

Rwanda   xx, xxx, 18

Massacres, Juawu   xxi, xxviii, 8, 10, 37, 38, 39, 40,41, 46, 51, 80, 82, 83, 85, 86, 87, 97, 100, 112

Massacres, Riachu   xxviii, 8, 11, 37, 38, 39, 40, 42

Massacres: Tete

Chaworha   xxi, xxv, xxvii, xxviii, 8, 9, 10, 12, 13, 14, 27, 37, 39, 42, 46, 71–7, 78, 79, 84, 85, 86, 87, 90, 101, 111, 112, 113, 117, 118, 155, 197, 199, 200, 202

Djemusse   xxi, xxv, xxviii, 8, 11, 37, 39, 40, 41, 45, 46, 70, 80, 82, 85, 87, 93, 97–100, 207

Estima   8, 33, 34

Inhaminga   9, 207

Juawu   xxi, xxviii, 8, 10, 37, 38, 39, 40, 41, 46, 51, 80, 82, 83, 85, 86, 87, 97, 100, 112

Mucumbura   xxiv, 4, 6, 8, 11, 12, 14, 26, 27, 28, 30, 32, 41, 116, 133, 134, 138, 154, 155, 192, 195, 196

Mueda   3, 60, 112

Riachu   xxviii, 8, 11, 37, 38, 39, 40, 42

Wiriyamu   xix–xx, xxi, xxiii–xxxi, 3, 6, 8, 9–10, 12–13, 15–18, 26, 29, 30, 36–46, 48, 52, 54–5, 62, 67, 71–2, 74, 78, 80, 82–9, 91–4, 96–8, 100, 103–5, 107, 111–13, 117–18, 120–2, 124, 126, 130, 132–7, 140, 143–5, 148–50, 153–64, 169–72, 175–6, 178, 181–2, 186–8, 192–3, 197–9, 206, 207–8

Massacres, The Immediate Aftermath   47

Massacres, The Revelation   133–6

Massacres, Wiriyamu   xix–xx, xxi, xxiii–xxxi, 3, 6, 8, 9–10, 12–13, 15–18, 26, 29, 30, 36–46, 48, 52, 54–5, 62, 67, 71–2, 74, 78, 80, 82–9, 91–4, 96–8, 100, 103–5, 107, 111–13, 117–18, 120–2, 124, 126, 130, 132–7, 140, 143–5, 148–50, 153–64, 169–72, 175–6, 178, 181–2, 186–8, 192–3, 197–9, 206, 207–8

Massacre victims, list   xxviii

mass violence   1–3, 8, 18, 141, 189
media publications
  BBC (British Broadcasting Corporation)   186
  CBS (Columbia Broadcasting System)   144
  Express, The Daily   159, 160, 167
  Famiglia Cristiana   159
  Guardian, The   147, 156, 160
  Herald, The Catholic   162
  Independent, The   187
  Independent Television Service (ITV)   159
  International, Kayhan   181
  ITN (Independent Television Network)
    171, 175
  Observer, The   146, 149, 160, 161, 162, 163, 187
  People, The   167
  Portsmouth Evening News, The   167
  Search Press, The   162
  SPCK (Society for Promoting Christian
    Knowledge)   162
  Spectator, The   187
  Sunday Times, The London   15, 16, 147, 157,
    158, 159, 160, 165, 167, 181, 182, 184,
    185, 186
  Telegraph, The Daily   157, 158, 159, 160, 167,
    182, 187
  Television, The Southern   167, 175
  Times, The London   xv, xix, xx, 8, 12, 14, 15,
    16, 17, 114, 135, 141, 144, 148, 149, 156,
    157, 158, 159, 160, 161, 162, 167, 168, 169,
    170, 171, 172, 173, 177, 179, 182, 198,
    199, 208
  Times, The London Financial   146
Mozambican nationalist organizations
  COREMO (Comité Revolucionário de
    Moçambique, Revolutionary Committee of
    Mozambique)   23, 153
  MANU (Mozambique African National
    Union)   23
  UDENAMO (União Democrática Nacional
    de Moçambique, the National Democratic
    Union of Mozambique)   23
  UNAMI (União Africana de Moçambique
    Independente, National African Union of
    Independent Mozambique)   23
Mozambique place names
  Aluiro   26
  Beira   3, 4, 6, 12, 13, 14, 16, 21–2, 24, 25, 32,
    47, 60, 63, 131, 135, 139, 140, 152, 162, 170,
    172, 173, 183, 192, 205
  Cachembere   28
  Cahora Bassa   6, 23, 26, 29, 32, 33, 67, 113
  Chaworha   xxi, xxv, xxvii, xxviii, 8, 9, 10, 12,
    13, 14, 27, 37, 39, 42, 46, 71–7, 78, 79, 84,
    85, 86, 87, 90, 101, 111, 112, 113, 117, 118,
    155, 197, 199, 200, 202

  Chimoio   13, 131
  Chioco   26, 31, 33, 40, 78, 192
  Cruzamento Dezoito   48, 49, 80
  18th Parallel   42
  Fingoé   25, 78
  Gama   42, 82, 87, 113
  Inhangoma   103, 138
  Kabvumbo   90
  Kabwiri   93
  Luenha   6, 8, 30, 37, 87
  Luenha River   40, 41, 42, 48, 82, 83, 87, 94
  M'Thane   89, 9
  Machangazi   40
  Maconde Plateau   26, 31
  Maconia   57
  Macúti   12, 131, 132, 133, 162
  Magoé   26
  Manga   131
  Manica-e-Sofala   19, 25, 26, 29, 30, 32, 33,
    41, 207
  Maputo   xxi, xxii, xxiv, 12, 25, 28, 52, 89, 110,
    125, 128, 139, 190
  Marara   4, 26, 28, 78, 114, 116, 197, 200
  Marques, Lourenço   12, 25, 60, 131, 132,
    133, 140, 170, 172, 173, 175, 182, 183,
    184, 205
  Massigo hills   82
  Matola   26
  Mavuzi   47, 48, 55
  Mazoe   103
  Montepuez   47, 48, 57, 59, 60
  Mpharhamadwe   10
  Mtwara   79
  M'Bewa River   43
  M'Phadwe   31, 37, 38, 42, 46, 72, 73, 74, 75,
    76, 77, 78, 80, 81, 95, 96, 100, 105, 119, 121,
    200, 202, 204
  Nacala   24, 25, 60
  Nampula   49, 57, 60, 63, 122, 123, 125, 152,
    161, 162, 163, 205
  Nhampha   66
  Nhantambarha   66
  Porto Amelia   57, 60
  Raul, Cantina   102, 103, 104
  Saquala River   89
  Selinda, Mount   34, 35
  Shiússaquala   89
  Sofala   22, 30, 31, 32
  Tete   xx, xxi, xxii, xxv, xxvii, 3–6, 8, 10–13,
    15–16, 21, 23–35, 37, 40,42–3, 47–8, 50,
    52, 57, 60–2, 65–7, 71, 73, 75, 78–9, 83–4,
    97–105, 107–11, 114, 116, 118–19, 121–3,
    125, 130, 135–6, 138–40, 154, 160, 165,
    170, 172–5, 179, 183–4, 187, 189, 191–3,
    195–202, 204–8

Index

Williamo 15, 177
Zambezi River 8, 12, 23, 25, 26, 28, 29, 77, 195

Nationalsozialistische Deutsche Arbeiterpartei (the National Socialist German Workers' Party) 193

Operation Marosca 17, 19, 47–9, 58, 101, 207

Portuguese Air Force 23, 49, 119, 200
Portuguese cattle rraders
  Senhor Aguiar 83, 84
  Senhor Gonçalves 38, 45, 76, 83, 84
  Senhor Miranda 83, 84, 95
  Senhor Monteiro 83
  Senhor Saize 45
Portuguese military leaders
  Arriaga, Kaúlza de 4, 6, 24, 25, 164, 173
  Machado, General Tomás Basto 25, 124, 125
  Spínola, António Sebastião Ribeiro de 1, 25
  Videira, Brigidier Armindo 6, 8, 170, 171
Portuguese military strategy
  Operation Gordian Knot 6, 25
  Operation Marosca 17, 47–9, 58, 101, 207
Portuguese military units
  GE (Grupos Especiais), Special Forces 41
  MFA (Movimento das Forças Armadas) 1, 152, 163
  OPV (Organização Provincial de Voluntários), Provincial Organization of Volunteers 67, 75
  OPVDC (Organização Provincial de Voluntários para Defesa Civil), Provincial Organization of Volunteers for Civil Defense 28
  ZOT (Zona Operacional de Tete) 8, 49, 201
Portuguese political emissary
  Jardim, Jorge 22, 24, 116, 117, 136, 192
Portuguese security agents
  António, Santo 68
  Kachavi, Chico xxi, 9, 19, 41, 59, 65, 74, 91, 98, 107, 197, 207
  Kongorhogondo, Johnny 9, 73, 99, 103–4, 107, 197
  Kongorhogondo, Thai 41
  Nhungwe, Galiciano 99
  Sabino, Joaquim 16, 115–16, 183–4, 197, 198, 202–6
Portuguese security police
  DGS Direção-Geral de Segurança, General Directorate For Security 41, 73, 103, 172

PIDE Polícia Internacional e de Defesa do Estado, International Police for the Defense of the State 22, 78, 109, 131, 164, 197

Portuguese Tete strategy xx, xxi, xxii, xxv, xxvii, 3–6, 8, 10–13, 15–16, 21, 23–35, 37, 40, 42–3, 47–8, 50, 52, 57, 60–2, 65–7, 71, 73, 75, 78–9, 83–4, 97–105, 107–11, 114, 116, 118–19, 121–3, 125, 130, 135–6, 138–40, 154, 160, 165, 170, 172–5, 179, 183–4, 187, 189, 191–3, 195–202, 204–8

Sheehy, Tim 143, 147, 148, 156
sorcerers and rain makers
  Chinzongha 82
  Mirhos 84–5
  Pirhoti 82
  Senhor Soda 38, 42, 43, 82
  Shingambo 82
South African security police
  BOSS South African Bureau for State Security 185
Southern African nationalist organizations
  ANC (African National Congress) 27
  ZANU (Zimbabwe African National Union) 27
  ZAPU (Zimbabwe African People's Union) 27
special terms
  cachaço 38, 90
  chimbawas 42
  kabandazi 38
  kadembo 41, 42, 43, 72, 88, 93
  lenha 96
  m'zungo 84
  machamba 19, 28, 37, 38, 42, 45, 46, 48, 80, 83, 85, 86, 89, 90, 94, 104
  massa 40
  mfumo 37, 40, 75, 82, 83, 85, 86, 94
  mphondorho 38–9, 42, 82, 83, 86, 96
  ngozi 72
  Nhungwe xxi, xxiii, 22, 39, 46, 51, 66, 73, 74, 77, 83, 84, 98, 99, 102, 103, 106
  parada xxviii, 70, 96
  pombe 38, 42, 66, 82, 85, 90, 91, 95
  poço 75
  thundo 38
  turras 86, 87, 99, 199
statesmen
  Banda, Hastings Kamuzu 24
  Caetano, Marcelo 1, 2, 14, 15, 16, 17, 26, 66, 121, 122, 134, 141, 145, 148, 149, 153–4, 156, 157, 164, 169, 192, 193, 208
  Franco, General Francisco 129
  Heath, Edward 14
  Kaunda, Kenneth 6
  Nyerere, Julius 169
  Salazar, António de Oliveira 152

Smith, Ian   6, 14, 159, 160
Soares, Mário   144, 149, 152, 154, 164
Tanaka, Akihiko   160
Wilson, Harold   157
Sudworth, Eileen   143

Tenente, Enéria   xxi, xxv, xxvi, xxvii, 70, 207
tortures   108–10
Totten and Ubaldo   xxx

Vatican II   4, 6, 8, 141, 150, 151, 152

Wall, Patrick   145
Ward, Dr. Jonathan   170, 171, 175, 176
Wiriyamu, Nonica   41–2, 73
Wiriyamu London revelations   208

Young, Hugo   143, 147, 148, 157